ECONOMIC ISSUES, PROBLEMS AND PERSPECTIVES

Additional books in this series can be found on Nova's website under the Series tab.

Additional E-books in this series can be found on Nova's website under the E-books tab.

AMERICAN POLITICAL, ECONOMIC, AND SECURITY ISSUES

Additional books in this series can be found on Nova's website under the Series tab.

Additional E-books in this series can be found on Nova's website under the E-books tab.

ECONOMIC ISSUES, PROBLEMS AND PERSPECTIVES

REFLECTIONS ON THE TROUBLED ASSET RELIEF PROGRAM (TARP)

DONNA C. HAYWORTH
EDITOR

Nova Science Publishers, Inc.

New York

NOTICE TO THE READER

The Publisher has taken reasonable care in the preparation of this book, but makes no expressed or implied warranty of any kind and assumes no responsibility for any errors or omissions. No liability is assumed for incidental or consequential damages in connection with or arising out of information contained in this book. The Publisher shall not be liable for any special, consequential, or exemplary damages resulting, in whole or in part, from the readers' use of, or reliance upon, this material. Any parts of this book based on government reports are so indicated and copyright is claimed for those parts to the extent applicable to compilations of such works.

Independent verification should be sought for any data, advice or recommendations contained in this book. In addition, no responsibility is assumed by the publisher for any injury and/or damage to persons or property arising from any methods, products, instructions, ideas or otherwise contained in this publication.

This publication is designed to provide accurate and authoritative information with regard to the subject matter covered herein. It is sold with the clear understanding that the Publisher is not engaged in rendering legal or any other professional services. If legal or any other expert assistance is required, the services of a competent person should be sought. FROM A DECLARATION OF PARTICIPANTS JOINTLY ADOPTED BY A COMMITTEE OF THE AMERICAN BAR ASSOCIATION AND A COMMITTEE OF PUBLISHERS.

Additional color graphics may be available in the e-book version of this book.

LIBRARY OF CONGRESS CATALOGING-IN-PUBLICATION DATA

Reflections on the Troubled Asset Relief Program (TARP) / editor, Donna C. Hayworth.
    p. cm.
 Includes index.
 ISBN 978-1-61209-519-6 (hbk.)
 1. Troubled Asset Relief Program (U.S.)--Evaluation. 2. Economic stabilization--United States. 3. Economic assistance, Domestic--United States--Evaluation. I. Hayworth, Donna C.
 HB3743.R37 2011
 338.5'430973--dc22
2011003564

Published by Nova Science Publishers, Inc. † New York

CONTENTS

PREFACE

Alongside the actions of the Federal Reserve and the FDIC, and the tax cuts and investments set forth in the American Recovery and Reinvestment Act, the financial actions authorized under TARP were critical in preventing a devastating collapse of our financial system and restarting economic growth. Hundred of billions of unused authority have been returned to the taxpayer to help reduce the debt and future budget deficits. This new book examines the TARP program, two years after its implementation, as well as the current status and estimated costs of the program.

Chapter 1- October 3, 2010 marked the second anniversary of the Emergency Economic Stabilization Act (EESA) that created the Troubled Asset Relief Program (TARP) and the end of the authority to make new financial commitments.

EESA was an integral part of the government's program to resolve the financial crisis of 2008 and early 2009. Alongside the actions of the Federal Reserve and the FDIC, and the tax cuts and investments set forth in the American Recovery and Reinvestment Act, the financial actions authorized under EESA were critical in preventing a devastating collapse of our financial system and restarting economic growth.

We now have recovered most of the investments we made in the banks. Taxpayers will likely earn a profit on the investments the government made in banks and AIG, with TARP losses limited to investments in the automobile industry and housing programs. And we have already returned hundreds of billions of unused authority to the taxpayer to help reduce our debt and future budget deficits.

Chapter 2- Congress created the Troubled Asset Relief Program (TARP) to restore liquidity and stability in the financial system. The Department of the Treasury (Treasury), among other actions, established the Capital Purchase Program (CPP) as its primary initiative to accomplish these goals by making capital investments in eligible financial institutions. This chapter examines (1) the characteristics of financial institutions that received CPP funding and (2) how Treasury implemented CPP with the assistance of federal bank regulators. GAO analyzed data obtained from Treasury case files, reviewed program documents, and interviewed officials from Treasury and federal bank regulators.

Chapter 3- The Troubled Asset Relief Program (TARP) was created by the Emergency Economic Stabilization Act (EESA; P.L. 110-343) in October 2008. EESA was passed by Congress and signed by President Bush to address an ongoing financial crisis that reached near-panic proportions in September 2008. EESA granted the Secretary of the Treasury authority to either purchase or insure up to $700 billion in troubled assets owned by financial institutions. This authority was granted for up to two years from the date of enactment and was very broad. In particular, the definitions of both "troubled asset" and "financial institution" allowed the Secretary wide leeway in deciding what assets might be purchased or guaranteed and what might qualify as a financial firm.

Chapter 4- The Supervisory Capital Assessment Program (SCAP) was established under the Capital Assistance Program (CAP)—a component of the Troubled Asset Relief Program (TARP)—to assess whether the 19 largest U.S. bank holding companies (BHC) had enough capital to withstand a severe economic downturn. Led by the Board of Governors of the Federal Reserve System (Federal Reserve), federal bank regulators conducted a stress test to determine if these banks needed to raise additional capital, either privately or through CAP. This chapter (1) describes the SCAP process and participants' views of the process, (2) assesses SCAP's goals and results and BHCs' performance, and (3) identifies how regulators and the BHCs are applying lessons learned from SCAP. To do this work, GAO reviewed SCAP documents, analyzed financial data, and interviewed regulatory, industry, and BHC officials.

In: Reflections on the Troubled Asset Relief Program (TARP)   ISBN: 978-1-61209-519-6
Editor: Donna C. Hayworth   © 2011 Nova Science Publishers, Inc.

Chapter 1

TROUBLED ASSET RELIEF PROGRAM: TWO YEAR RETROSPECTIVE

United States Department of the Treasury

". . . if there's one thing that has unified Democrats and Republicans, and everybody in between, it's that we all hated the bank bailout. I hated it. You hated it. It was about as popular as a root canal.

But when I ran for President, I promised I wouldn't just do what was popular – I would do what was necessary. And if we had allowed the meltdown of the financial system, unemployment might be double what it is today. More businesses would certainly have closed. More homes would have surely been lost.

So I supported the last administration's efforts to create the financial rescue program. And when we took that program over, we made it more transparent and more accountable. And as a result, the markets are now stabilized, and we've recovered most of the money we spent on the banks."

President Obama, January 27, 2010

TARP Summary Table

As of September 30, 2010	Maximum Allocation	Total Spent	Repayments	% Repaid	Income
Bank capital programs	$ 250	$ 245	$ 192	78%	$ 26.8
Automotive companies	$ 82	$ 80	$ 11	14%	$ 2.6
AIG	$ 70	$ 48			
Credit Markets					
Public Private Investment Program[1]	$ 22.4[1]	$ 14.2	$ 0.43	3%	$ 0.2
Term Asset-Backed Loan Facility	$ 4.3	$ 0.1			
SBA 7a Securities Purchase Program	$ 0.4	$ 0.4			*
Community Development Capital Initiative	$ 0.8	$ 0.6			
Treasury housing programs[2]	$ 45.6[3]	$ 0.5[4]	n/a	n/a	n/a
Totals	**$ 475**	**$ 388**	**$ 204**	**53%**	**$30**

*Less than $10 million as of 8/31/2010

1/ Amount was $30 billion, but was reduced to $22 billion in July 2010.

2/ Treasury's housing expenditures are not expected to be repaid and Treasury does not receive income or warrants related to these programs.

3/ Amount was $50 billion, but was reduced to approximately $46 billion in July 2010.

4/ Expenditures under the housing programs are made incrementally over time.

1. MESSAGE FROM THE ACTING ASSISTANT SECRETARY FOR FINANCIAL STABILITY

October 5, 2010

Ladies and Gentlemen:

October 3, 2010 marked the second anniversary of the Emergency Economic Stabilization Act that created the Troubled Asset Relief Program TARP) and the end of the authority to make new financial commitments. Therefore, this is an appropriate time to reflect on what TARP has accomplished.

The TARP was, and is, an enormous commitment of taxpayer money. And TARP has been unpopular for good reason -- no one likes using tax dollars to rescue financial institutions. However, by objective measures, TARP worked. Two years later, our financial system is stable, more than $204 billion of TARP funds have been repaid, only a quarter of the original $700 billion authorization remains outstanding, the total estimated cost of TARP has been cut by more than three-fourths, taxpayers have received $30 billion in income, and the TARP bank programs are on track to make solid returns for taxpayers.

The ultimate cost of TARP and our other financial policies will depend on how financial markets and the economy perform in the future. If financial and economic conditions deteriorate, prospects for TARP investments will also deteriorate. But in light of the recently-announced AIG restructuring and when valued at current market prices, Treasury now estimates that the total cost of TARP will be about $50 billion. In addition, using the same assumptions, we estimate that the combined cost of TARP programs and other Treasury interests in AIG will be about $30 billion. The costs are expected to come from losses related to TARP investments in auto companies and initiatives to help responsible omeowners avoid foreclosure.

Going forward, the Department of the Treasury will continue to manage the investments prudently while working with the companies to recover a much of the taxpayers' funds as possible. We will also continue our efforts to help distressed homeowners. And we will take these steps while maintaining comprehensive accountability and transparency for the TARP programs.

This milestone also marked the departure, on September 30, 2010, of Herbert M. Allison, Jr. as the Assistant Secretary for Financial Stability. As Secretary Geithner has said, "the fact that TARP is now regarded by many experts as one of the most effective emergency programs in financial history is a direct result of Herb's leadership."

Sincerely,

Timothy G. Massad
Acting Assistant Secretary for Financial Stability

2. EXECUTIVE SUMMARY

October 3, 2010 marked the second anniversary of the Emergency Economic Stabilization Act (EESA) that created the Troubled Asset Relief Program (TARP) and the end of the authority to make new financial commitments.

EESA was an integral part of the government's program to resolve the financial crisis of 2008 and early 2009. Alongside the actions of the Federal Reserve and the FDIC, and the tax cuts and investments set forth in the American Recovery and Reinvestment Act, the financial actions authorized under EESA were critical in preventing a devastating collapse of our financial system and restarting economic growth.

We now have recovered most of the investments we made in the banks. Taxpayers will likely earn a profit on the investments the government made in banks and AIG, with TARP losses limited to investments in the automobile industry and housing programs. And we have already returned hundreds of billions of unused authority to the taxpayer to help reduce our debt and future budget deficits.

TARP, of course, was not the answer to all of America's challenges, and we have many still ahead. The U.S. economy is healing, but at a slower pace than we need. Millions of Americans are still out of work and at risk of losing their homes. Small businesses in many parts of the country still find it very hard to get access to credit. American families are still working to reduce debt and rebuild their savings.

And although the direct fiscal cost of the emergency financial programs will likely be a very small fraction of initial projections and significantly lower than the savings and loan crisis of the 1980s, the overall fiscal and economic costs of this crisis are substantial, and will take significantly more time to address.

The record of the financial programs is defined by the following key accomplishments:

1. TARP was remarkably effective in helping to unfreeze the markets for credit and capital, bring down the cost of borrowing, restore confidence in the financial system, and restart economic growth.

At the peak of the crisis, banks were not making new loans to businesses, or even to one another. Businesses could not get financing in our capital markets. Municipalities and state governments could not issue bonds at reasonable rates. The securitization markets—which provide financing for credit cards, student loans, auto loans and other consumer financing—had basically stopped functioning. The economy was contracting at an accelerating rate, with millions of Americans losing their jobs.

By the middle of 2009, because of the combined impact of the government's financial programs, borrowing rates had fallen sharply for businesses, individuals, and state and local governments. Companies were able to fund themselves in private markets by issuing equity and long-term debt. Housing prices began to stabilize. The value of the savings of American workers had begun to recover. And economic growth turned from negative to positive.

2. The projected costs of TARP have fallen by about $300 billion.

Independent observers, such as the Congressional Budget Office, initially projected that TARP would cost $350 billion or more. Now, because of the success of the program, TARP will likely cost a fraction of this amount.

We expect that TARP investments in the banks and the credit market programs will be profitable. The recently announced restructuring of AIG will accelerate the government's exit on terms that are likely to lead to an overall profit on the government's support for AIG, including the value of Treasury's interests in AIG held outside of TARP. Most of the cost of TARP is expected to come from two sources: expected losses related to TARP investments in auto companies and initiatives to help responsible homeowners avoid foreclosure.

The ultimate cost of TARP and our other financial policies will depend on how financial markets and the economy perform in the future. If financial and economic conditions deteriorate, prospects for TARP investments will also deteriorate. But in light of the recently-announced AIG restructuring and when valued at current market prices, Treasury now estimates that the total cost of TARP will be about $50 billion. In addition, using the same assumptions, we estimate that the combined cost of TARP programs and other Treasury interests in AIG will be about $30 billion.

Outside of TARP, we expect to incur substantial losses from Fannie Mae and Freddie Mac (Government Sponsored Enterprises, or GSEs), through capital injections from Treasury to the GSEs through the Preferred Stock Purchase Agreements (PSPAs). These losses stem from poor credit choices and bad risk management decisions before the Federal Housing Finance Agency (FHFA) placed the GSEs in conservatorship in late 2008-- not actions taken in 2009 or 2010.

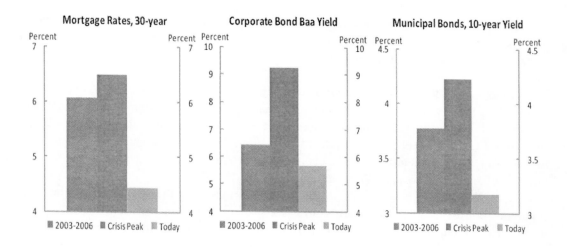

Figure 2-A.

	($U.S. billions)
TARP Bank Programs	16 [2]
AIG (TARP)	-5 [3]
TARP Credit Market Programs [4]	1 [2]
TARP Auto Programs	-17 [2]
TARP Housing Programs	-46 [2]
Total TARP Cost	-51
Other Treasury AIG Investments	22 [5]
Total Treasury Cost	-29

[1] Estimates for AIG reflect the impact of the recently announced restructuring of the government's interests in the firm. Treasury and the Federal Reserve made several investments in AIG. These investments have been restructured over time and are closely intertwined. In particular, Treasury holds investments in AIG in two forms: equity investments made through TARP and equity provided to a trust for Treasury's benefit in connection with the Federal Reserve's creation of a credit facility for AIG.

[2] Preliminary estimates for end August. Change for autos from previously-published estimate primarlly reflects increase in valuation of investments in Ally Financial Inc. (formerly known as GMAC, Inc.). due to improved market conditions.

[3] After the proposed restructuring of AIG, TARP will hold 1.09 billion shares of AIG common stock, plus preferred equity interests in SPVs of approximately $22.3 billion, against a cost basis of $69.8 billion. Valuing the common equity at the market close for October 1 of $38.86 per share implies a net cost of -$5.1 billion.

[4] Includes PPIP, TALF, CDCI and SBA.

[5] After the proposed restructuring of AIG, Treasury will receive 563 million shares of AIG common in connection with the wind-down of the Federal Reserve credit facility, in addtion to the shares noted in footnote 3. Valuing those shares at the market closing price for October 1 of $38.86 per share implies a profit to the Treasury of $21.9 billion.

Figure 2-B. Preliminary Treasury Estimates of the impact of TARP Programs and Other Treasury Investments in AIG on the Federal Budget [1]

However, a substantial part of the government's projected losses on its support for the GSEs will be offset by revenue from two sources. Under authority provided by the Housing and Economic Recovery Act (HERA), Treasury purchased more than $200 billion in mortgage-backed securities guaranteed by the GSEs. Those investments are generating notable returns. In addition, as a result of its emergency financial programs, remittances from Federal Reserve operations to the Federal Budget have increased sharply in 2009 and 2010, and they are projected to remain elevated for some time. While considerable uncertainty remains, revenues from these two sources will significantly offset to likely losses elsewhere.

We currently expect that the overall direct fiscal cost of all our financial interventions will be less than one percent of GDP. This result is notable compared past systemic financial crises. An International Monetary Fund study found that the average net fiscal cost of resolving roughly 40 banking crises since 1970 was 13 percent of GDP. And according to the Government Accountability Office (GAO), the net fiscal cost of cleaning up the U.S. savings and loan crisis was 2.4 percent of GDP.

These estimates provide a meaningful way to compare the direct fiscal cost of resolving financial crises across countries and time. However, our estimates do not reflect the full economic and fiscal costs of this crisis, whether measured in the millions of Americans still searching for work, the lost income for business, or the impact of the recession on Federal and State budgets. But because TARP was so effective at much lower cost than expected, we are in a much stronger position than we would otherwise have been to address the very substantial economic challenges we still face as a country.

3. We are moving quickly to recover the government's investments and to withdraw from the financial system.

We have already made substantial progress in recovering taxpayer investments, ending emergency government programs, and exiting from the financial system.

In the most acute phase of the crisis at the end of 2008, TARP preferred stock investments were made in financial institutions that held approximately 88 percent of the total assets of our banking system. Today, we hold preferred stock investments in financial institutions that hold approximately 10 percent of the total assets of the system.

In just two years, we have already recovered three-fourths of the TARP funds invested in banks, and we have generated $27 billion in income from our investments in banks.

We will finish selling our investment in Citigroup early next year. We will also exit from government investments in AIG and the automotive industry much faster than anyone predicted. General Motors is planning an initial public offering for later this year that will allow us to begin to sell down, and AIG has announced a restructuring plan that will accelerate the timeline for repaying the government and put taxpayers in a considerably stronger position to recoup our investment in the company.

We have closed or are in the process of winding down nearly all other emergency government programs. Treasury terminated the Money Market Fund Guarantee program last year, resulting in a profit to taxpayers. The FDIC's Temporary Liquidity Guarantee Program (TLGP) for debt is closed to new commitments, and the level of participation in the TLGP for transaction accounts has fallen to roughly one quarter of its peak. Nearly all of the Federal Reserve's liquidity programs have been shut down and generated significant revenues.

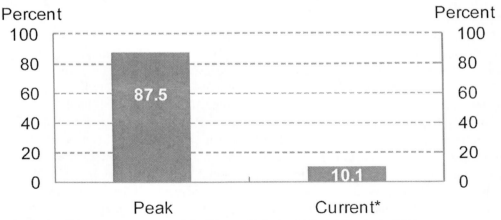

*   Excludes Citigroup common stock holdings which should be sold by early 2011.

Figure 2-C. Share of Bank Holding Company Assets Held by Firms with Outstanding CPP Prefered Equity

4. Two critical elements of the Obama Administration's strategy were the "stress test" to force banks to raise private capital and a series of innovative programs to jumpstart credit markets and financing for consumers, businesses, and homeowners.

When President Obama took office many were convinced that the only way to stabilize the banking system was with large additional injections of public capital or nationalization – steps that would have entailed significant risks and costs. The President chose a different path, subjecting major U.S. financial institutions to a "stress test" and forcing them to strengthen capital through private fundraising. Since the results of the tests were released last May, those institutions have raised in the aggregate over $150 billion in private capital. Only one of the 19 institutions subjected to the tests needed to access TARP after the results were released. And all but six of those institutions have repaid all TARP funds they received—at a profit to taxpayers.

One popular misconception is that Treasury under the Obama Administration injected massive amounts of TARP funds into large banks. In fact, since January 20, 2009, Treasury has provided only $11 billion to banks under CPP, a large part of which went to over four hundred small and community banks. Meanwhile, the government has gotten out of the business of guaranteeing newlyissued - bank debt. Nearly 50 percent of such new issuance was guaranteed by the government in January 2009. The government has not guaranteed one dollar of new issuance in 2010.

When the Administration took office, the credit markets that help provide access to loans to consumers and businesses had frozen. Treasury efforts to unfreeze these markets – including through the Term Asset-Backed Securities Loan Facility (TALF), the Public Private Investment Program (PPIP), and the SBA 7(a) Securities Purchase Program – have helped to make credit more available and are expected to generate revenues—not costs—for taxpayers. Since the government launched TALF in March 2009, prices for securities backed by consumer and business loans have improved significantly and new issuance of such asset-backed securities has averaged $12 billion per month, compared to less than $2 billion per month in the six months prior to the program's launch. Similarly, since the announcement of PPIP in March 2009, prices for eligible residential and commercial mortgage-backed securities (i.e., RMBS and CMBS) have increased by as much as 75 percent. As a result, both programs have helped remove significant impediments to new credit for consumers, businesses, and homeowners.

In addition, under TARP, Treasury launched the Making Home Affordable Program (MHA), which includes the Home Affordable Modification Program (HAMP).

After 18 months, HAMP has helped more than 1.3 million homeowners by reducing their mortgage payments to more affordable levels. This includes more than 460,000 homeowners whose mortgage terms have been modified permanently. These homeowners have experienced a 36 percent median reduction in their mortgage payments—more than $500 per month—amounting to a total, program -wide savings for homeowners of more than $3.2 billion. MHA has also spurred the mortgage industry to adopt similar programs that have helped millions more at no cost to the taxpayer.

In addition, Treasury launched the Housing Finance Agency (HFA) Innovation Fund for the Hardest Hit Housing Markets (HFA Hardest Hit Fund, or HHF) to help state housing finance agencies provide additional relief to homeowners in the states hit hardest by unemployment and house price declines, and Treasury and the Department of Housing and

Urban Development (HUD) enhanced the FHA Short Refinance program to enable more homeowners whose mortgages exceed the value of their homes to refinance into more affordable mortgages if their lenders agree to reduce principal by at least 10%.

The U.S. Financial System Is Much Stronger Today, and in a Strong Position to Support Economic Recovery

The policy response to the crisis has brought about an essential restructuring of the financial system.

The weakest parts of the financial system no longer exist. Of the 20 largest financial institutions in the fall of 2008, four no longer exist as independent entities, five were subject to major interventions by regulators, two agreed to become subject to much greater oversight, and 10 have had significant changes in senior management. The firms that remain had to meet a market test for viability – they had to demonstrate they could raise substantial amounts of private capital.

Today, our financial system has substantially higher levels of capital relative to risk than before the crisis and more capital relative to global competitors. At the same time, we led the effort, working with other countries, to design and impose higher capital requirements internationally so that banks will not become so undercapitalized again.

And the Dodd-Frank Wall Street Reform and Consumer Protection Act of 2010 (the Dodd-Frank Act) will significantly reduce the threat of future financial crises. No longer will a major non-bank firm escape comprehensive supervision and capital requirements. No longer will the government be left without the tools it needs to wind down a major firm in the event of a major financial crisis. No longer will derivatives or the shadow banking system be left in the dark. And no longer will consumers be left without adequate protection or the basic information they need to make sound choices.

The Next Stage of Financial Repair

Even though the most dangerous phase of the financial crisis is behind us, we still have substantial work to do to repair the damage.

The Administration will continue to help responsible but atrisk-homeowners, while reforming the U.S. housing finance system. In addition to the MHA, the HFA Hardest Hit Fund and FHA Short Refinance programs discussed above, Treasury continues to support new housing credit through the Preferred Stock Purchase Agreements with Fannie Mae and Freddie Mac (the GSEs). Treasury is also working with HUD and other agencies to develop proposals to reform U.S. housing finance and restructure the GSEs. In recent months, we have received input from a variety of stakeholders to inform that process, and have held conferences to hear the views of citizen advocacy groups, economists, investors, market researchers, originators, securitizers, servicers, and private mortgage insurers on reform. We will provide a comprehensive reform proposal to Congress by January 2011 and will work to ensure the new system will deliver a more stable housing market with stronger regulation and a clearer role of government with less risk borne by the American taxpayer. Where guarantees or support is provided, it will be explicit and priced appropriately.

Beyond the measures taken under EESA, we are continuing to provide support for small businesses, many of which are still struggling to access credit, expand and hire new workers. Last week, the President signed into law the Small Business Jobs Act. This legislation establishes two new and separate Treasury lending initiatives: a Small Business Lending Fund that will provide up to $30 billion in capital to community banks with incentives to increase their small business lending, and a State Small Business Credit Initiative that will spur $15 billion in private sector lending by strengthening small business programs threatened by state budget cuts. The Small Business Jobs Act also includes enhancements to SBA programs that will help creditworthy small businesses access loans, as well as eight new small business tax cuts that provide incentives for small businesses to invest and expand.

Finally, there is still work to be done in managing our remaining TARP commitments. Foreclosure-mitigation programs will continue to require substantial oversight of mortgage servicers to ensure that these initiatives are effectively implemented. While most of the largest banks have repaid their obligations to TARP, we still have investments in over 600 banks. We will work with these institutions, and their regulators, to accelerate repayment where appropriate. We will also work to ensure that restructuring plans for our investments in AIG and the auto industry are executed successfully. And we will continue to be transparent in all of our efforts.

When TARP was created, the world around us was falling apart. And in that moment, when families and businesses were worried like never before about their basic economic security, leaders from both parties stood up, stood together, and as Americans, did what was best for the country. They did something unpopular, but necessary. And we are much better off as a result.

In this overview, we discuss why TARP was necessary, the results and current status of the actions taken under TARP, its costs, its effect on achieving stabilization of financial markets, and Treasury's plans to wind down the program.

A. The Financial Crisis and the Need for the Troubled Asset Relief Program

In September 2008, the nation was in the midst of one of the worst financial crises in our history. The financial institutions and markets that Americans rely upon to protect their savings, help finance their children's education, and help pay their bills, and that businesses rely upon to make payroll, build inventories, fund new investments, and create new jobs, were threatened unlike at any time since the Great Depression. Across the country, people were rapidly losing confidence in our financial system and in the government's ability to safeguard their economic future.

The causes of the crisis will be studied for years, and this chapter is not meant to provide a comprehensive analysis of why the crisis occurred. But some reasons are clear. Over the two decades preceding the crisis, the financial system had grown rapidly in an environment of economic growth and stability. Risks grew in the system without adequate transparency. Lax regulations and loopholes in supervision let firms become highly leveraged and take on too much risk. Ample credit around the world fueled an unsustainable housing boom in the first half of the last decade. When the housing market inevitably turned down, starting in 2006, the pace of mortgage defaults accelerated at an unprecedented rate. By mid-2007, rising mortgage defaults were undermining the performance of many investments held by major financial institutions.

The crisis began in the summer of 2007 and gradually increased in intensity and momentum over the course of the following year. A series of major financial institutions, including Countrywide Financial, Bear Stearns, and IndyMac, failed; and Fannie Mae and Freddie Mac, the largest purchasers and guarantors of home loans in the mortgage market, came under severe stress.

By September 2008, for the first time in 80 years, the U.S. financial system was at risk of collapse. A growing sense of panic was producing the classic signs of a generalized run on the banks. Peoples' trust and confidence in the stability of major institutions, and the capacity of the government to contain the damage, were vanishing.

Our system of regulation and supervision had failed to constrain the excessive use of leverage and the level of risk in the financial system, and the United States entered this crisis without adequate tools to manage it. The Executive Branch did not have existing options for managing failures of systemically important non-bank financial institutions.

The Treasury Department, the Federal Reserve, the FDIC, and other government bodies undertook an array of emergency actions to prevent a collapse and the dangers posed to consumers, businesses, and the broader economy. However, the severe conditions our nation faced required additional resources and authorities. Therefore, the Bush Administration proposed EESA in late September, and with the support of Democrats and Republicans in Congress, it was enacted into law on October 3, 2008.

B. The Bush Administration's Actions under TARP

The TARP was originally proposed as a means for the government to buy mortgage loans, mortgage backed securities and certain other assets from banks. The fact that it was not used for this purpose promptly after passage has led to criticism of the program. However, by early October 2008, lending even between banks had practically stopped, credit markets had shut down, and many financial institutions were facing severe stress. It was also clear that there was not sufficient time to implement a program to buy mortgage-related assets, given the challenges of valuing troubled assets and quickly building the administrative infrastructure to purchase large volumes of those assets.

In this context, immediate capital injections were needed to stabilize the banks and avert a potential catastrophe. The law provided for this approach, because the authorities had been broadened in the legislative process to cover the purchase of any financial instrument if the Secretary of the Treasury, after consultation with the Chairman of the Federal Reserve, determined this was necessary to promote financial stability. This was also the approach that many other countries took at that time. Therefore, the Bush Administration launched the Capital Purchase Program and later the Targeted Investment Program to provide this support.

Under the Bush Administration, during the fall and winter of 2008, TARP funds were used as follows:

- $234 billion was invested in banks and thrifts, including $165 billion in eight of the largest financial institutions in the country, and additional funds were committed to guarantee assets of two of the largest banks;
- $40 billion was invested in American International Group (AIG), along with additional funds from the Federal Reserve; and
- Approximately $20 billion in loans was provided to the auto industry.

C. The Obama Administration's Actions under TARP

In January 2009, President-elect Obama faced a combination of acute financial and economic challenges. The economy was in a full-fledged recession. The nation had lost over 3.5 million jobs in 2008, and was losing additional jobs at the rate of roughly 750,000 per month in the first quarter of 2009. Businesses around the world were cutting back investments that are essential to growth. Trade among nations had contracted sharply. Home prices were falling, and foreclosures were increasing. Instead of catalyzing recovery, the financial system was working against recovery. The system was still fragile, and the recession was putting even greater pressure on banks. This dangerous dynamic needed to be halted immediately.

Together with the fiscal stimulus enacted under the American Recovery and Reinvestment Act, the Financial Stability Plan announced in February 2009 laid out the Obama Administration's comprehensive, forceful and sustained commitment to ensure the stability of the financial system, assist in the cleanup of legacy assets, jumpstart the provision of new credit for households and businesses, and support distressed housing markets. As part of that plan, the Treasury Department has taken the following actions under TARP over the last 20 months:

1. Recapitalizing the Banking System

Our financial system needed to be recapitalized. But private capital could not be raised until the condition of the major financial institutions was made clear. Treasury worked with the federal banking regulators to develop a comprehensive, forward-looking "stress test" for the nineteen largest bank holding companies to determine which ones would need more capital to remain well-capitalized if economic conditions deteriorated significantly more than expected. The stress test was conducted with unprecedented openness and transparency, which helped restore market confidence in our financial system. Since completion of the stress test, these banks have raised an aggregate of more than $150 billion in private capital, and twelve of the stress test banks that had TARP investments have repaid the government in full. Treasury allowed banks needing capital to apply for further assistance from the government, but only one did so.

Treasury estimates that the capital programs developed under TARP to support all banks, taken together, will result in a gain to the taxpayer. See Section 5 – Program Descriptions, pages 22 – 33.

2. Jumpstarting the Credit Markets that are Critical to Providing Financing to Consumers and Businesses

Because the crisis had frozen credit markets, Treasury launched three programs to help restart them:

- The Term Asset-Backed Securities Loan Facility (TALF), a joint program with the Federal Reserve, helped to restart the asset-backed securitization markets that provide credit to consumers and small businesses;
- The Legacy Securities Public Private Investment Program (PPIP), matched TARP funds with private capital to purchase legacy mortgage-related securities; and
- The SBA 7(a) Securities Purchase Program, in which Treasury committed to help unlock credit for small businesses by providing capital in exchange for securities backed by small business loans.

Treasury estimates that these programs, taken together, will result in minimal or no costs under TARP. See Section 5 – Program Descriptions, pages 34 – 43.

3. Stabilizing the Automotive Industry and AIG

Treasury provided additional assistance to GM and Chrysler on the condition that those companies fundamentally restructure their businesses. These restructurings involved sacrifices from all stakeholders—shareholders, unions, auto dealers, and creditors—and have enabled the companies to become more competitive. This assistance also helped the many suppliers and ancillary businesses that depend on the automotive industry.

Treasury also took steps to restructure the assistance that had been provided to the American International Group, Inc. (AIG) under the Bush Administration. This involved making an additional commitment of support and working with AIG toward repaying the government by selling non-core businesses and completing other restructuring initiatives.

In Treasury's most recent official estimate, these investments will result in a portion of the costs under TARP. However, the prospects for repayment to the taxpayer are improving as the companies continue to strengthen. See Section 5 – Program Descriptions, pages 44–57.

4. Support for Small and Mid-Sized Banks

While the Obama Administration made no further investments in the nation's largest banks, Treasury invested $11 billion in more than 400 other banks and thrifts, most of which were small and community banks. In recognition of the fact that they had fewer alternatives to raise capital, the smallest banks were also given additional time to apply for assistance. Because community development financial institutions serve small businesses and consumers in the communities hardest hit by the recession, communities which are typically underserved by large financial institutions, a special program was established to help these institutions.

See Section 5 – Program Descriptions, page 33.

5. Helping Responsible but Struggling Homeowners

When the Obama Administration took office, the nation's housing market had been in broad decline for 18 months. EESA authorities enabled Treasury to develop a voluntary program that would support servicers' efforts to modify mortgages, consistent with the protection of taxpayers. While the serious effects of the recession and financial crisis on the housing market and foreclosures persist, this Administration has taken aggressive action on many fronts, including under TARP, and has made considerable progress in helping to stabilize the housing market.

- Treasury launched the Making Home Affordable (MHA) program, which includes the Home Affordable Modification Program (HAMP), under TARP. HAMP has helped hundreds of thousands of responsible homeowners reduce their mortgage payments by an average of $500 per month and avoid foreclosure. MHA has also spurred the mortgage industry to adopt similar programs that have helped millions more at no cost to the taxpayer.

As the housing crisis has evolved, Treasury has responded to the unemployment and negative equity problems by adjusting HAMP and instituting additional programs. For example:

- Treasury launched the Housing Finance Agency (HFA) Hardest Hit Fund to help state housing finance agencies provide additional relief to homeowners in the states hit hardest by unemployment and house price declines.
- Treasury and the Department of Housing and Urban Development (HUD) enhanced the FHA Short Refinance program to enable more homeowners whose mortgages exceed the value of their homes to refinance into more affordable mortgages.

To protect taxpayers, MHA housing initiatives have pay-forsuccess -   incentives: funds are spent only when transactions are completed and thereafter only as long as those contracts remain in place. Therefore, funds will be disbursed over many years. The total cost of the housing programs cannot exceed—and may be less than—$46 billion, which is the amount committed to that purpose.

See Section 6 – Retrospective on the TARP Housing Initiatives, pages 58 – 79.

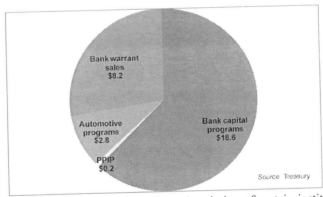

See Section 5 – Program Descriptions, page 26, for a description of certain institutions in the Capital Purchase Program that represent losses on TARP investments.

Figure 3-A. TARP Income as of September 30, 2010

6. Recovering TARP Funds

One of Treasury's primary objectives has been to get TARP dollars back. So far, more than $200 billion has been returned. In addition, TARP investments have generated $30 billion of proceeds to taxpayers, in the form of dividend and interest payments and sales of warrants.

The sales of warrants have been particularly successful. The law that created TARP requires, in most cases, an institution receiving TARP funds to give Treasury warrants that allow taxpayers to participate in potential additional returns when the institution regains financial stability. By negotiating effectively with banks seeking to repurchase their warrants directly, and by effectively auctioning the warrants of banks that elect not to repurchase, Treasury has received over $8 billion in additional revenue for taxpayers.

7. Implementing Executive Compensation Restrictions

The law that created TARP (as amended by the American Recovery and Reinvestment Act of 2009 (ARRA)) imposes restrictions on the executive compensation of top management of those institutions that received TARP funds. Treasury implemented regulations to enforce these restrictions, which included creating the Office of the Special Master for Executive Compensation. The Special Master has taken steps to ensure that executive pay at the TARP firms receiving exceptional assistance promotes long-term value creation and financial stability.

8. Comprehensive Accountability and Transparency

Treasury has operated the TARP programs with comprehensive standards for accountability and transparency. Voluminous data and information have been made public and available to taxpayers, observers and Congress on the websites – www.FinancialStability.gov and www.MakingHomeAffordable.gov. This includes all contracts governing any investment or expenditure of TARP funds, and more than 275 reports over two years. Treasury will also publish in November comprehensive audited financial statements for the TARP programs, for the fiscal year ending September 30, 2010, as we did for the previous fiscal year.

D. TARP Will Cost a Fraction of What Was Expected

It is clear that TARP will cost taxpayers a fraction of the $700 billion originally authorized. The Treasury Department's efforts have consistently reduced the program's cost. We will not use more than $475 billion of TARP funds, including amounts already expended and recovered, and we expect to recover most of those funds, other than the funds spent on housing programs, which were not intended to be returned.

- In July 2010, the Obama Administration and Congress capped the amount that could be invested under TARP at $475 billion, a one-third reduction from the original commitment authorized by Congress.
- More than $204 billion of TARP funds expended have been repaid — including more than seventy-five percent of the money invested in large banks.

- TARP investments have already generated returns to taxpayers from dividends, interest and sales of warrants and other securities of $30 billion.
- The pay-for-success features of TARP's MHA housing programs assure that taxpayer funds are used only to the extent that programs achieve intended results. In addition, the TARP housing programs have also caused mortgage servicers to adopt similar programs that have helped millions more homeowners at no cost to the taxpayer.

The ultimate cost of TARP and our other financial policies will depend on how financial markets and the economy perform in the future. If financial and economic conditions deteriorate prospects for TARP investments will also deteriorate. But the most up-to-date Treasury estimates for TARP programs, including the impact of the AIG restructuring, now suggest that total fiscal impact of TARP will be to increase the Federal deficit by about $50 billion. Moreover, other Treasury investments in AIG are expected to generate a positive return of about $20 billion. See Figure 2-B "Preliminary Treasury Estimates of the Impact of TARP Programs and Other Treasury Investments in AIG on the Federal Budget" in Section 2 – Executive Summary, page 4.

E. Exit Strategy and Wind Down

Final purchase authority to make commitments under TARP expired on October 3, 2010. This means no new commitments to invest funds can be made. The Department of the Treasury will continue to wind down TARP and manage the remaining TARP investments prudently in order to recover as much of taxpayers' funds as possible.

1. TARP Investments

As of September 30, 2010, Treasury has approximately $184 billion in TARP investments and commitments outstanding, in over 600 banks, the automotive industry, AIG, the Public Private Investment Program funds and the purchased SBA 7(a) securities[1], but exclusive of the housing initiatives. Treasury intends to recover or dispose of these investments as soon as practicable. But generally, Treasury cannot demand repayment, so recovery requires that the institutions replace government support with private capital. This means that the timing of repayments by various institutions will differ, as will the times when the various TARP programs terminate. For example, under the bank capital support programs, some financial institutions are thriving and have the ability to repay Treasury now or in the very near future. Other institutions will need more time to recover and repay Treasury, as expected given the uneven impact of this financial crisis. Exit from the largest remaining investments – which are in the automotive industry and AIG – will also take time in order to protect the returns for the taxpayer.

In most cases, the TARP investment is in the form of non-voting preferred stock, for which Treasury cannot demand repayment. In certain cases, Treasury owns common stock: in GM (61 percent of the outstanding shares) – for which an initial public offering is expected before year-end; Ally Financial (formerly GMAC, 56 percent); Chrysler (9 percent); and Citigroup (12.4 percent as of September 30, 2010). Upon consummation of the restructuring plan for AIG announced on September 30, 2010, Treasury will be the majority shareholder of AIG.

2. Housing Initiatives

In this next phase of TARP, Treasury will also complete the implementation of the housing initiatives. HAMP, the principal TARP housing program, is designed so that most funds are disbursed over a five year period, on a "pay for success" basis. This ensures that taxpayer dollars are used only as long as mortgage modifications remain in effect and borrowers continue to fulfill their responsibilities.

Servicers that participate in HAMP can continue to make mortgage modifications through the end of 2012. The HFA Hardest Hit Fund permits participating state housing agencies to provide support through their programs until as late as 2017, depending on available funding. And the FHA Short Refinance program is designed to enable homeowners to refinance their mortgage loans and reduce their overall mortgage debt through the end of 2012. In much the same way that HAMP's first lien modification program has provided a national blueprint for mortgage modifications, these new programs will continue to reshape the mortgage servicing industry and promote industry standardization of short sale, refinance and principal reduction programs. However, their cost cannot exceed—and may be less than—the $46 billion allocated.

F. Financial Regulatory Reform

The actions taken to combat the financial crisis were, in part, the result of a fundamental failure of the structure of financial regulation. Regulators did not have the tools to break apart or wind down a failing financial firm without putting the entire financial system at risk. The FDIC's resolution authority was limited to insured depository institutions and did not include their holding companies. Without changes to the system, there is a risk that TARP and other government actions had created "moral hazard". That is, because the federal government stepped in to provide assistance, the private sector may assume federal government support will be there if they again cause a systemic risk to our financial system. Therefore, beginning in 2009, the Obama Administration fought to pass a comprehensive financial reform law to rein in excessive risk in our financial system so that we will not have to again resort to a TARP like program. In July this year, Congress passed and President Obama signed into law the comprehensive financial reform legislation, the DoddFrank-Wall Street Reform and Consumer Protection Act of 2010. The rules to implement the Dodd-Frank Act are currently being written. Among other things, the legislation will:

- Give the federal government the authority to shut down and break apart large non-bank financial firms whose imminent failure might threaten the broader system;
- Put in place a Consumer Financial Protection Bureau to promote transparency and consumer choice, and to prevent abusive and deceptive practices;
- Give financial regulators the tools they need to collect data and analyze risk in the entire financial system, beyond individual firms and markets, and to identify and curb reckless risk -taking, so that we can help prevent future crises; and

- Create a safer, more transparent derivatives market.

4. Stabilization of the Financial Markets

"There is broad consensus that the TARP was an important part of a broader government strategy that stabilized the U.S. financial system by renewing the flow of credit and averting a more acute crisis…it eventually proved decisive enough to stop the panic and restore market confidence."
>   -Congressional Oversight Panel, "Taking Stock: What Has the Troubled Asset Relief Program Achieved?", (December 2009), page 4.

A. TARP Contributed to Financial Stability

The Troubled Asset Relief Program has succeeded—faster, and at a much lower cost, than expected. TARP has played a critical role in helping to stabilize the financial system and in putting the economy in a better position to confront the challenges that lie ahead. Emergency government programs helped to stabilize financial markets by rebuilding confidence in our financial system, making it possible for U.S. homeowners, consumers, and businesses to borrow at lower costs and the U.S. to recover more rapidly from a severe recession. Financial market data shows that conditions have significantly improved since the fall of 2008.

- Fear that our major financial institutions could fail has receded.
- Credit markets important to consumers and small businesses have reopened.
- Businesses are able to raise record amounts of capital in private markets.
- Mortgage rates have been brought down to historical lows.
- Municipalities are able to borrow at historically low rates.

While substantial progress has been made, our economy still has a long way to go to get back to normal. Unemployment is unacceptably high and the housing market has not yet stabilized. In the banking system, charge-offs for residential, consumer, and commercial loans are still high, and the FDIC projects that the rate of bank failures will remain high for some time. Despite offering relatively low borrowing costs, banks continue to report falling loan balances. This reflects the fact that we have endured a difficult recession and many borrowers and lenders are reducing debt after a period of aggressive growth in leverage. But it means that many responsible consumers and businesses are still finding it difficult to get new credit.

Nevertheless, thanks to the coordinated and forceful actions of Congress, the Obama Administration, the Federal Reserve, the FDIC, and other regulatory agencies, the U.S. financial system is much stronger today than it was in the fall of 2008 and early 2009.

1. TARP Restored Confidence In The Financial System, Lowering Borrowing Costs For Businesses, Homeowners, And Municipalities

The primary purpose of TARP was to restore the liquidity and stability of our financial system. That system plays a critical role in our economy, for example, by helping businesses raise funds and pay employees, providing consumers with convenient forms of credit, financing education, and allowing millions of Americans to own homes.

In September 2008, banks were not making new loans to businesses, or even to one another. Businesses could not get financing in our capital markets. Municipalities and state governments could not issue bonds at reasonable rates. The securitization markets—which provide financing for credit cards, student loans, auto loans and other consumer financing— had basically stopped functioning.

TARP provided the buffer that the system needed. In conjunction with the "stress tests" of our major banks, it helped force the system to raise private capital. And more broadly TARP provided a backstop that allowed the credit markets to start working again.

Figure 4-A shows bank borrowing costs relative to Treasury borrowing cost over the course of the crisis. During the financial crisis in 2008, there was a drastic spike in cost of bank borrowing costs, followed by an improved, lower cost of borrowing after implementation of the TARP and the Obama Administration's Financial Stability Plan.

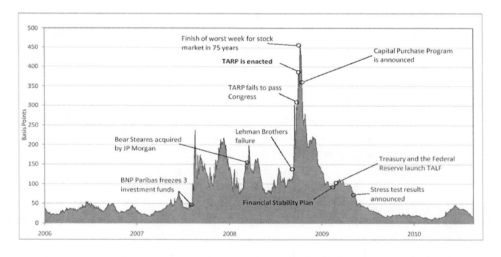

Figure 4-A. Spread Between Inter-Bank Deposit Rates and Yields on Short-term Treasury Bills

Figure 4-B.

Following the passage of TARP and the announcement or implementation of TARP programs, borrowing costs declined for many businesses, homeowners, and municipalities. Investment-grade corporate bond spreads fell by almost 70 percent in 2009. Yields on high quality municipal bond rates fell to three percent in 2009, down from five percent in fall 2008. That translated into real savings for Americans and enabled our economy to begin to recover.

2. Lower Borrowing Costs Have Allowed Businesses To Tap Private Funding Sources And Major Financial Institutions To Recapitalize With Private Funds

As borrowing costs have come down, businesses have raised substantial capital from private sources in 2009 and 2010. Corporations, for example, raised over $1 trillion in investment-grade debt and over $180 billion in high-yield debt in 2009. While much of the new issuance in early 2009 was supported by government guarantees, private investors funded most new corporate debt without public support in late 2009 and in 2010. Nearly 50 percent of new issuance was guaranteed by the government in January 2009. No new issuance has been government guaranteed in 2010.

The overall strength in the funding markets has continued into 2010. The pace of high yield issuance so far this year is actually higher than in 2009.

It is important to note that, banks managed to raise substantial private capital following the release of the results from the federal government "stress test" of major U.S. financial institutions. In the months after the results were released, banks issued over $100 billion in new common equity. As a result, the U.S. banking system is much better capitalized today

3. Securitization Markets Have Come Back To Life As A Result Of TALF And Other Initiatives

Securitization markets that provide important channels of credit for consumers and small businesses have also improved, in large part because of programs launched under the TARP. Announcements about the Term Asset-Backed Securities Loan Facility (TALF) helped narrow spreads in these markets even before the program began operating. In 2009, spreads on TALF-eligible asset-backed securities (ABS) fell back to pre-crisis levels and spreads on non-TALF-eligible ABS were down more than 90 percent from their peaks in the fall of 2008. Since the government launched TALF in March 2009, issuance of ABS backed by consumer and business loans have averaged $12 billion per month, compared to less than $2 billion per month in the six months prior to the program's launch. And as with corporate bonds, new issuance in the ABS market has shifted from public support to purely private financing.

Prices for impaired securities that constrain bank lending also improved significantly starting in 2009. This was due in part to general market improvement and in part to announcements for the Public Private Investment Program, which was designed to remove these securities from banks. Most of the Public Private Investment Funds were formed by the end of 2009 and had started to purchase legacy securities. Since the announcement of PPIP in March 2009, prices of benchmark indices for the non -agency residential mortgage backed securities and commercial mortgage backed securities have appreciated between 60 percent and 100 percent. These positive developments reduced the need for PPIP at the levels originally contemplated.

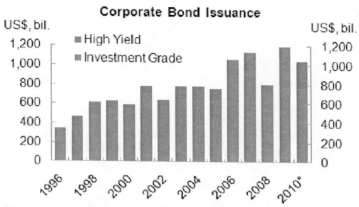

Figure 4-C.

4. Housing Markets Stabilized To Some Degree

Following the implementation of TARP, housing markets began showing some signs of stabilizing and wealth recovery, which should stimulate consumer spending – vital to American economic growth. Thanks in part to federal government financial policies, mortgage rates remain near historic lows. Home prices stabilized in March 2009, following consistent declines since 2006. For example, the S&P/Case -Shiller U.S. 20-City Composite Home Price Index experienced a 3 percent year-to-year increase in July, compared to a 19 percent year-to-year decline in March 2009.

The Obama Administration's housing initiatives under TARP were intended to help prevent avoidable foreclosures and stabilize the housing market. Eighteen months into the HAMP program, over 1.3 million homeowners have seen their monthly mortgage payments reduced to affordable levels, including over 460,000 who are in permanent modifications.

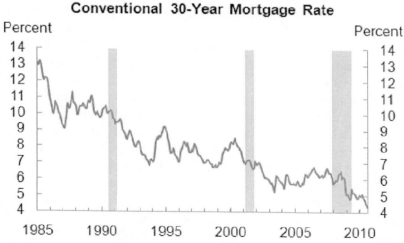

Source:Federal Reserve

Figure 4-D.

The TARP housing initiatives have also spurred mortgage servicers to adopt similar programs, enhancing their capacity to engage with homeowners to modify mortgages and provide additional solutions to avoid foreclosure. This has helped millions more homeowners at no cost to the taxpayer.

5. *The Investments In The Automotive Industry And AIG Accomplished Their Purpose-- They Were Critical To Maintaining Financial Stability*

The Bush Administration provided loans to GM and Chrysler in December 2008 to avoid uncontrolled liquidations in the industry that could have resulted in millions of job losses. The Obama Administration provided additional assistance to GM and Chrysler on the condition that those companies would fundamentally restructure their businesses. In the 14 months since GM and Chrysler emerged from bankruptcy, the auto industry has increased employment by 62,100 jobs and is much stronger. Some TARP funds have already been returned, and GM is poised for an initial public offering, which will allow the government to begin selling down its TARP investment.

Before the crisis there was insufficient regulation and oversight of AIG, and none of the government agencies with supervisory authority had a mechanism to provide for the orderly unwinding, dismantling, sale, or liquidation of a global, nonbank-financial institution like AIG. But, today, the risks to our economy posed by AIG have been reduced. On September 30, 2010, AIG and the government announced a restructuring plan that will accelerate the government's exit and puts us in a stronger position to recover taxpayers' investments.

B. TARP Was Part of the Government's Coordinated Efforts

As credit conditions have improved, the U.S. economy has stopped contracting and started to grow again. The number of jobs is also growing, although at a slow pace. After four consecutive quarters of negative growth, the economy expanded at an annual rate of 1.6 percent in the third quarter of 2009 and has continued to grow since. The unemployment rate has fallen from a peak of 10.1 percent in October 2009 to 9.6 percent in August.

Economic experts Alan Blinder and Mark Zandi[2] find that TARP has been a substantial success in helping the economy snap back more rapidly than would be expected from early 2009 when the U.S. was suffering a severe economic downturn. Blinder and Zandi estimate that without government intervention U.S. real GDP would have fallen roughly three times what we actually experienced, and the unemployment rate would have peaked at 16.5 percent.

C. Challenges Lie Ahead to Achieving a Full Recovery

The financial and economic recovery still faces significant headwinds. TARP and the broader response to the financial crisis have been successful in critical ways. Those policies have contained the most significant financial crisis our country has faced since the Great Depression. But the economy has a long way to go to recover fully from the deep contraction generated by the crisis.

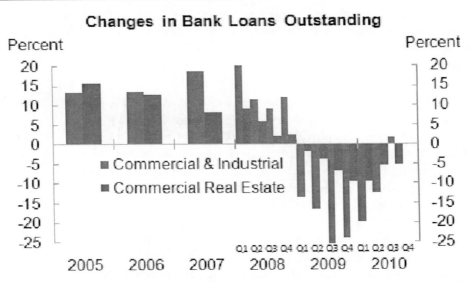

Source:Federal Reserve Assets and Liabilitiesof Banks (H.8). Note:Adjustedfor merger activity and accountingchanges

Figure 4-E.

The contraction in many categories of bank lending reflects a combination of persistent weak demand for credit and tight lending standards at the banks, amidst continued pressure on many bank balance sheets, particularly from commercial mortgage losses. Bank lending continues to contract overall, although the pace of contraction has moderated and some categories of lending are growing again. For example, commercial and industrial loans contracted at an annual rate of 27 percent in the third quarter of 2009, but they expanded in the third quarter of 2010. Such loans are particularly important for small businesses, which generally cannot raise money by issuing debt in securities markets.

Although RealtyTrac reports that July 2010 foreclosure activity was 10 percent lower than in July 2009, foreclosures were still up nearly 20 percent since July 2008, and July 2010 marked the seventeenth consecutive month of foreclosure activity exceeding 300,000 filings.

5. TARP INVESTMENT PROGRAM DESCRIPTIONS

A. Capital Purchase Program

EESA was originally proposed as a means to buy mortgage loans, mortgage-backed securities and certain other assets from banks. However, the authorities granted under EESA were broadened in the legislative process to cover any financial instrument whose purchase the Secretary of the Treasury, after consultation with the Chairman of the Federal Reserve, determines necessary to promote financial market stability. Shortly following passage of EESA, lending even between banks had practically stopped, credit markets had shut down, and many financial institutions were facing severe stress. Given the high level of uncertainty in financial markets and the economy, even strong financial institutions began to hoard capital. There was not sufficient time to implement a program to buy mortgage related assets, which posed difficulties related to valuing such assets and getting the holders of such assets to sell them at current prices. Based on market indicators, it became clear that financial institutions needed additional capital to sustain a normal flow of credit to businesses and consumers during the financial turmoil and economic downturn. In this context, immediate capital injections into financial institutions were a necessary step to avert a potential collapse of the system.

As a result, Treasury launched the Capital Purchase Program (CPP), the largest and most significant program under EESA, on October 14, 2008. Treasury initially committed over a third of the total TARP funding, $250 billion, to the CPP, which was later lowered to $218 billion in March 2009. At the close of the program, Treasury had invested approximately $205 billion under the Capital Purchase Program.

1. Program and Goals

The Capital Purchase Program was designed to bolster the capital position of viable institutions of all sizes and, in doing so, to build confidence in these institutions and the financial system as a whole. With the additional capital, CPP participants were better equipped to undertake new lending and continue to provide other services to consumers and businesses, even while absorbing writedowns and charge-offs on loans that were not performing.

Of the $250 billion in total possible commitments, Treasury invested $125 billion in eight of the country's largest financial institutions.[3] The remaining $125 billion was made available to qualifying financial institutions (QFIs) of all sizes and types across the country, including banks, savings and loan associations, bank holding companies and savings and loan holding companies. QFIs interested in participating in the program had to submit an application to their primary federal banking regulator. The minimum subscription amount available to a participating institution was one percent of risk -weighted assets. The maximum subscription amount was the lesser of $25 billion or three percent of riskweighted-assets.

In the months following announcement of the Capital Purchase Program, Treasury provided $205 billion in capital to 707 institutions in 48 states, including more than 450 small and community banks and 22 certified community development financial institutions (CDFIs) (see chart 5-A below). The largest investment was $25 billion and the smallest was $301,000. The final investment under the CPP was made in December 2009.

The CPP funds were not given as grants. Treasury received preferred stock or debt securities in exchange for these investments. There is no fixed date on which the banks must redeem the preferred stock—or repay Treasury. This is necessary for the investment to qualify as "Tier 1" capital under regulatory requirements. However, there are incentives for the banks to repay.[4] Institutions may repay Treasury after consultation with the appropriate federal regulator. To date, Treasury has received approximately $152 billion in CPP repayments.

Most banks participating in the Capital Purchase Program pay Treasury a dividend rate of five percent per year, which will increase to nine percent a year after the first five years. In the case of Subchapter S -corporations, Treasury acquires subordinated debentures. The subordinated debenture interest rate is 7.7 percent per year for the first five years and 13.8 percent thereafter; however, the total amount of S -corporation dividends payable per year is less than $40 million. To date, Treasury has received approximately $10 billion in CPP dividends and interest and $3 billion in other income from the sale of Citigroup common stock (in excess of the recovered principal amount).

Treasury also received warrants to purchase common shares or other securities from the banks at the time of the CPP investment. The purpose of the additional securities is to provide opportunities for taxpayers to reap additional returns on their investments as banks recover. To date, Treasury has received more than $8 billion in proceeds from the sale of CPP and TIP warrants. See page 32 for a description of the warrants and their sale by Treasury.

a. Role of bank regulators

Many have asked how Treasury decided which banks would receive funds. The program was open to all institutions and a process was established to ensure decisions were made in a fair, impartial and consistent manner. The process also helped ensure that the program fulfilled Treasury's statutory responsibilities to promote financial stability and protect the taxpayer. The process required that a QFI apply to the federal agency that is its primary regulator—the Federal Reserve, the FDIC, the Office of the Comptroller of the Currency or the Office of Thrift Supervision. The application had to receive the positive recommendation of the regulator.

The regulators are most familiar with these institutions because they perform periodic safety and soundness examinations that include detailed analyses of the banks' overall financial conditions and operations, e.g., capital, assets, management, earnings, liquidity, and sensitivity to market risk. Regulators also examine the institutions for compliance with applicable laws and regulations.

Nonetheless, Treasury did not defer entirely to the regulators. Treasury conducted its own review of every application that received a positive funding recommendation from the regulators. Treasury staff reviewed the successful applications and presented them to an internal TARP investment committee, which in turn made recommendations to the Assistant Secretary for Financial Stability for a final decision. This process was critical to ensuring objective decision making. The Special Inspector General for TARP did an extensive review of the process and concluded in its August 2009 report that that it was "a mostly clear process enhanced by multiple reviews and control mechanisms".

b. Small Institutions

The Capital Purchase Program is often characterized as a "big bank" program and many people erroneously believe that small institutions did not benefit from this program. In fact, smaller financial institutions make up the vast majority of participants in the CPP. Of the 707 applications approved and funded by Treasury through the Capital Purchase Program by the time it closed on December 31, 2009, 473 or 67 percent were institutions with less than $1 billion in assets.

Treasury recognized that, to allow small institutions to participate in CPP, the program would need to accommodate more than one corporate structure. To that end, Treasury prepared CPP transactional documents for private institutions, mutual organizations, and S-corporations in addition to the documents for publicly traded institutions. The variety of documents addressed the structural complexity of including large and small institutions.

The rate at which applications were submitted declined rapidly in early 2009 and over 650 banks withdrew new applications. Several reasons have been cited for this. One was that in February 2009, Congress adopted more restrictive executive compensation requirements on all TARP recipients. A second was that many banks felt there was a stigma associated with participation in the program. A third was that the severity of the crisis had lessened somewhat.

In May 2009, after many larger institutions started raising capital from the private debt and equity markets, Treasury re-opened the CPP application window for institutions with less than $500 million in assets. This initiative gave smaller institutions, which did not have the same access to the capital markets as larger institutions, an opportunity to receive additional CPP investments, and Treasury increased the amount of capital available to smaller institutions under the program. Originally, institutions were eligible for a CPP capital investment that represented up to three percent of risk -weighted assets. Upon re-opening the CPP for smaller institutions, Treasury raised the amount of funds available to five percent of riskweighted - assets, and did not require additional warrants for the incremental investment.

The chart below indicates the asset size of the banks participating in the Capital Purchase Program.

C. Tarp Bank Investments Were Structured As Non-Voting Preferred Stock, Which Provided Crucial Capital Support Without Creating Government Control

As described in Section 3 on page 10, in 2008 Treasury decided that the most effective way to try to stabilize the nation's financial system was to provide capital to banks. The vast majority of TARP investments were made in the form of nonvoting-preferred stock. In order to achieve the objective of providing capital support, and meet bank regulatory requirements for Tier 1 capital, TARP could not require that a bank repay Treasury at a fixed date, as one would with a loan.

Preferred stock generally is nonvoting (except in limited circumstances), while common stock has full voting rights. Therefore, most TARP investments are nonvoting. The preferred stock does not entitle Treasury to board seats or board observers, except in the event dividends are not paid for six quarters, in which case Treasury has the right to elect two directors to the board.

2. Status as of September 2010

A. Repayments – Getting Tarp Funds Back

Banks may repay Treasury under the conditions established in the purchase agreements as amended by the ARRA. Treasury also has the right to sell the securities. However, Treasury does not have the right to force repayment. The repayment price is equal to what Treasury paid for the shares, plus any unpaid dividends or interest.

CPP Initial Investment Profile ($ in billions)				
	CPP Participants		Investment	
Asset Range*	Number	Percent	Amount	Percent
<$1bn	473	66.9%	3.8	1.9%
$1bn -$10bn	177	25.0%	10.0	4.9%
>$10bn	57	8.1%	191.1	93.3%
Total	707	100%	204.9	100%

Source: SNL Financial; Treasury

Figure 5-A.

As of September 30, 2010, Treasury has received over $152 billion in CPP repayments. Of that amount, approximately $13.4 billion of repayments is from the sales of Citigroup common stock through September 30, 2010.

B. Returns For Taxpayers

1) Dividend and interest payments

As is typical for a preferred stock investment, banks must decide whether to pay the dividends; they can elect instead to conserve their capital. Treasury received "cumulative" dividends where permitted by applicable regulation. That is, if the dividends are not paid in any quarter, they are added to the liquidation preference, thus increasing the claim of the holder of the preferred. In other cases, the dividends were "noncumulative". CPP participants are allowed to make dividend payments with the approval of their primary federal regulator. But if a bank fails to pay dividends for six quarterly periods, Treasury has the right to appoint two directors to the bank's board.

As of September 30, 2010, total dividends and interest received from Capital Purchase Program investments is approximately $10 billion. In addition, the sales of Citigroup common stock through September 30, 2010 have generated $3 billion of income (in excess of the recovered principal amount of the Citigroup investment referred to above).

2) Overall returns

The CPP was a success not only in stabilizing the financial system. It will also generate a positive return to taxpayers, as will the bank support programs (Capital Purchase Program, Targeted Investment Program and Asset Guarantee Program) taken as a whole. Currently, Treasury estimates that the net gain for all three programs combined will be $16 billion. This is only an estimate and it will depend on several factors, including market conditions and performance of individual companies. Some initial observers of the CPP investments were critical, for example, that Treasury overpaid to make the investments in eight of the nation's largest financial institutions and/or that the institutions would not be able to repay. In fact, all of those institutions have repaid the government in full with the exception of Citigroup where part of the investment is in the form of common stock which the government is currently in the process of selling. In that case, the government expects to complete its exit by early next year. For the seven institutions which have fully repaid, our internal rate of return on a combined basis was 11 percent. We have also realized a gain on our Citigroup sales to date and expect to realize a gain overall based on the current market price.

3) Certain institutions; missed payments and appointment of directors

The returns realized from investments in the Capital Purchase Program will be partially offset by losses on investments in certain institutions. As of September 30, 2010, five institutions have been declared bankrupt or had their banking subsidiary placed in receivership (CIT Group Inc., UCBH Holdings, Inc., Midwest Banc Holdings, Inc., Sonoma Valley Bancorp, and Pacific Coast National Bancorp), which represent a total investment of $2.73 billion. To date, together with the $242 million of realized discount on sales, as described later in this chapter, losses on investments are approximately $3 billion.

For the quarterly dividend payment due in August 2010, 123 institutions missed payments[5], consisting of 96 cumulative dividend payments (approximately $41.5 million), 19 noncumulative-dividend payments (approximately $1.8 million), and eight S-corporation interest payments (approximately $1.6 million). To date, 21 banks have missed four payments, 15 banks have missed five, six banks have missed six, and one bank has missed seven.

Treasury has released guidance on the exercise of its contractual right to nominate members to an institution's board of directors. Directors cannot be government employees and by law they must act in the interests of all shareholders, not as Treasury's or the taxpayers' representative. Treasury will prioritize banks in part based on whether its investment exceeds $25 million. In addition, Treasury will seek a bank's permission to have an observer attend board meetings once an institution misses five dividends. The observers can be government employees. This proactive step will help Treasury determine where the appointment of directors would be most effective. If the right to nominate members to a board of directors of a bank becomes exercisable, Treasury will determine whether to nominate up to two members based on an evaluation of the condition of the institution and the functioning of its board of directors.

4) Exchanges and restructurings – to preserve value and protect taxpayer Interests

In limited cases, in order to protect the taxpayers' interest in the value of a CPP investment and to promote financial stability, Treasury may exchange the CPP preferred stock for other securities. Treasury evaluates whether to participate in an exchange of the CPP preferred stock on the basis of enabling the bank to get new investors to provide additional capital, to conduct a capital restructuring or to strengthen its capital position and financial condition. Exchanges made on this basis may be at a rate less than par, and sales by Treasury to a new investor may be made at a discount. Treasury has described the considerations for evaluating exchanges and restructurings in the Agency Financial Report for FY2009, page 41.

c. Use of funds by banks participating in the Capital Purchase Program

Treasury worked with the Office of the Special Inspector General for the Troubled Asset Relief Program (SIGTARP) on a Use of Capital Survey. The scope of the annual Use of Capital Survey covers lending, financial intermediation, and capital building activities of each financial institution after the investment of funds under the CPP from the date the funds were initially received until the end of the fourth quarter 2009. Treasury sent the Use of Capital Survey to CPP participants in March 2010, and received survey responses from the majority of CPP participants. Treasury posted all submitted surveys from individual CPP recipients and published the names of the financial institutions that failed to submit a survey response to Treasury, on the FinancialStability.gov website. Additionally, Treasury posted a summary of quantitative data (summary balance sheet and income statement information from each institution's regulatory filings) for each individual CPP recipient on the FinancialStability.gov website.

d. Comparative lending by CPP banks

The capital that remains in place at many small and medium-sized banks is facilitating new lending while they absorb losses from legacy assets. Indeed, at banks with less than $1 billion in assets that received TARP capital, median total loans have grown 3.3 percent since 2008Q3, compared with 1.6 percent for comparably-sized institutions that did not receive

TARP funds. The difference is even larger for commercial and industrial loans, and for commercial real estate loans, which are especially important for small businesses.

B. Supervisory Capital Assessment Program ("Stress Test") and Capital Assistance Program

While the investments made under the Capital Purchase Program helped prevent a collapse, Treasury also focused on how to recapitalize the system with private capital, so that government support could be paid back. But in late 2008 and early 2009 confidence in our financial system had been severely eroded; investors questioned whether institutions were healthy enough to survive, and doubted whether many institutions really knew their true condition. Therefore, a critical part of the Financial Stability Plan announced by the Obama Administration was to conduct a "stress test" on the major banks to determine their health, and to do so in an open and transparent manner so that the market would know which banks needed more capital. In conjunction with this forward-looking test, Treasury announced that it would provide capital under TARP through the Capital Assistance Program (CAP) to banks that needed additional capital but were unable to raise it through private sources.

1. Program and Goals

In early 2009, Treasury worked with the Federal banking agencies to develop the one-time, forward -looking assessment or "stress test"—known as the **Supervisory Capital Assessment Program (SCAP)**—on the nineteen largest U.S. bank holding companies (BHCs). The design of the tests and their results were made public, a novel step that was taken because of the unprecedented need to restore confidence. By identifying and quantifying potential capital shortfalls and requiring that additional capital be raised to eliminate any deficiencies, the SCAP ensured that these financial institutions would have sufficient capital to sustain their role as intermediaries and continue to provide loans to creditworthy borrowers even if economic conditions suffered a severe and extended deterioration.

The stress test found that nine of the largest bank holding companies had adequate capital to withstand more severe economic conditions. Of the ten bank holding companies that were identified as needing to raise more capital, nine met or exceeded the capital raising requirements through private efforts. Only one institution, Ally Financial (formerly GMAC), required additional funds under TARP to meet its SCAP requirements, which was provided through the Automotive Industry Financing Program, not CAP.

2. Status as of September 2010

Since the results of the SCAP were released in May 2009, in the aggregate, the stress test firms have increased requisite capital by over $150 billion. Importantly, that capital raising has enabled more than 80 banks to repay the TARP investments made by Treasury.

The Capital Assistance Program was offered to all banks and QFIs, not solely to those banks that underwent the SCAP. Another measure of the effectiveness of SCAP and the CPP, as well as other government efforts, is that Treasury did not receive any applications for CAP which terminated on November 9, 2009.

C. Targeted Investment Program

Treasury established the Targeted Investment Program (TIP) in December 2008. The program gave the Treasury the necessary flexibility to provide additional or new funding to financial institutions that were critical to the functioning of the financial system. The TIP was considered "exceptional assistance" for purposes of executive compensation requirements (see Section 7).

1. Program and Goals

Through the Targeted Investment Program, Treasury sought to prevent a loss of confidence in critical financial institutions, which could result in significant financial market disruptions, threaten the financial strength of similarly situated financial institutions, impair broader financial markets, and undermine the overall economy. Eligibility to participate in the TIP was determined on a case-by-case basis, and depended on a number of factors. Treasury considered, among other things:

- The extent to which the failure of an institution could threaten the viability of its creditors and counterparties because of their direct exposures to the institution;
- The number and size of financial institutions that are perceived or known by investors or counterparties as similarly situated to the failing institution, or that would otherwise be likely to experience indirect contagion effects from the failure of the institution;
- Whether the institution is sufficiently important to the nation's financial and economic system that a disorderly failure would, with a high probability, cause major disruptions to credit markets or payments and settlement systems, seriously destabilize key asset prices, or significantly increase uncertainty or loss of confidence, thereby materially weakening overall economic performance; and
- The extent and probability of the institution's ability to access alternative sources of capital and liquidity, whether from the private sector or other sources of government funds.

Treasury invested $20 billion in each of Bank of America and Citigroup under the Targeted Investment Program, which investments were in addition to those that the banks received under the CPP. Like the Capital Purchase Program, Treasury invested in preferred stock, and received warrants to purchase common stock in the institutions. However, the TIP investments provided for annual dividends of eight percent, which was higher than the CPP rate, and also imposed greater reporting requirements and more onerous terms on the companies than under the CPP terms, including restricting dividends to $0.01 per share per quarter, restrictions on executive compensation, restrictions on corporate expenses, and other measures.

2. Status as of September 2010

In December 2009, both participating institutions repaid their TIP investments in full, with dividends. Total dividends received from Targeted Investment Program investments was $3 billion. Treasury also received warrants from each bank which provide the taxpayer with additional gain on the investments. As a consequence, the program is closed and resulted in a positive return for taxpayers.

D. Asset Guarantee Program

1. Program and Goals

Under the Asset Guarantee Program (AGP), Treasury acted to support the value of certain assets held by qualifying financial institutions, by agreeing to absorb a portion of the losses on those assets. The program was conducted jointly by Treasury, the Federal Reserve and the FDIC. Like the Targeted Investment Program, it was designed for financial institutions whose failure could harm the financial system and reduce the potential for "spillover" to the broader financial system and economy. More specifically, the Asset Guarantee Program was used to help certain financial institutions facing a potential loss of market confidence due in large part to their holdings of distressed or illiquid assets. By helping to limit the institution's exposure to losses on illiquid or distressed assets, the Asset Guarantee Program helped the institution maintain the confidence of depositors and other funding sources and continue to meet the credit needs of households and businesses. The AGP was used in a limited fashion to assist Bank of America and Citigroup in conjunction with the Targeted Investment Program investments in those institutions.

a. Bank of America

In January 2009, Treasury, the Federal Reserve and the FDIC agreed in principle to share potential losses on a $118 billion pool of financial instruments owned by Bank of America, consisting of securities backed by residential and commercial real estate loans and corporate debt and derivative transactions that reference such securities, loans and associated hedges. If the arrangement had been finalized, Treasury and the FDIC would have received preferred stock and warrants as a premium for the guarantee. The announcement of the transaction (and the Citigroup transaction discussed below) was widely welcomed by the markets and contributed immediately to helping restore investor confidence in the financial institution and the banking system generally. In May 2009, before the transaction was finalized, Bank of America announced its intention to terminate negotiations with respect to the losssharing - arrangement and in September 2009, the government and Bank of America entered into a termination agreement. Bank of America agreed to pay a termination fee of $425 million to the government, $276 million of which went to Treasury. The fee compensated the government for the value that Bank of America had received from the announcement of the government's willingness to guarantee and share losses on the pool of assets from and after the date of the term sheet. The termination fee was determined by reference to the fees that would have been payable had the guarantee been finalized. No claims for loss payments were made to the government, nor were any TARP or other funds spent. Thus, the fee is a net gain to the taxpayer.

b. Citigroup

In January 2009, Treasury, the Federal Reserve and the FDIC similarly agreed to share potential losses on a $301 billion pool of Citigroup's covered assets. The arrangement was finalized and, as a premium for the guarantee, Treasury and the FDIC received $7.1 billion of preferred stock, with terms that were similar to those in the TIP investment and more onerous than in the CPP, including a dividend rate of eight percent. Treasury also received warrants to purchase 66.5 million shares of common stock. Although the guarantee was originally designed to be in place for five to ten years, Citigroup requested that it be terminated in December 2009 in conjunction with Citigroup's repayment of the $20 billion TIP investment. This was because Citigroup's financial condition had improved and the bank raised over $20 billion of private capital. The banking regulators approved this request.

In connection with the termination, Treasury and the FDIC kept most of the premium paid. That is, the government retained a total of $5.3 billion of the $7.1 billion of preferred stock (which had since been converted to trust preferred securities). Of this amount, Treasury retained $2.23 billion, and the FDIC and Treasury agreed that, subject to certain conditions, the FDIC would transfer up to $800 million of trust preferred securities to Treasury at the close of Citigroup's participation in the FDIC's Temporary Liquidity Guarantee Program.

For the period that the Citigroup asset guarantee was outstanding prior to termination in December 2009, Citigroup made no claims for loss payments to the government, and consequently Treasury made no guarantee payments of TARP funds to Citigroup. Thus, all payments received to date, and the income received from the sale of the securities described above, will constitute a net gain to the taxpayer. As of September 30, 2010, total dividends received from the securities were approximately $440 million. On September 30, 2010, Treasury sold the trust preferred securities for proceeds of approximately $2.25 billion. Treasury still holds its Citigroup warrants and expects to receive another $800 million in trust preferred securities from the FDIC, both of which should provide the taxpayer with an additional gain.

2. Status as of September 2010

The Asset Guarantee Program is now closed. No payments were made. The fee from Bank of America, and securities and dividends received from Citigroup, will result in a positive return for taxpayers.

E. Warrant Dispositions

1. Program and Goals

As required by EESA, Treasury received warrants from TARP banks to provide taxpayers with an additional return on the government's investment. For each CPP and TIP investment in a publicly traded company, Treasury received warrants to purchase, at a fixed exercise price, shares of common stock equal to 15 percent of the aggregate liquidation preference of the senior preferred investment. The per share exercise price was set at the 20-trading day trailing average of the bank's common stock price as of the time it was given preliminary approval for the TARP investment.

The warrants may be exercised at any time over a ten year period. These public warrants include certain customary anti-dilution provisions to protect their value to Treasury in the event the company issues more stock or takes certain other actions. For CPP investments in a privately-held company, an S -corporation, or certain mutual institutions, Treasury received warrants to purchase, at a nominal cost, additional preferred stock (these securities are referred to as "warrant preferreds") or subordinated debentures (these securities are referred to as "warrant sub debt") equivalent to five percent of the aggregate liquidation preference of the primary CPP investment. These warrant preferreds and warrant sub debt securities pay a higher dividend or interest rate than the primary CPP investment. Treasury immediately exercised these kinds of warrants at the closings of the investments.

Upon repaying its TARP preferred stock investment, a financial institution may repurchase its warrants at an agreed upon fair market value. In all cases, Treasury follows a consistent evaluation process to ensure that taxpayers receive fair market values for the warrants. If an institution decides not to repurchase its warrants, Treasury has the contractual right to sell the warrants. Treasury has followed a policy of disposing of warrants as soon as practicable if no agreement is reached on a repurchase. Thus far, Treasury has utilized a modified Dutch public auction methodology to dispose of warrants that are not repurchased by the bank.

2. Status as of September 2010

To date, the disposition of warrants has succeeded in significantly increasing taxpayer returns on the Capital Purchase Program and Targeted Investment Program preferred investments that have been repaid. As of September 30, 2010, Treasury has received more than $8 billion in gross proceeds from the disposition of warrants associated with 58 CPP investments and one (1) TIP investment, consisting of approximately (i) $3 billion from issuer repurchases at agreed upon fair market values and (ii) $5 billion from auctions. In the auctions, clearing prices have been set through robust competition among large numbers of bidders. For those investments, which represent approximately $140 billion in capital, Treasury has received an absolute return of 4.2 percent from dividends and an added 5 percent return from the sale of the warrants for a total absolute return of 9.2 percent. For the $20 billion TIP investment in Bank of America Corporation, Treasury received an internal rate of return of 15.3 percent. These returns are not predictive of the eventual returns on the entire CPP and TIP portfolios.

Treasury has released two semi-annual Warrant Disposition Reports that provide additional information regarding the disposition process and the results of the warrant sales. The reports can be found on our website at www.FinancialStability.gov/latest/reportsanddocs.html.

F. Community Development Capital Initiative

Communities underserved by traditional banks and financial services providers have found it more difficult to obtain credit in the current economic environment. Community Development Financial Institutions (CDFIs) exist to provide financing to these communities. CDFIs offer a wide range of traditional and innovative financial products and services designed to help their customers access the financial system, build wealth and improve their lives and the communities in which they live. In particular, CDFIs focus on providing financial services to low -and moderate -income, minority, and other underserved communities. CDFIs are certified by Treasury's CDFI Fund, which was created for the purpose of promoting economic revitalization and community development in lowincome - communities.

1. Program and Goals

Most CDFIs have been adversely affected by the financial crisis. Treasury launched the Community Development Capital Initiative to help viable certified CDFIs and the communities they serve cope with effects of the financial crisis.

Under this program, CDFI banks and thrifts received investments of capital with an initial dividend or interest rate of 2 percent, compared to the 5 percent rate offered under the Capital Purchase Program. CDFI banks and thrifts applied to receive capital up to 5 percent of risk-weighted assets. To encourage repayment while recognizing the unique circumstances facing CDFIs, the dividend rate will increase to 9 percent after eight years, compared to five years under CPP.

CDFI credit unions could also apply to receive secondary capital investments at rates equivalent to those offered to CDFI banks and thrifts and with similar terms. These institutions could apply for up to 3.5 percent of total assets, which is an amount approximately equivalent to the 5 percent of risk-weighted assets available to banks and thrifts.

Treasury established a process for reviewing CDCI applications that relied on the appropriate federal regulators, similar to that described under *"CPP Role-of bank regulators"* above. For this program, viability was determined by the CDFI's federal regulator on a pro-forma basis. That is, pro forma viability took into account additional capital injections from private investors made prior to, or concurrently with, Treasury's investment. CDFIs were not required to issue warrants under this program. In addition, CDFIs that participated in CPP and were in good standing could exchange securities issued under CPP for securities under this program.

2. Status as of September 2010

Treasury completed funding under this program in September 2010. The total investment amount for the CDCI program under TARP is approximately $570 million for 84 institutions. Of this amount, approximately $363.3 million from 28 banks was exchanged from investments under the Capital Purchase Program into the CDCI.

Programs Designed to Unlock Credit for Small Businesses and Consumers

Credit was extremely constrained for small businesses and consumers during the financial crisis. Availability of credit is critical for small businesses to grow and for consumers to make home improvements, buy a new car, or send their children to college. Recognizing the vital importance that small businesses and consumers have for the overall economy, Treasury launched three programs to address the credit constraints faced by these groups: the Term Asset-Backed Securities Loan Facility (TALF), the Public Private Investment Program (PPIP) and the SBA 7(a) Securities Purchase Program. Although the specific goals and implementation methods of each program differed, the overall goal of these three programs was the same – to restart the flow of credit to meet the critical needs of small businesses and consumers.

G. Term Asset-Backed Securities Loan Facility

The Term Asset-Backed Securities Loan Facility is a key part of the Obama Administration's Financial Stability Plan and the major initiative under the TARP's Consumer and Business Lending Initiative (CBLI). TALF is a joint Federal Reserve-Treasury program that was designed to restart the asset-backed-securitization markets that had ground to a virtual standstill during the early months of this financial crisis. The ABS markets historically have helped to fund a substantial share of credit to consumers and businesses. The effects of this issuance standstill were many: limited availability of credit to households and businesses of all sizes, an unprecedented widening of interest rate spreads, sharply contracting liquidity in the capital markets and a potential to further weaken U.S. economic activity.

1. Program and Goals

a. Program design

Pursuant to its Federal Reserve Act Section 13(3) authority, the Federal Reserve Bank of New York (FRBNY) agreed to extend up to $200 billion in non-recourse loans to borrowers to enable the purchase of AAA-rated asset-backed securities (ABS), including those backed by consumer loans, student loans, small business loans, and commercial real estate loans. In return, the borrowers pledged the eligible collateral as security for the loans, including the amount of the equity "haircut" provided by the individual borrower. Should a borrower default upon its TALF loan or voluntarily surrender the collateral, the collateral would be seized and sold to TALF LLC, a special purpose vehicle created by FRBNY to purchase and hold seized or surrendered collateral.

Treasury's role in TALF is to provide credit protection for the program through the purchase of subordinated debt in TALF LLC. The funds would be used to purchase the underlying collateral associated with TALF loans in the event the borrower surrendered the collateral or defaulted upon its loan. Treasury originally committed to purchase $20 billion in subordinated debt from TALF LLC, or 10 percent of the maximum amount of loans that could be issued. This commitment was later reduced to $4.3 billion after the program closed to new lending in June 2010 with $43 billion in loans outstanding, so that the commitment remained at 10 percent of the outstanding loans.

Although TALF was designed to provide up to $200 billion in loans secured by eligible collateral, the positive effects of TALF on liquidity and interest rate spreads resulting from the announcement of TALF made utilization of the full amount unnecessary. As TALF positively impacted the market for asset -backed securities, investors became able to access cheaper funds in the restarted capital markets. The program was at first extended past the original termination date of December 2009 to March 2010, for non-mortgage-backed ABS and legacy CMBS collateral, and to June 2010, for newly issued CMBS collateral. Given the improvements in the markets, by program close the FRBNY had approximately $70 billion in loans under TALF. Of that amount, $33 billion (or 47 percent) in TALF loans remained outstanding as of September 8, 2010.

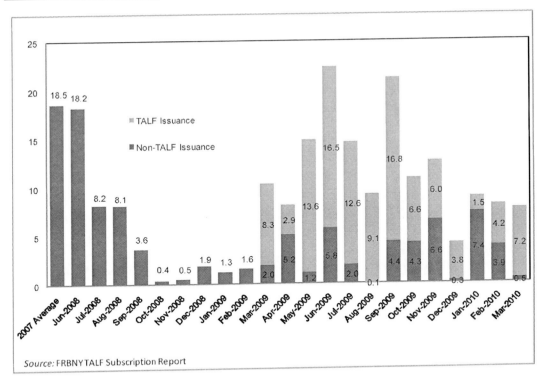

Source: FRBNY TALF Subscription Report

Figure 5-B. Total Consumer ABS Issuance during TALF

B. Protection Of Taxpayer Interests

TALF was designed to provide borrowers with term loans of up to five years against highly rated securities, which are forfeited in the event a loan is not repaid. TALF employs a number of other safeguards to protect taxpayers' interests including the following:

- TALF borrowers bear the first loss risk in all securities pledged as collateral for TALF loans due to the substantial haircuts (set by reference to borrower's equity in the securities) required of those borrowers. Haircuts ranged from 5 percent to 20 percent based on asset quality thereby further limiting risk.
- Eligible securities must have received two AAA ratings from the major rating agencies, and none of the major rating agencies can have rated the security below AAA or placed the security on watch for a downgrade.
- Protection is provided by the risk premium included in the TALF loan rates. The interest rate spread provides accumulated excess interest in TALF LLC as a first loss position. The available excess spread to fund forfeited loans is $476 million as of August 2010.
- Each ABS issuer must engage an external auditor to offer an opinion that supports management's assertion that the ABS is TALF eligible. Further protection is provided by FRBNY and their collateral monitors that assess the risk associated with ABS and CMBS collateral and perform due diligence.

2. *Status as of September 2010*

TALF is widely credited for achieving its purpose of encouraging lending to consumers and businesses while operating under a conservative structure that protects taxpayer interests. The facility has ceased making new loans as noted above. By improving credit market functioning and adding liquidity to the system, TALF has provided critical support to the financial system. This has allowed lenders to meet the credit needs of consumers and small businesses, and has strengthened the overall economy.

Specifically, TALF achieved its objectives of increasing credit availability and liquidity in the securitization markets and reducing interest rate spreads. Secondary spreads narrowed significantly across all eligible asset classes by 60 percent or more. For instance, spreads on AAA-rated auto receivables fell sharply from a peak of 600 basis points in the fourth quarter of 2008 to 21 basis points over their benchmarks today. Spreads in the secondary market for CMBS have declined from 1500 basis points over its benchmark to 210 basis points as of September 16, 2010.

Moreover, the improvements in the secondary credit market contributed to the restart-of the new -issue market. According to the Federal Reserve Bank of New York, issuance of non-mortgage asset -backed securities jumped to $35 billion in the first three months of TALF lending in 2009, after having slowed to less than $1 billion per month in late 2008.[6]

In November 2009, TALF funds also facilitated the first issuance of commercial mortgage-backed securities since June 2008. This helped re-open the market for such securities. Following that deal, there have been additional commercial mortgage-backed deals funded without assistance from TALF.

As the liquidity premium on securitized credit has decreased and credit conditions have improved, TALF has become a less attractive source of financing. The cost of funds for borrowers who utilized the TALF has in many cases become more expensive than the cost of funds in the private sector. This is reflected in the high amount of borrower prepayments which have totaled $35.3 billion one-- third of aggregate TALF loans in -spite of the longer maturity three--and fiveyear-terms-of TALF loans. If these trends continue, and prepayments continue, this may lead to an earlier than originally expected exit from the program.

The maturity date on the Treasury loan to the TALF LLC is March 2019. Treasury's engagement may extend beyond this period if collateral is sold to TALF LLC which will require active management of the assets. To date, the TALF program has experienced no losses and all outstanding TALF loans are well collateralized. Treasury and FRBNY continue to see it as highly likely that the accumulated excess interest spread will cover any loan losses that may occur without recourse to the dedicated TARP funds. Therefore, Treasury does not expect any cost to the taxpayers from this program.

H. Public Private Investment Program

The Legacy Securities Public Private Investment Program (PPIP), another key component of the Financial Stability Plan, was designed to purchase troubled legacy securities (i.e., non-agency residential mortgage-backed securities ("RMBS") and commercial mortgage-backed securities ("CMBS")) that were central to the problems facing the U.S.

financial system, and thereby help ensure that credit is available to households and businesses and ultimately drive the U.S. toward economic recovery.

1. Program Goals and Design

A. The Goal: Unlock Credit Markets For Legacy Securities To Allow Financial Institutions To Repair Their Balance Sheets And Extend New Credit

During the crisis, many financial institutions and investors were under extreme pressure to reduce indebtedness. This de-leveraging process pushed down the market prices for many financial assets, including troubled legacy RMBS and CMBS, below their fundamental value. Institutions and investors were trapped with hard-to-value assets, marked at distressed prices on their balance sheets, which constrained liquidity and the availability of credit in these markets.

The purpose of PPIP was to draw new private capital into the market for legacy RMBS and CMBS by providing financing on attractive terms as well as a matching equity investment made by the Treasury Department. By providing this financing, PPIP was designed to help restart the market for these securities, thereby helping financial institutions begin to remove these assets from their balance sheets and allowing for a general increase in credit availability to consumers and small businesses.

The key objectives of the Public Private Investment Program include:

- Support market functioning by acting as a catalyst to bring private capital back to the market for legacy RMBS and CMBS;
- Facilitate price discovery in the markets for mortgage-backed securities, thereby reducing the uncertainty regarding the value of such securities among the banks and other financial institutions holding them and enabling these financial institutions to sell such assets and raise new private capital;
- Restore confidence in and create an environment conducive to new issuance of new credit; and
- Protect taxpayer interests and generate returns through long-term investments in eligible assets by following predominantly a buy and hold strategy.

b. Program Design

Following the completion of fundraising, Treasury has committed approximately $22 billion of equity and debt financing to eight Public Private Investment Funds (PPIFs). These funds were established by private sector fund managers for the purpose of purchasing eligible RMBS and CMBS from eligible financial institutions under EESA. This represented a reduction from Treasury's initial allocation of $30 billion in potential capital commitments, because there was less aggregate demand from private sector investors due to improved market conditions for legacy non-agency RMBS and CMBS.[7]

The equity capital raised from private investors by the PPIP fund managers has been matched by Treasury. Treasury has also provided debt financing up to 100 percent of the total equity committed to each PPIF. PPIFs have the ability to invest in eligible assets over a three-year investment period from their initial closing. They then have up to five additional years, which may be extended for up to two more years, to manage these investments and return the proceeds to Treasury and the other PPIF investors. PPIP fund managers retain control of asset selection, purchasing, trading, and disposition of investments.

The profits generated by a PPIF, net of expenses, will be distributed to the investors, including Treasury, in proportion to their equity capital investments. Treasury also receives warrants from the PPIFs, which gives Treasury the right to receive a percentage of the profits that would otherwise be distributed to the private partners that are in excess of their contributed capital. The program structure spreads risk between the private investors and Treasury, and provides taxpayers with the opportunity for substantial gain.

The following fund managers currently participate in PPIP:

- AllianceBernstein, LP and its sub-advisors Greenfield Partners, LLC and Rialto Capital Management, LLC;
- Angelo, Gordon & Co., L.P. and GE Capital Real Estate;
- BlackRock, Inc.;
- Invesco Ltd.;
- Marathon Asset Management, L.P.;
- Oaktree Capital Management, L.P.;
- RLJ Western Asset Management, LP.; and
- Wellington Management Company, LLP.

In addition, PPIP fund managers have established meaningful partnership roles for small, minority, and women-owned businesses. These roles include, among others, asset management, capital raising, broker-dealer, investment sourcing, research, advisory, cash management and fund administration services. Collectively, PPIP fund managers have established relationships with ten leading small-, minority-, and women-owned firms, located in five different states.

2. Status as of September 2010

a. PPIF status

The PPIFs have completed fundraising and closed on approximately $7.4 billion of private sector equity capital, which was matched 100 percent by Treasury, representing $14.7 billion of total equity capital. Treasury also committed to provide $14.7 billion of debt capital, representing $29.4 billion of total purchasing power to the program. As of September 30, 2010, PPIFs have drawn-down approximately $18.6 billion of total capital (63 percent of total purchasing power), which has been invested in eligible assets and cash equivalents pending investment.[8] The reduction of Treasury's maximum commitment from $30 billion to $22 billion, after the announcement of the program contributed to improved market conditions, allowed Treasury to accomplish its objectives with an efficient use of taxpayer funds.

B. Support Market Functioning

The announcement and subsequent implementation of PPIP were keys to reducing the illiquidity discount embedded in these legacy securities and the uncertainty associated with their value, which created an environment conducive for financial institutions to begin trading and selling their holdings of such assets. According to the National Information Center[9], the nonagency - RMBS and CMBS holdings of the top 50 bank holding companies holdings were $237 billion as of June 30, 2010, approximately $47 billion or 17 percent lower than levels from a year earlier. We believe that PPIP played a role in helping restart the market for such securities, thereby allowing banks and other financial institutions to begin reducing their holdings in such assets at more normalized prices.

C. Facilitate Price Discovery

Since the announcement of PPIP in March 2009, prices for representative legacy securities have increased by as much as 75 percent for RMBS and CMBS. As illustrated in the chart below[10], benchmark indices for a standardized basket of subprime non-agency RMBS reference obligations from the 2006 vintage, originally rated AAA, and a standardized basket of CMBS reference obligations from the 2007 vintage, originally rated AAA, have appreciated between 50 percent and 80 percent.

d. Extending New Credit

Since the announcement of the program in March 2009, approximately ten new CMBS and RMBS transactions have been brought to market, collectively representing approximately $5 billion in new issuance to date. Although smaller than the annual issuance prior to the financial crisis, we believe that these transactions, particularly in CMBS, represent meaningful steps toward new credit formation in the marketplace.

e. Returns to Taxpayers

Although the PPIFs have been in operation for only a short time, each of the eight PPIFs has generated positive investment returns for Treasury, with net internal rates of return since inception ranging from 13 percent to 37 percent as of June 30, 2010. The PPIFs have generated cumulative unrealized equity gains in excess of funded capital contributions of more than $600 million as of June 30, 2010 to all investors (Treasury and private investors). As of September 30, 2010, the PPIFs also have made approximately $215 million of interest and dividend payments and distributions to Treasury. Because the PPIFs are still in the early stages of their investment life cycles, it would be premature to draw any meaningful long-term conclusions regarding the performance of individual PPIFs or the program in general. However, Treasury has been encouraged by the performance of the PPIP fund managers to date.

f. PPIP Going Forward

The PPIFs are still in their first year of investing, having only drawn approximately 63 percent of their potential purchasing power as of September 30, 2010, and are expected to continue deploying and reinvesting their capital in eligible assets through 2012. As time progresses, Treasury anticipatesthat the PPIP fund managers will continue to make prudent investment decisions that are consistent with their long-term, buy and hold strategy, and that the PPIFs will serve as a stabilizing force in the market.

I. SBA 7(a) Securities Purchase Program

Small businesses have played an important role in generating new jobs and growth in our economy. The Small Business Administration's (SBA) 7(a) Loan Guarantee Program assists start-up and existing small businesses that face difficulty in obtaining loans through traditional lending channels. SBA 7(a) loans help finance a wide variety of business needs, including working capital, machinery, equipment, furniture and fixtures.

The initiative to unlock credit for small business included support for the primary market (i.e. loan origination) and secondary market support (i.e. securities market). The primary market support, an initiative separate from TARP, included temporarily increasing loan guarantees from 75 percent to 90 percent of an SBA 7(a) loan balance, as well as eliminating certain loan origination fees. These actions, which were part of the Recovery Act, made it easier for small businesses to obtain SBA 7(a) loans.

1. Program and Goals

To ensure that credit flows to entrepreneurs and small business owners, Treasury took measures to complement the Obama Administration's actions to help small businesses recover and grow, including a program to purchase SBA guaranteed securities ("pooled certificates"). Treasury developed the SBA 7(a) Securities Purchase Program to purchase SBA guaranteed securities from pool assemblers. By purchasing in the open market, Treasury injected liquidity providing cash to pool assemblers enabling those entities to purchase additional loans from loan originators. In this manner, Treasury acted as a patient provider of incremental liquidity to foster a fluid secondary market, which in turn benefits small business lending.

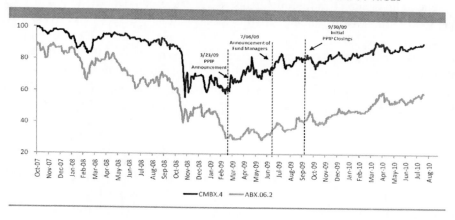

Figure 5-C.

The design and the launch of the program experienced delays due to the reluctance of pool assemblers (sellers) to participate in the program, citing concerns about EESA restrictions, general hesitancy in doing business with the government and 'TARP stigma'. Notwithstanding these initial hurdles, secondary market purchases of SBA 7(a) securities originated on or after July 1, 2008 commenced in March 2010. This coincided with the expiration of the ABS portion of the TALF, which had helped to fund SBA 7(a) loans, along with credit card, automotive and student loans, among others. The SBA 7(a) Securities Purchase Program extended the liquidity assistance for the credit markets supporting small business loans. The SBA 7(a) secondary market support is intended to create an effective, fluid secondary market, which promotes additional lending in the primary market by providing originators an avenue to sell their issuances and obtain cash for additional lending, and thus improve the capital inflows to fund small businesses.

Since the launch of the program Treasury has conducted transactions with two pool assemblers. An external asset manager purchases the SBA 7(a) securities on behalf of Treasury directly from those pool assemblers (sellers) in the open market. Treasury utilized independent valuation service providers to gain additional market insight in order to make informed purchases.

2. Status as of September 2010

The SBA 7(a) Securities Purchase Program was focused in scope and appropriate in scale relative to the market. Currently, there are approximately $15 billion[11] SBA 7(a) securities outstanding, of which $5 billion[12] were issued on or after July 1, 2008 (the eligible universe for the SBA 7(a) Securities Purchase Program). The market has received the program well based on comments from the market participants and the fact that secondary market prices have strengthened.

Securities purchased by Treasury comprised about 700 loans ranging across approximately 17 diverse industries including: retail, food services, manufacturing, scientific and technical services, health care and educational services. The program has supported loans from 39 of the 50 states in the country, indicating a broad geographic impact.

As of September 30, 2010, Treasury has conducted 31 transactions totaling approximately $357 million. The program ceased purchasing securities in conjunction with the expiration of purchase authority under the Act. Treasury will continue to manage existing positions.

J. Automotive Industry Financing Program (AIFP)

The Automotive Industry Financing Program (AIFP) was begun in December 2008 to prevent a significant disruption of the U.S. automotive industry, because the potential for such a disruption posed a systemic risk to financial market stability and would have had a negative effect on the economy. In 2008, the auto industry lost nearly 35 percent of its sales volume and almost 400,000 jobs, and both GM and Chrysler were on the verge of disorderly liquidations. This could have caused millions of additional job losses.

Recognizing the danger, Treasury extended temporary loans to GM and Chrysler in December 2008. After the Obama Administration took office, it agreed to provide additional investments conditioned on each company and its stakeholders participating in a fundamental restructuring. Sacrifices were made by unions, dealers, creditors and other stakeholders, and the restructurings were achieved through bankruptcy court proceedings in record time. As a result, GM and Chrysler are more competitive and viable companies, supporting American jobs and the economy. Operating results have improved, the industry has added jobs, and the TARP investments have begun to be repaid.

1. Programs and Goals

a. Automotive companies

Short-term funding was initially provided to General Motors (GM) and Chrysler on the condition that they develop plans to achieve long-term viability. In cooperation with the Obama Administration, GM and Chrysler developed satisfactory viability plans and successfully conducted sales of their assets to new entities in bankruptcy proceedings. Chrysler completed its sale process in 42 days and GM in 40 days. Treasury provided additional assistance during these periods.

In total, Treasury has provided approximately $80 billion in loans and equity investments to GM, GMAC (now known as Ally Financial), Chrysler, and Chrysler Financial. The terms of Treasury's assistance impose a number of restrictions including rigorous executive compensation standards, limits on luxury expenditures, and other corporate governance requirements.

While some have questioned why TARP was used to support the automotive industry, both the Bush and Obama Administrations determined that Treasury's investments in the auto companies were consistent with the purpose and specific requirements of EESA. Among other things, Treasury determined that the auto companies were and are interrelated with entities extending credit to consumers and dealers because of their financing subsidiaries and other operations, and that a disruption in the industry or an uncontrolled liquidation would have had serious effects on financial market stability, employment and the economy as a whole.

b. Supplier and warranty support programs

In the related Auto **Supplier Support Program (ASSP)**, Treasury provided loans to ensure that auto suppliers receive compensation for their services and products, regardless of the condition of the auto companies that purchase their products. In the **Auto Warranty Commitment Program (AWCP)**, Treasury provided loans to protect warranties on new vehicles purchased from GM and Chrysler during their restructuring periods.

In early 2009, auto suppliers faced the risk of uncontrolled liquidations across the sector. Fiftyfour-(54) supplier-related bankruptcies occurred in 2009 as the industry went through a painful restructuring. Today, in part due to the support provided by Automotive Supplier Support Program (ASSP), the auto supply base appears to have stabilized. Suppliers are now breaking even at a lower level of North American production.[13]

2. General Motors

Treasury provided $50 billion under TARP to General Motors. This began in December 2008, with a $13.4 billion loan by the Bush Administration to General Motors Corporation

(GM or Old GM) to fund working capital. Under the loan agreement, GM was required to submit a viable restructuring plan. The first plan GM submitted failed to establish a credible path to viability, and the deadline was extended to June 2009 for GM to develop an amended plan. Treasury loaned an additional $6 billion to fund GM during this period.

To achieve an orderly restructuring, GM filed for bankruptcy on June 1, 2009. Treasury provided $30.1 billion under a debtor-in-possession financing agreement to assist GM during the restructuring. A newly formed entity, General Motors Company (New GM), purchased most of the assets of Old GM under a sale pursuant to Section 363 of the bankruptcy code (363 Sale). When the sale to New GM was completed on July 10, Treasury converted most of its loans to 60.8 percent of the common equity in the New GM and $2.1 billion in preferred stock. At that time, Treasury held $6.7 billion in outstanding loans.

Approximately $986 million remained with Old GM (now known as Motors Liquidation Company) for wind-down costs associated with its liquidation.

a. Repayments

New GM has repaid the $6.7 billion loan in full. (The rest of the investment is equity which will be sold as described below.) In December 2009, New GM began quarterly repayments of $1 billion on the loan. In January 2010, New GM and Treasury amended the loan agreement to require cash that New GM held in an escrow account to be applied to repay the loan by June 30, 2010. After New GM repaid Treasury $1 billion on March 31, 2010, the outstanding loan balance fell to approximately $4.7 billion, all of which was repaid on April 21, 2010, from the escrowed funds.

b. Ownership structure

New GM currently has the following ownership: Treasury (60.8 percent), GM Voluntary Employee Benefit Association (VEBA) (17.5 percent), the Canadian Government (11.7 percent), and Old GM's unsecured bondholders (10 percent). As part of the restructuring, GM issued warrants to acquire additional shares of common stock to VEBA and Old GM (for distribution to the creditors of Old GM following confirmation of a plan of liquidation by the bankruptcy court).

c. General Motors initial public offering

Treasury has indicated the most likely exit strategy for the AIFP equity investments is a gradual sale beginning with an initial public offering of New GM. In June 2010, Treasury provided guidance on its role in the exploration of an IPO by New GM. The following are excerpts from the statement:

- The exact timing of an IPO will be determined by New GM in light of market conditions and other factors.
- The overall size of the offering and relative amounts of primary and secondary shares will be determined at a later date.
- The selection of the lead underwriters was made by New GM, subject to Treasury's agreement that the selection was reasonable. Treasury will determine the fees to be paid to the underwriters.

In August 2010, New GM filed a registration statement on Form S-1 with the U.S. Securities and Exchange Commission (SEC) for a proposed IPO consisting of common stock to be sold by certain of its stockholders, including Treasury, and the issuance by the company of its Series B mandatory convertible junior preferred stock. Treasury will retain the right, at all times, to decide whether and at what level to participate in the offering.

3. Chrysler

Treasury has provided a total commitment of approximately $14 billion to Chrysler and Chrysler Financial of which more than $12 billion has been utilized.[*] In January 2009, Treasury loaned $4 billion to Chrysler Holding (the parent of Chrysler Financial and Old Chrysler). Under the loan agreement, Chrysler was required to implement a viable restructuring plan. In March 2009, the Administration determined that the business plan submitted by Chrysler failed to demonstrate viability and concluded that Chrysler was not viable as a stand-alone company. President Obama subsequently laid out a framework for Chrysler to achieve viability by partnering with the international car company Fiat. As part of the planned restructuring, in April 2009, Chrysler filed for bankruptcy protection. In May 2009, Treasury provided $1.9 billion to Chrysler (Old Chrysler) under a debtorin-- possession financing agreement for assistance during its bankruptcy proceeding.

a. New Chrysler

In June 2009, a newly formed entity, Chrysler Group LLC (New Chrysler), purchased most of the assets of Old Chrysler under a 363 Sale. Treasury provided a $6.6 billion loan commitment to New Chrysler, and received a 9.9 percent equity ownership in New Chrysler. Fiat transferred valuable technology to Chrysler and, after extensive consultation with the Obama Administration, committed to building new fuel efficient cars and engines in U.S. factories.

Treasury's remaining investments in New Chrysler consist of 9.9 percent of common equity and a $7.1 billion loan (including undrawn commitments and $500 million assumed from Chrysler Holding). New Chrysler currently has the following ownership: Chrysler Voluntary Employee Benefit Association (VEBA) (67.7 percent), Fiat (20 percent), Treasury (9.9 percent), and the Government of Canada (2.5 percent).

b. Old Chrysler

In April 2010, the bankruptcy court approved Old Chrysler's Plan of Liquidation. As a result, the $1.9 billion debtor-in-possession loan provided to Old Chrysler in May 2009 was extinguished and the assets remaining with Old Chrysler, including collateral security attached to the loan, were transferred to a liquidation trust. Treasury retained the right to recover the proceeds from the liquidation of the specified collateral, but does not expect a significant recovery from the liquidation proceeds.

c. Settlement with Chrysler Holding

The original $4 billion loan made to Chrysler Holding in January 2009 went into default when Old Chrysler filed for bankruptcy. In July 2009, $500 million of that loan was assumed by New Chrysler. In May 2010, Treasury accepted a settlement payment of $1.9 billion as

---

[*] Correction made as of October 7, 2010.

satisfaction in full of the remaining debt obligations associated with the original loan. The final repayment, while less than face value, was significantly more than Treasury had previously estimated to recover following the bankruptcy and greater than an independent valuation provided by Keefe, Bruyette and Woods, Treasury's adviser for the transaction.

d. Chrysler Financial

In January 2009, Treasury announced that it would lend up to $1.5 billion to a special purpose vehicle (SPV) created by Chrysler Financial to enable the company to finance the purchase of Chrysler vehicles by consumers. In July 2009, Chrysler Financial fully repaid the loan, including the additional notes that were issued to satisfy the EESA warrant requirement, together with interest.

4. Ally Financial (formerly GMAC)

Treasury has invested approximately $17 billion in Ally Financial. This began with an investment by the Bush Administration of $5 billion in December 2008. Treasury also lent $884 million of TARP funds to GM (one of GMAC's owners) for the purchase of additional ownership interests in a rights offering by GMAC. In May 2009, federal banking regulators required GMAC to raise additional capital by November 2009 in connection with the SCAP/stress test. Treasury exercised its option to exchange the loan with GM for 35.4 percent of common membership interests in GMAC. Treasury also purchased $7.5 billion of convertible preferred shares from GMAC, which enabled GMAC to partially meet the SCAP requirements. Additional Treasury investments in GMAC were contemplated to enable GMAC to satisfy the SCAP requirements. These were completed in December 2009, when Treasury invested an additional $3.8 billion in GMAC. Today, Treasury's investment consists of 56.3 percent of the common stock, $11.4 billion of mandatorily convertible preferred securities (which may be converted into common stock at a later date) and $2.7 billion of trust preferred securities.

5. Status as of September 2010

A. Auto Supplier Support And Warranty Commitment Program

Treasury has recovered all amounts invested under the supplier and warranty programs. With the emergence of New GM and New Chrysler from bankruptcy proceedings and with the threat of liquidation greatly reduced, credit market access for suppliers improved. In July 2009, Treasury reduced the base commitment under the supplier support program to $3.5 billion. As scheduled, the program closed in April 2010 after full repayment of all loans, which had totaled not more than $413 million, with interest. The warranty program was terminated in 2009, and the $640 million advanced under the program was assumed and/or repaid in the bankruptcy sale transactions by New GM and New Chrysler.

B. Outlook On Automotive Industry Following Restructurings And Repayments

Today, the domestic auto industry continues to recover. U.S. sales improved in the first half of 2010 with annualized auto sales running at 11.1 million vehicles (compared to 9.6 million in the first half of 2009 and 10.4 million for the full year of 2009). Since the GM and

Chrysler bankruptcies concluded last year, U.S. auto industry employment has increased by 62,100 jobs.

As the outlook for the domestic auto industry has improved and the estimated value of Treasury's investments has increased, the projected cost of AIFP has decreased (from approximately $28.2 billion as of November 2009, to $17 billion as of August 2010).

- GM repaid $7 billion to Treasury, and is currently preparing for an initial public offering in which Treasury may elect to sell shares. In the first six months of 2010, GM achieved two consecutive quarters of positive operating profit and net income – its first quarterly profits since 2007.
- Likewise, after taking one-time charges last year associated with its restructuring, Chrysler posted two consecutive quarters of operating profit. With respect to Old Chrysler, Treasury was repaid $1.9 billion, which was significantly more than Treasury had previously estimated to recover.
- Each of Ally Financial's four operating businesses has generated a profit so far this year.

K. American International Group, Inc. (AIG) Investment Program

"We acted because the consequences of AIG failing at that time, in those circumstances, would have been catastrophic for our economy and for American families and businesses."

-Secretary Geithner, Written Testimony before the House Committee on Oversight and Government Reform (January 27, 2010), *available at*: http://www.treas.gov /press/releases/tg514.htm.

In September of 2008, panic in the financial system was deep and widespread. Fannie Mae and Freddie Mac were placed into conservatorship; Lehman Brothers filed for bankruptcy; and Merrill Lynch was acquired by Bank of America in a last-minute rescue. Major banks, such as Washington Mutual and Wachovia, experienced debilitating deposit withdrawals, eventually collapsed, and were acquired. Money market funds also suffered a broad run, threatening what was considered one of the safest investments for Americans. The commercial paper market was also disrupted, threatening a vital source of funding for many businesses. No one knew how deeply the markets and the economy would fall, and private lenders massively retrenched risk.

Amidst these events, on Friday, September 12, American International Group (AIG) officials informed the Federal Reserve and Treasury that the company was facing potentially fatal liquidity problems. Although it was neither AIG's regulator nor supervisor, the Federal Reserve Bank of New York (FRBNY) immediately brought together a team of people from the Federal Reserve, the New York State Insurance Department, and other experts to consider how to respond to AIG's problems. Congress gave the Federal Reserve authority to provide liquidity to the financial system in times of severe stress, and it acted to fulfill that responsibility.

At the time, AIG was the largest provider of conventional insurance in the world, with approximately 75 million individual and corporate customers in over 130 countries. AIG's assets exceeded $1 trillion. It was significantly larger than Lehman Brothers. It insured

180,000 businesses and other entities employing over 100 million people in the U.S. It was a large issuer of commercial paper and the second largest holder of U.S. municipal bonds. AIG's parent holding company, which was largely unregulated, engaged in financial activities that strayed well beyond the business of life insurance and property and casualty insurance. Its financial products unit was a significant participant in some of the newest, riskiest, and most complex parts of the financial system.

In the chaotic environment of September 2008, the Federal Reserve and Treasury concluded that AIG's failure could be catastrophic. Among other things, if AIG had failed, the crisis would have almost certainly spread to the entire insurance industry, and its failure would have directly affected the savings of millions of Americans in ways that Lehman's failure did not. Therefore, the government took action to protect the financial system.

AIG needed a durable restructuring of both its balance sheet and its business operations. Falling asset prices generated substantial losses on the company's balance sheet. They also increased the payments to counterparties that AIG was required to make under the terms of credit protection contracts it had sold. AIG's insurance subsidiaries experienced significant cash outflows related to a securities lending program, as the value of residential mortgage-backed securities that they had purchased and loaned against cash collateral continued to fall.

The government faced escalating and unprecedented challenges on many different fronts of the financial crisis during September, October, and November. During that time, the Federal Reserve and Treasury took a series of steps to prevent AIG's disorderly failure and mitigate systemic risks.

1. Program and Goals

The initial assistance to AIG was provided by the FRBNY before the passage of EESA and the creation of TARP. The FRBNY provided loans to AIG under the section 13(3) authority of the Federal Reserve Act to lend on a secured basis under "unusual and exigent" circumstances to companies that are not depository institutions:

- In September 2008, the FRBNY provided an $85 billion credit facility to AIG, and received preferred shares which currently have approximately 79.8 percent of the voting rights of AIG's common stock (known as Series C). The FRBNY created the AIG Credit Facility Trust (the Trust) to hold the shares for the benefit of the U.S. Treasury but the Department of the Treasury does not control the Trust and cannot direct its trustees.

After TARP was enacted, the Treasury and the Federal Reserve continued to work together to address the challenges posed by AIG:

- In November 2008, the Federal Reserve and Treasury jointly announced a package of actions designed to address the continuing vulnerabilities in AIG's balance sheet that threatened its viability and its credit ratings. Treasury invested $40 billion in senior preferred stock of AIG under the authority recently granted by EESA (the preferred stock was subsequently exchanged in April 2009, for face value plus accrued dividends, into $41.6 billion of a different series of preferred stock), and it also received warrants to purchase common shares in the firm. The funds were used immediately to reduce the loans provided by the FRBNY. As part of the restructuring, the FRBNY also agreed to lend up to $22.5 billion to a newly created entity, Maiden Lane II LLC, to fund the purchase of residential mortgage -backed securities from the securities lending portfolio of several of AIG's regulated U.S. insurance subsidiaries, and up to $30 billion to a second newly created entity, Maiden Lane III LLC, to fund the purchase of multi-sector collateralized debt obligations from certain counterparties of AIG Financial Products Corp. (AIGFP).

- In April 2009, Treasury created an equity capital facility, under which AIG may draw up to $29.8 billion as needed in exchange for issuing additional shares of preferred stock to Treasury. As of September 30, 2010, AIG has drawn $7.5 billion from the facility and the remainder will be used in connection with the restructuring plan discussed below.

- In December 2009, the Federal Reserve received preferred equity interests in two special purpose vehicles (SPVs) formed to hold the outstanding stock of AIG's largest foreign insurance subsidiaries, American International Assurance Company (AIA) and American Life Insurance Company (ALICO), in exchange for a $25 billion reduction in the balance outstanding and maximum credit available under AIG's revolving credit facility with the FRBNY. The transactions positioned AIA and ALICO for initial public offerings or sale.

2. The AIG Restructuring Plan and Taxpayer Exit

On September 30, 2010 AIG announced that it had entered into an agreement-in-principle with the U.S. Department of the Treasury, the FRBNY, and the Trust designed to repay all of the company's obligations to American taxpayers. The restructuring plan will accelerate the timeline for AIG's repayment of the government and will put taxpayers in a considerably stronger position to recoup their investment in the company. At current market prices the value of the 1.655 billion of shares that Treasury will receive is approximately $64.3 billion,[14] versus the $47.5 billion that Treasury has invested in the company to date.

The basic terms of the restructuring plan are straightforward in concept: sell sufficient assets to pay off AIG's obligations to the FRBNY, streamline AIG's business portfolio, and recapitalize AIG's balance sheet to support investment grade status without the need for ongoing government support.

More specifically, the plan is premised on three key steps:

a. Repaying and terminating the FRBNY Credit Facility with AIG

Today, AIG owes the FRBNY approximately $21 billion in senior secured debt under the FRBNY credit facility. Under the plan, AIG will repay this entire amount and terminate the FRBNY senior secured credit facility. Funding for this will come primarily from the proceeds of the initial public offering of the company's Asian life insurance business (AIA) and the pending sale of its foreign life insurance company (ALICO) to MetLife.

B. Facilitating The Orderly Exit Of The U.S. Government's Interests In Two Special Purpose Vehicles (Spvs) That Hold Aia And Alico

Today, the FRBNY holds preferred interests in two AIG-related SPVs totaling approximately $26 billion. Under the plan, AIG will use the remaining $22 billion of TARP funds available to it (under the Series F preferred stock facility provided in April 2009) and Treasury will receive an equal amount of the FRBNY's preferred interests in the SPVs. Over time, AIG will repay the FRBNY and the Treasury for these preferred interests through proceeds from the sales of AIG Star Life Insurance and AIG Edison Life Insurance, the monetization of the remaining equity stake in AIA, the sale of MetLife equity securities that AIG will own after the close of the ALICO sale, and the monetization of certain other designated assets. The aggregate value of the assets underlying the preferred interests in the SPVs significantly exceeds the liquidation preference of the preferred interests. Treasury does not anticipate incurring any loss from its purchase of the SPV preferred interests.

c. Retiring AIG's remaining TARP support

To date, Treasury has invested approximately $47.5 billion of TARP funds in AIG. Under the plan, Treasury is expected to receive approximately 1.1 billion shares of AIG common stock in exchange for its existing TARP investments in AIG, and an additional 563 million shares of common stock from the exchange of the Series C preferred shares held by the Trust. After the exchange is completed, it is expected that Treasury will sell its stake in AIG into the public markets over time.

The plan is still subject to a number of conditions, and much work remains to be done to close the transactions. Nevertheless, the plan reflects the substantial progress that AIG and the government have made in restructuring the company and reducing the systemic risk that it once posed. The plan also represents a significant step towards ending the government's role in providing assistance to the company.

Treasury Positions in AIG, post-Restructuring[1]

	TARP	Other (Series C)	Total Treasury
Funds Invested ($B)	$69.8	-	$69.8
Common Equity			
Number of Shares (B)	1.092 [2]	0.563 [3]	
Value ($B)	$42.4 [4]	$21.9 [4]	$64.3
Preferred Interest In AIG SPVs ($B	$22.3 [5]	-	$22.3
Treasury Net Value ($B)	**($5.1)**	**$21.9**	**$16.8**

Note: This table shows only Treasury's investments in AIG and does not reflect FRBNY's loans to or interests in AIG. The restructuring plan provides for payment in full of the FRBNY Credit Facility. In addition, the value of the assets held by Maiden Lane II and Maiden Lane III currently exceeds the amounts of the FRBNY loans to those entities, and it is expected that each of those loans will be paid in full.

[1] Treasury holds investments in AIG in two forms: equity investments made through TARP and equity provided to the AIG Credit Facility Trust for Treasury's benefit and in connection with the Federal Reserve's creation of the FRBNY Credit Facility in September 2008.

[2] After the proposed restructuring of AIG TARP will hold 1.092 billion shares of AIG common stock.

[3] After the proposed restructuring of AIG Treasury will receive 563 million shares of AIG common in connection with the wind-down of the AIG Credit Facility Trust.

[4] Common equity is valued at the market closing price on October 1, 2010 of $38.86 per share.

[5] After the proposed restructuring of AIG, TARP will hold up to $22.3 billion of preferred interests in two AIG-related SPVs. The estimated aggregate value of the assets underlying the preferred interests in the SPVs significantly exceeds the liquidation preference of the TARP preferred interests. Therefore, Treasury does not anticipate incurring any loss from its purchase of the SPV preferred in connection with the AIG restructuring. For further details see the 8-K filed by AIG with the SEC on September 30, 2010.

Over the past two years, the government has worked with AIG to recruit a new CEO, a new Chief Risk Officer, a new General Counsel, a new Chief Administrative Officer, and an almost entirely new Board of Directors. All of these executives and directors are committed to the objective of executing the restructuring plan and paying back taxpayers as promptly as practicable. In addition, the profitability of the AIG's core business – its insurance subsidiaries – has been steadily improving, as has the market's perception of the value of these subsidiaries. The improvement in the value of these businesses and their ultimate sale are central to the AIG restructuring plan.

Upon completion of the restructuring plan, AIG will be a simplified life, property and casualty insurer with solidly capitalized insurance subsidiaries, adequate liquidity, and a stable balance sheet.

3. Protecting the Taxpayer

Since the rescue of AIG, there have been a number of criticisms leveled at the actions the government took and the decision-making process that resulted in those actions. Representatives of Treasury, the Federal Reserve Board, and the FRBNY have testified on several occasions about the actions that the government took and have provided written responses for the public record.[15] That record should be read by anyone who wants to obtain a full understanding of the government's actions. In this chapter, we summarize some of the issues that have been raised in that public discussion. We focus on three key questions that have been asked:

- Should AIG have been allowed to fail and go bankrupt?
- Were all other options exhausted before assistance was provided to AIG?
- Were the payments made by AIG to its derivative counterparties appropriate?

A. Should Aig Have Been Allowed To Fail And Go Bankrupt?

Some observers have argued that AIG should have been left to fail and file for bankruptcy. However, by virtue of both the size of its balance sheet and the nature of its liabilities, an AIG bankruptcy in September of 2008 would have been catastrophic to global financial and insurance markets. AIG was one of the largest life insurers in the United States. AIG's failure would have directly threatened the savings of millions of Americans. AIG had provided financial protection to municipalities, pension funds, and other public and private entities through guaranteed investment contracts and products that protect participants in 401(k) retirement plans. Doubts about the value of AIG life insurance products could have generated doubts about similar products provided by other life insurance companies, and opened an entirely new channel of contagion and panic.

In addition, upon the filing of a bankruptcy petition by AIG, holders of hundreds of billions of dollars of financial assets "insured" by AIGFP would have been entitled to: (i) immediately terminate their insurance contracts with AIG, (ii) apply the collateral AIG had previously posted with them to their termination claims against AIG, and (iii) offset remaining contractual claims they had against AIG against any other obligation they might owe AIG on any other qualified financial contract. The consequences of this rapid unwinding of AIG's credit insurance would have been severe. Having lost the benefit of AIG's insurance or "wrap" on hundreds of billions of dollars of credit instruments, AIG's counterparties would have sought to replace the insurance if it were available, or (because such insurance was largely unavailable in September of 2008) to sell the underlying credit instruments so as to mitigate future losses.

The widespread sale of hundreds of billions of dollars of a concentrated class of financial assets would have created significant additional downward selling pressure on financial assets, amplifying the selling panic that had already started following the Lehman bankruptcy. Of equal concern, the default by AIG and AIGFP on more than $100 billion of institutional indebtedness, including $15 billion of commercial paper and $85 billion of short-term repurchase obligations, would have exacerbated the stresses in the money market and repo markets.

This damage of AIG's collapse would have rapidly spread beyond Wall Street. Borrowing costs for all businesses would have increased severely, the value of pension funds would have fallen even more sharply, and job losses would have skyrocketed. While the decision to save AIG was not an easy one, it was a better choice for the American people than facing the catastrophic risks of letting it fail given the state of the financial system at the time.

B. Were All Other Options Exhausted?

Some have suggested that the government should have pursued other options more aggressively, such as a rescue by private firms or a "hybrid" option involving both public and private assistance. However, no one has identified a particular private or "public-private hybrid" solution that could have been achieved in the circumstances, or even a potential specific one that should have been explored. Others have suggested that a pre-packaged bankruptcy might have been possible, even though there was no legal tool available to manage the orderly wind-down of the company. In particular, the government did not have the ability to quickly separate the stable, underlying insurance businesses from the complex and dangerous financial activities carried out primarily by AIGFP.

1) Private Or A Hybrid Privatepublic -Rescue

The basic fact is that AIG needed over $60 billion in September 2008 to avoid failure. No private firm was willing to provide it, despite the efforts of AIG and the government to secure support. AIG had already reached out to the private sector for funding but was unable to find companies willing to lend it the amount that it needed to avoid bankruptcy. The government also worked to facilitate a private solution. A series of major investors considered taking action and refused to do so, including Warren Buffett, two of the largest banks, and some of the largest private equity firms in the world.

At the time AIG needed assistance, banks were shrinking credit and were reluctant to lend even to one another. Large private investors were hoarding cash. In short, it was simply not possible, under the circumstances, to prevent the failure of AIG without having the government step in.

2) Prepackaged - bankruptcy

Others have suggested that the government should have explored the option of a pre-packaged bankruptcy for AIG. A pre-packaged bankruptcy typically requires months of planning and preparation. By contrast, in September 2008, the FRBNY, having had no previous regulatory or supervisory authority over AIG or AIGFP, did not have time to organize AIG's thousands of creditors and hundreds of regulators (in over 100 countries) into an effective negotiating committee, let alone structure a plan of reorganization with them and implement it.

The impracticality of a pre-packaged plan process for AIG was not merely about timing, however, as there was a more fundamental problem. AIG's business depends on its customers' and lenders' perception of its longterm-viability. Unlike a manufacturing or retail company, the stability of a financial institution like AIG depends on its customers' and counterparties' confidence that it will be "good for the money". A manufacturer or a retailer can continue to sell its products during the restructuring of its balance sheet so long as it has physical goods to sell. A financial institution like AIG cannot. A balance sheet restructuring involving the compromise of its obligations, whether in or out of formal bankruptcy proceedings, is fundamentally inconsistent with the basic commitment that an insurance company gives to its customers: that it will honor its longterm-payment obligations.

Similarly, even with an announced government facility to "bridge" AIG to and through bankruptcy, at the first hint that AIG had commenced negotiations with its creditors over the potential restructuring of their debt, AIG's ability to sell new insurance policies would likely have evaporated. Equally damaging, redemptions of old policies would have further accelerated. Together, the loss of new sales and the increase in redemptions would have created a huge drain on the insurance subsidiaries' liquidity. Similarly, shortterm-creditors, such as AIG's securities lending counterparties, would have likely refused to roll over their loans, demanding immediate payment instead. That "run" on AIG and its subsidiaries' liquidity would have forced regulators to protect all policyholders in their jurisdictions by ringfencing ,the insurers' assets or, in the extreme case, forcing the insurer into wind-down proceedings. In addition, it is probable that in order to effectuate a pre-packaged bankruptcy, the size of a government "bridge" facility would have needed to be much larger than the amount of assistance the government actually provided to stabilize the company.

Moreover, at the time there existed no "resolution authority" to resolve AIG, such as the manner in which the FDIC resolves banks. AIG's liquidity position and the value of its underlying insurance subsidiaries were inextricably linked to the rating of the parent company. So with no other "resolution" alternative, the only way to avoid the systemic risks associated with a chapter 11 filing of AIG was to provide AIG with (i) sufficient liquidity to meet its obligations to its creditors and counterparties in the ordinary course of business in full (so as to avoid any defaults that might trigger insolvency proceedings), and (ii) sufficient equity to maintain AIG's investment grade rating (so as to preserve the viability of its insurance subsidiaries and to avoid further collateral calls at AIGFP).

By contrast, commencement of bankruptcy proceedings for those subsidiaries of AIG that were eligible for chapter 11 relief would have triggered ratings downgrades at each of AIG's major insurance subsidiary groups and would almost certainly have resulted in the commencement of receivership, rehabilitation or wind-down proceedings by local insurance regulators, affecting the redemption and surrender rights of more than 100 million life insurance and annuity policyholders, globally. With its insurance subsidiaries in separate regulatory proceedings in 130 countries, any sale of AIG's major insurance business units as integrated wholes would have been extremely difficult.

These further downgrades by the rating agencies would also have triggered additional collateral calls at AIGFP, putting AIG's liquidity under even greater stress. In all likelihood, the policyholder run on AIG's insurance subsidiaries and the counterparty run on AIGFP would have started in earnest before any prepackaged plan could have been put to a vote.

3) Conditional lending

Some have suggested that the government should have made its assistance to AIG conditional on certain creditors taking discounts on their claims. There are a number of reasons why the government did not do so which are discussed in the testimony referred to earlier. Most important, had the government conditioned its assistance on AIG's coercion of certain creditors to reduce their amounts due and owed from AIG, the government would have created the very conditions of default that it was seeking to avoid. The coercion would have undercut the government's primary goal in providing AIG with necessary liquidity – enabling AIG to pay its customers and creditors, maintain confidence, and avoid further rating downgrades and default. The tactic has been used in certain sovereign debt restructurings, but it can be used there only because sovereigns cannot go bankrupt, and it generally requires months of planning.

In addition, any attempt to condition the government's lending would have created further uncertainty as to which of AIG's counterparties would have been paid and which would have been forced to take losses. More generally, conditional lending would have undermined the public's trust in the government's commitment to the broader range of extraordinary financial stability initiatives underway during that very fragile period. One of the objectives at the time was to calm market participants. The market uncertainty (and the potential allegations of favoritism) that would have followed from conditional lending would have undermined that aim. Such an action would have caused confusion and doubt about what the government might do. For instance, would the government force the creditors of other institutions to take haircuts as a condition of assistance and, if so, which ones?

Finally, conditional lending might not necessarily have even worked: would a creditor who was pressed for a discount simply refuse and declare a default? In sum, conditional lending would have heightened the risk of an AIG default, which is what the government was trying to – and did – avoid.

C. Was The Treatment Of AIG's Derivative Counterparties Appropriate?

Various questions have been raised about how AIG's counterparties were treated when Maiden Lane III was established. While the financial contracts involved were complex, basically, AIG had agreed to insure the value of certain risky securities called multi-sector CDOs. The value of these securities was tied to pools of other assets, mostly subprime mortgages. As the financial crisis intensified, the value of the securities fell sharply, and AIG had to post collateral or make payments on the insurance.

The problem was that AIG had written billions of dollars of insurance on these CDOs without sufficient capital. AIG was fine as long as the prices of the assets it insured didn't fall, and its own credit rating didn't fall. But if either happened, it would be in trouble. In the fall of 2008, both events occurred. The value of the assets and AIG's credit rating fell, bringing AIG to the brink of bankruptcy.

By August of 2008, AIG had already paid out over $16 billion to counterparties on contracts similar to the ones that Maiden Lane III was designed to address. When the Federal Reserve established the initial credit facility on September 16, 2008, it knew that there could be further demands of this sort. In the midst of the ongoing financial crisis, the underlying mortgage securities were likely to continue to decline in value.

The government faced the following options: let AIG default on these contracts; continue to lend AIG money so it could meet its short-term obligations; or restructure the contracts to stop the hemorrhaging, and potentially recover value on them in the future. If the government had let AIG default, it would have gone into bankruptcy, triggering all the disastrous economic consequences described earlier. If the government had simply continued to lend AIG money, it would have fed a vicious cycle. AIG could have made its current payments, but this would have increased AIG's debt at a time when the rating agencies felt AIG already had too much. Any resulting downgrade by the rating agencies would have further threatened AIG's viability, driving more uncertainty and panic through the entire financial system, and requiring even more financial support.

Instead, the government sought to restructure the contracts. The counterparties held insurance contracts entitling them to full or par value of the contract. Some have suggested that the FRBNY should have used its regulatory authority, or some other means, to coerce AIG's counterparties to accept discounts. This was not a viable option either. If the FRBNY had sought to force counterparties to accept less than they were legally entitled to, market participants would have lost confidence in AIG, customers would have sought other places to do business, and the ratings agencies would have downgraded AIG again. This would likely have led to AIG's collapse and threatened the government's efforts to rebuild confidence in the financial system. This would have likely meant a deeper recession, more financial turmoil, and a much higher long-term cost for American taxpayers.

Operating with these constraints, the FRBNY and AIG initiated discussions with the major counterparties about whether they would be prepared to accept concessions on the prices of the securities. The government knew that the likelihood of success was modest. Relatively quickly, most firms declared that they would not, on any condition, provide such a concession. One said that it was willing to accept a small discount, but only if everybody else would agree to equal concessions on their prices.

In order to cancel the insurance, the CDOs were purchased for fair market value, which at the time was about 48 cents on the dollar.[16] The counterparties also kept the cash that they had already received from AIG. Taken together, these two amounts approximately equaled the original par value that the banks had insured. In designing and implementing this transaction the Federal Reserve's objective was, as it always is, to get the best deal for the taxpayer. The Federal Reserve made judgments about these transactions carefully with the advice of outside counsel and financial experts. Because Maiden Lane III can hold the underlying CDOs to maturity, it is largely immune from short-term volatility and liquidity needs, and is therefore in a better position to maximize the value of the CDO portfolio.

In fact, since Maiden Lane III purchased the securities, they have generated significant cash flows. These have been used to pay down the FRBNY's loan by over $9 billion. It is likely that Maiden Lane III (as well as Maiden Lane II) will pay the FRBNY back in full and generate a profit for U.S. taxpayers. While the immediate objective was to prevent AIG's collapse, the government believes that strategy that the Federal Reserve and the Treasury pursued in establishing Maiden Lane III will generate a better long -term outcome for taxpayers than would have any alternative available at that time.

6. RETROSPECTIVE ON THE TARP HOUSING INITIATIVES

This section examines the development, accomplishments, challenges and evolution of Treasury's housing initiatives under TARP. The basic terms of these programs are summarized in the subsection titled "Summary Description of Housing Programs" on page 77.

A. The Crisis

In the beginning of 2009, the U.S. economy was facing the fallout from a housing bubble that by some measures had doubled home prices in a period of six years. During the heady days of the bubble, lenders had migrated to riskier mortgage products and borrowers had extracted equity from their homes. From 2003 through 2006, the share of mortgages that met the relatively conservative underwriting guidelines of Fannie Mae, Freddie Mac, and the government fell roughly in half, from two -thirds to one-third, while riskier products such as subprime and "Alternative A" (Alt-A) loans gained market share.

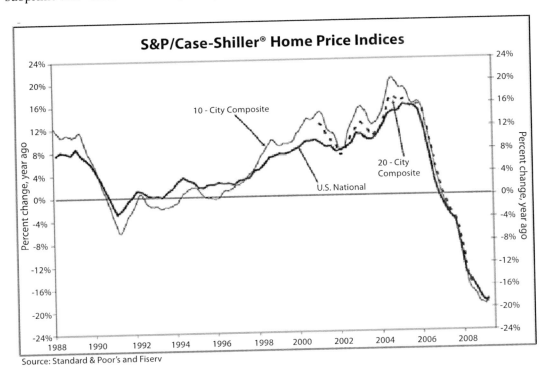

Source: Standard & Poor's and Fiserv

Figure 6-A.

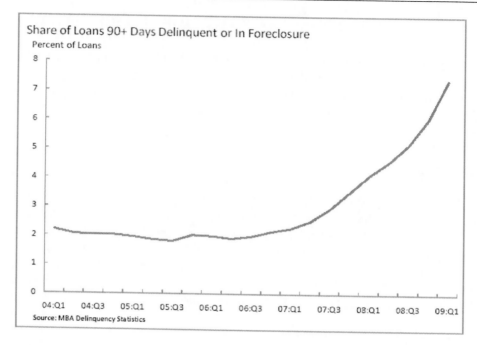

Figure 6-B.

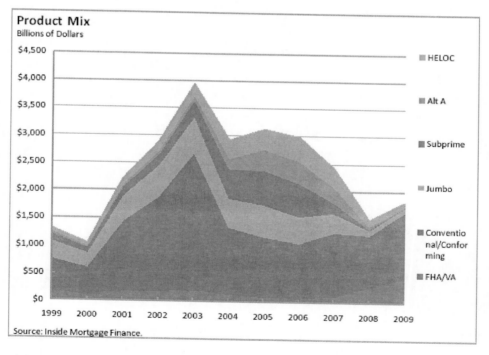

Figure 6-C.

Delinquency rates on mortgages had risen significantly, particularly on riskier products; loans were defaulting at over three times their early-2004 rate. Alt-A and subprime loans, which comprised a combined 19 percent of OCC-regulated banks' portfolios in early 2009, accounted for nearly half of the seriously delinquent loans.

A backlog of seriously delinquent loans had developed, through a combination of state foreclosure moratoria and the inability of servicers to manage the unprecedented volume of defaults.

Stresses in the financial system had reduced the supply of mortgage credit, limiting the ability of Americans to buy homes. Fannie Mae and Freddie Mac had been in conservatorship for over four months. And millions of responsible American families who were making their monthly payments—despite having lost jobs or income—had seen their property values fall, and were unable to sell or refinance at lower mortgage rates. The combination of falling home prices and economic contraction had sharply increased the financial strains on many responsible homeowners. At the beginning of 2009, nearly one-quarter of homeowners owed more on their mortgages than their homes were worth.

B. Policy Responses

During its first month in office, the Obama Administration took aggressive action to address the housing crisis. In February 2009, President Obama announced the Homeowner Affordability and Stability Plan. As part of this plan and through other housing initiatives, the Administration took the following actions to strengthen the housing market:

- Launched the Home Affordable Modification Program (HAMP), which would permanently reduce mortgage payments to affordable levels for qualifying borrowers;
- Provided strong support to Fannie Mae and Freddie Mac to ensure continued access to affordable mortgage credit across the market;
- Purchased, through Treasury and with the Federal Reserve, more than $1.4 trillion in agency mortgage backed securities, which helped keep mortgage rates at historic lows, allowing homeowners to access credit to purchase new homes and refinance into more affordable monthly payments;
- Through the Federal Housing Administration (FHA), provided liquidity for housing purchases at a time when private lending had declined, playing an important counter-cyclical role;
- Supported expanding the limits for loans guaranteed by Fannie Mae, Freddie Mac, and FHA from previous limits up to $625,500 per loan to $729,750;
- Expanded refinancing options for Fannie Mae and Freddie Mac loans, particularly for borrowers with negative equity, to allow more Americans to refinance;
- Supported a tax credit for first time homebuyers, which helped 2.5 million American families purchase homes; and
- Through ARRA, provided more than $5 billion in support for affordable rental housing through low income housing tax credit programs and $6.92 billion in support for a neighborhood stabilization program to restore neighborhoods suffering concentrated foreclosures.

As Mark Zandi (a former economic adviser for Senator John McCain's 2008 presidential campaign) and Alan S. Blinder (a former economic adviser for President Clinton) noted in a paper released in July 2010, the government's financial and fiscal policies tend to reinforce each other, such that the combined effect exceeds the sum of the parts. For example, providing housing tax credits as part of the stimulus boosts housing demand and therefore house prices. Foreclosures decrease, and the financial system suffers smaller losses, which, in turn, enhances the effectiveness of the government's efforts to stabilize the financial system.

C. Design of HAMP

As part of that Homeowner Affordability and Stability Plan, pursuant to the authority granted in EESA, the Obama Treasury Department began work on a program that would improve the affordability of mortgages for responsible homeowners, consistent with the mandate of EESA to promote financial stability while protecting taxpayers. Developing the program posed very difficult and challenging policy tradeoffs—how to make meaningful interventions that yield a high probability of participation and broadly support borrower success while minimizing the cost to the government, moral hazard, adverse selection, and operational and financial risks and complexity.

In addition, legal and other constraints required Treasury to develop a voluntary program that would support servicers' efforts to modify mortgages. TARP had originally been conceived as a program to purchase troubled assets directly from the balance sheets of banks, and to the extent Treasury acquired mortgages, it had authority to modify them directly. TARP was not primarily used for this purpose. EESA authorized certain types of programs to assist homeowners but constrained Treasury's ability to set up a mandatory modification program. Direct assistance to borrowers would not be consistent with the law, and valid mortgage contracts would have to be respected by any program Treasury established. Consequently, these legal constraints forced Treasury to seek the voluntary cooperation of mortgage servicers and investors.

While designing a program to improve the affordability of mortgages for responsible homeowners was difficult, the problem facing the mortgage industry was clear: loan servicers were simply unequipped to manage the magnitude of the crisis before them. The servicers were structured and staffed to perform a limited role: collecting payments and foreclosing on delinquent mortgages. They did not have the systems, staffing, operational capacity or incentives to engage with homeowners on a large scale and offer meaningful relief from unaffordable mortgages. Moreover, the expansion of private securitizations during the housing boom left servicers in a complicated legal situation; contractual language designed during the heady days of the bubble vaguely bound them to maximize investor returns, but little specific guidance existed on how that might be accomplished if the environment turned sour. At the time, there was no consensus among loan servicers about how to respond to responsible borrowers who were willing to continue making payments but were in need of some mortgage assistance.

In August 2008, Sheila C. Bair, Chairman of the FDIC, announced a plan for the FDIC to systematically modify troubled mortgages owned or serviced by IndyMac Federal Bank. The program would use a standardized modification process, including interest rate reduction, term extension, and principal forbearance, to achieve a mortgage affordability target, defined as a monthly mortgage payment of no more than 38 percent of gross monthly income, which was later lowered to 31. The FDIC program also proposed a decisionmaking - framework that explicitly compared the difference in cash flows a mortgage-holder would receive with and without an FDIC modification, and the probability the borrower would ultimately suffer foreclosure in either case.

Though the scale of the FDIC/IndyMac program was small relative to the national crisis, the introduction of a standardized modification objective, a method for achieving it, and a decision-making framework marked a breakthrough in the mortgage investing and servicing industries' approach to foreclosure avoidance. Toward the end of 2008, a group of counselors, mortgage companies, investors, and other mortgage market participants called the Hope Now Alliance proposed a streamlined loan modification approach, which represented its best plan to offer relief to borrowers and to preserve its members' investments in mortgages. Shortly thereafter, Fannie Mae and Freddie Mac adopted the streamlined loan modification as policy. This standardized modification would reduce the borrower's obligation to no more than 38 percent of the borrower's income through any combination of interest rate reduction, term extension, and principal forbearance.

The Hope Now Alliance framework demonstrated the private sector's willingness to work toward finding solutions to improve borrower and investor outcomes. But the program had serious drawbacks. The proposed modification framework lacked a mechanism for deciding when to apply the mortgage modification. Servicers' legal obligations toward modifying securitized loans remained uncertain, and servicers continued to be paralyzed by the need to seek approval from investors on a mortgageby--mortgage basis. There were no accepted timeframes for servicer decisions. As a result, the streamlined loan modification was applied irregularly, and repayment plans – rather than more permanent modification solutions – remained a favored tool for servicers. In the first quarter of 2009, only half of modifications lowered borrowers' payments, and nearly 40 percent of servicers' home retention efforts took the form of repayment plans rather than modifications or modification trials. As a result, hundreds of thousands of responsible American families simply lost their homes.

The Obama Administration recognized the momentum in the private sector reflected in Hope Now's efforts and sought to build upon it. Understanding that the solution was incomplete, the Administration concluded that government had a crucial role to play in clarifying legal arrangements between servicers and securitized trusts, creating uniformity in the decision-making process, and subsidizing more generous modifications that would better stabilize borrowers.

The Administration challenged itself to develop a program that would protect taxpayers at the same time that it broadly offered responsible, but struggling, homeowners the opportunity to remain in their homes at more affordable payment levels. The Administration determined that in order to achieve these objectives simultaneously, it was critical to leave the financial risk of modification redefault with the investors. Ultimately, the program should offer the opportunity to many, but the taxpayer should pay only to the extent the distressed borrower is assisted by a permanent modification that remains in effect.

HAMP was built around four core principles, designed to help the large segment of at-risk homeowners for whom foreclosure is avoidable and who want to stay in their homes.

First, the program focused on affordability, in an effort to ensure that borrowers who hope to remain in their homes would be able to afford the modified mortgage payment. Every modification under the program would be required to lower the borrower's monthly mortgage payment to 31 percent of the borrower's monthly gross income, a level estimated to provide reasonable assurance that the modification would be sustainable. The borrower's modified monthly payment would remain in place for five years, which Treasury expected would provide sufficient time for the housing market and the financial system to recover.

Second, HAMP would protect the taxpayer by employing an innovative pay-for-success structure and requiring the investor in the mortgage to retain the risk of future redefault. This structure aligned the interests of servicers, investors, borrowers and taxpayers and encouraged loan modifications that would be both affordable for borrowers over the long term and cost-effective for taxpayers. Servicers would receive an up-front payment of $1,000 for each successful modification after completion of the trial period, and "pay for success" fees of up to $1,000 per year for three years, if the borrower continued to make payments on time and in full. Homeowners would earn up to $1,000 in principal reduction each year for five years if they remained current. HAMP also matches reductions in monthly payments dollar -for-dollar with the lender/investor as they are reduced from 38 percent of the borrower's income (a 38 percent debt-to-income ratio, or "DTI") to 31 percent DTI. This requires the lender/investor to share with the Treasury the first loss in reducing the borrower's payment down to a 38 percent DTI, requiring lenders/investors to share in the burden of achieving affordability. To encourage the modification of current loans expected to default, HAMP provides additional incentives to servicers and lenders/investors after current loans are modified. These incentives were deemed crucial to the success of a program that, under EESA, would have to elicit the voluntary participation of servicers, investors and homeowners.

Third, while participation in HAMP would be voluntary for mortgage servicers, servicers who chose to participate would be prevented from "cherry-picking" loans to modify in a manner that might deny assistance to qualified borrowers at greatest risk of foreclosure. Any servicer that signed up for the program would be required to evaluate every eligible loan using a standard net present value (NPV) test. If the test was positive, the servicer would be required to modify the loan.

Fourth, unemployed borrowers would be allowed to participate in the program. Unemployed borrowers who had nine months or more of unemployment insurance remaining would be eligible to include it in their income for consideration in the NPV calculation. Unemployed borrowers are also allowed to include other sources of passive income like rental income and income from an employed spouse.

The basic HAMP terms were as follows: a participating HAMP servicer applies a series of modification steps to reduce the homeowner's monthly mortgage payment to 31 percent of the homeowner's gross (pre-tax) income, in the following order: rate reduction to as low as two percent; term extension up to 40 years; and principal deferral (or forbearance, at the servicer's option). The modified interest rate is fixed for a minimum of five years. Beginning in year six, the rate may increase no more than one percentage point per year until it reaches the Freddie Mac Primary Mortgage Market Survey rate (essentially the market interest rate) at the time the permanent modification agreement was prepared.

Before a mortgage is permanently modified, the homeowner must make the new, reduced monthly mortgage payment on time and in full, and submit the necessary documentation, during a trial period of three months to demonstrate that the modified monthly payment is sustainable. Homeowners who make payments on permanently modified loans on time accrue an incentive of $1,000 per year to reduce the amount of principal they owe up to a maximum of $5,000.

Any modification offer will provide a binding reduction in payments for borrowers who continue to meet the full terms of the modification, whether in the trial phase or after having converted to a permanent modification.

D. HAMP Targeting

Protecting taxpayers required that the new program not aim to prevent all foreclosures. It would be unfair to ask taxpayers to subsidize mortgages for speculators and owners of million dollar homes or vacation homes. Homeowners were facing foreclosure for a number of reasons, many of them outside the control of the borrowers: some were put in unsustainable loans; many saw their incomes decline. In addition, Treasury recognized that homeowners who could not afford to remain in their homes even after receiving a substantial reduction in payments could be served better by assistance in relocating to more affordable housing. Furthermore, Treasury recognized that preventing all foreclosures would be extremely expensive, would further increase the "shadow" inventory of housing stock, and would delay the stabilization of housing prices at realistic levels reflecting a rebalancing of supply and demand.

The Administration therefore identified four separate groups, and took a different approach toward each:

1. Homeowners who either are likely to find ways to remain in their homes without government assistance or, for policy reasons, the government should not assist. This group includes homeowners with jumbo mortgages, non-owner occupied homes and speculative properties. The program would not assist these homeowners.
2. Homeowners who are very likely to lose their homes, even with government assistance. This group includes homeowners who purchased homes that they simply could not afford, either as a result of poor underwriting or because they provided incomplete or misleading information (often at the urging of originators). It also includes homeowners who lost their jobs, are unlikely to regain employment with compensation comparable to their prior incomes and, due to high debt-to-income ratios, would likely default even with a lower monthly payment. The program would assist these homeowners in relocating, but trying to prevent foreclosure would not be a justified or constructive intervention.
3. Homeowners who have made the decision that they no longer want to remain in their homes, regardless of affordability, did not respond to repeated efforts to contact them and were willing to walk away from their mortgages. The program would not assist these homeowners.
4. Middleclass-working homeowners in owner-occupied homes who are at risk of losing their homes but for whom government assistance would significantly improve the odds they would avoid foreclosures. Helping these homeowners would prevent unnecessary pain and suffering and would help to stabilize housing markets. **This was the target group for loan modifications through HAMP.**

The program that Treasury developed, HAMP, was therefore an important part – but only one part – of the Obama Administration's comprehensive response to the financial and housing crisis. Based on economic conditions at the time, HAMP was expected to offer up to three to four million responsible American homeowners at risk of foreclosure reduced monthly mortgage payments that were sustainable over the long-term, providing these homeowners with a chance to modify their mortgages and avoid foreclosure.

It is important to emphasize that HAMP was not intended to help all borrowers. As noted above, it was intended to help an important segment of borrowers who were currently atrisk-of foreclosure or who would be at risk prior to the end of 2012, including only those homeowners who:

- owned and occupied their homes as a primary residence; had loan balances less than $729,750; took out their mortgages prior to Jan. 1, 2009;
- had contractual mortgage payments that were greater than 31 percent of their gross monthly income;
- could afford to make reasonable payments on modified mortgages;
- could provide documentation of income and hardship; and
- wanted to remain in their homes and were willing to remain current on their payments and comply with program terms.

The Administration originally projected that the new program would offer help to three to four million families through the end of 2012, expecting most of these to families to act on the offer of help and to receive a permanent modification. Treasury developed other strategies to transition borrowers out of homeownership in the manner least disruptive to them or their communities, when a trial modification did not convert to a permanent solution. Among this target population, Treasury also expected that there would unfortunately still be some borrowers who would not respond to outreach efforts or who would not act on trial modification offers when extended, though every effort was planned to reach out to this population. Despite recognizing that not every trial modification would be successful, working with servicers, housing counselors and others, Treasury would strive to reach as many eligible borrowers as possible.

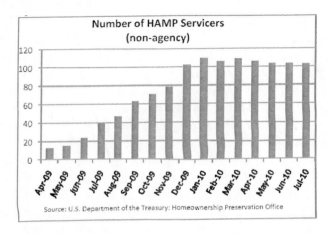

Figure 6-D.

E. Early Successes and Challenges

In the first year of the HAMP program, Treasury made substantial progress in many key areas. Treasury brought all stakeholders to the table-- servicers, investors, lenders, homeowners-- to assist as fast as possible. Treasury set a goal of 500,000 trial modifications by November 1, 2009. Even though participation was voluntary in accordance with EESA, Treasury quickly recruited servicers to the program. Over one hundred non-agency servicers signed up for HAMP, in addition to the many hundreds servicing loans on behalf of Fannie Mae and Freddie Mac. Close to ninety percent of mortgage loans nationwide were quickly covered by participating servicers.

Almost one month ahead of the November 1, 2009 benchmark, HAMP reached the 500,000 trial loan modifications milestone. This goal had pushed servicers to ramp up program implementation and sustain a faster pace of modifications; trial modifications were being issued at a faster rate than new homeowners were becoming eligible, helping to address the backlog of distressed homeowners who had received little assistance since the housing crisis became apparent in mid-2007. As of the end of February 2010, 822,000 borrowers had been in the trial phase of the modification process for more than three months and could be otherwise eligible for conversion subject to document submission and remaining current on payments. Of these, 32 percent had received permanent modifications or had been approved for permanent modification (170,000 permanent and another 92,000 approved for permanent).

Nearly 1.4 million borrowers were in contact with their servicers and were approved for and extended a modification offer, with 1.1 million of these approved offers resulting in modification trials. The run rate of eligible borrowers approved for and starting modifications was at or above the target rate set internally by Treasury of 20,000 – 25,000 per week. The 1.1 million borrowers who started modifications had their payments reduced by a median amount of more than $500. And even those borrowers who did not ultimately obtain a permanent modification received real relief as a result of reduced payments during the trial period, along with the opportunity to become current or pursue a foreclosure alternative like a short sale.

While the overall number of borrowers in permanent modifications rose substantially, the conversion rate to permanent modifications was below anticipated levels. When the program launched in May 2009, servicers were explicitly provided flexibility to approve borrowers for trial modifications without documentation of income in order to reach more borrowers more quickly. This approach was intended to provide more immediate relief and allow the program meet pentup-demand for modifications after two years of crisis conditions, "buy time" for many homeowners to find permanent solutions outside of the foreclosure process and facilitate housing market stabilization. Though some servicers required some documents up front, in practice most servicers started trials on the basis of a verbal income statement from the borrower. In the early fall and over the coming months, as the first large numbers of borrowers reached a trial length that would allow them to become eligible for conversion to a permanent modification, servicers experienced substantial difficulty in collecting and processing applications and making decisions based on the documentation provided. The modification conversion process was much more challenging than Treasury originally anticipated as a result of several factors, including insufficient capacity and execution at most servicers, a lack of borrower willingness or ability to provide necessary documentation, frequent inconsistencies between verbal and verified income that resulted in borrowers being deemed ineligible for the program (e.g., a borrower's verified income demonstrated that a borrower already had a contract payment below 31 percent of the borrower's monthly income), and a process that proved more complex administratively than originally conceived.

Therefore, Treasury's most immediate and critical challenge became working with servicers to increase the rate at which trial modifications were converted to permanent modifications as quickly as possible. As the first round of modifications reached the deadline to convert, Treasury caused servicers to implement an aggressive conversion campaign to address the challenges that borrowers were confronting in receiving permanent modifications. To prevent homeowners from losing their residences during the extended trial period, Treasury issued guidance prohibiting servicers from foreclosing on homeowners before their eligibility for a modification had been determined.

On January 28, 2010, Treasury issued new guidance requiring servicers to begin collecting documents upfront no later than June 1, 2010. This was done in direct response to the challenges of collecting documents during the trial period, and to help better ensure that more borrowers who start modifications are able to convert to permanent status.

As noted, the program made substantial progress in many key areas through early 2010. The 1.4 million offers and 1.1 million trial modifications put Treasury on track to meet the initial goal of offering help to up to three to four million borrowers via a modification. The pace over most of the first year of roughly 100,000 modification starts per month suggested a final total of over four million trial modifications.

In the spring of 2010, the move to collect documents upfront to achieve better overall conversions reduced the pace of modification offers materially; however, Treasury expects that requiring documentation up front will substantially improve the success rate of trial modifications and speed determinations.

Treasury also expects that the number of borrowers who do not complete trial modifications but ultimately transition to other forms of assistance will grow substantially and will ultimately number in the many hundreds of thousands. A cancelled trial modification does not mean that the program has completely failed a homeowner or that the borrower will inevitably face foreclosure: HAMP explicitly requires servicers to consider these borrowers for other foreclosure prevention options including proprietary modifications or other options like a short sale or deedin-- lieu of foreclosure that also prevent a foreclosure sale. The broader HAMP program provides borrowers with a range of assistance; success can only be measured on an aggregate basis, taking account of homeowners' individual situations and outcomes. Based on survey data from the eight largest servicers, it is estimated that a majority of borrowers who are turned down for a trial modification are offered some sort of foreclosure alternative – usually a modification proprietary to the servicer, or a short sale – rather than proceeding directly to foreclosure.

There are a range of important measures of success; keeping in mind the measures mentioned above, as well as others like the effect of HAMP on neighborhood and housing market stabilization, Treasury continues to monitor progress and push for improved results. HAMP has had a substantial impact on avoiding foreclosures so far (foreclosure sale is prohibited for the 200,000 borrowers still active in HAMP trial modifications), and very few borrowers that have qualified for HAMP (including the ability to make a reasonable payment on a modified loan as measured by income sufficient to pass an NPV model) have gone through foreclosure sale to date. In addition, HAMP has transformed the way the mortgage servicing industry treats borrowers in distress. Because of HAMP, servicers have developed constructive private-sector options. Where there was once no consensus plan among loan servicers about how to respond to borrowers in need of mortgage assistance, HAMP has established a universal affordability standard, a 31 percent debt-to-income ratio. This has enhanced servicers' ability to reduce mortgage payments to sustainable levels while simultaneously providing investors with a justification for modifications.

Taking into account HAMP's effect on standardizing and expanding proprietary modifications in the mortgage industry, the number of mortgage modifications has been double the number of foreclosure completions: More than 3.35 million modifications were arranged from April 2009 through the end of July 2010. This includes more than 1.3 million HAMP trial modifications started, more than 510,000 Federal Housing Administration (FHA) loss mitigation and early delinquency interventions, and nearly 1.6 million private sector modifications performed by members of the HOPE Now alliance. Given the complexity of the mortgage modification process and the number of government and non-government modification programs available, homeowners often receive more than one modification arrangement. Therefore it is difficult to determine the exact number of homeowners assisted by multiple programs.

On the measure of neighborhood and housing market stabilization, the substantial number of foreclosure sales avoided has contributed to a material improvement in market expectations for house prices and to many successive months of stability in home prices in much of the country. But, as discussed, efforts must continue to capitalize on early encouraging signs and overcome remaining challenges. There are still a number of risk factors that will challenge the stability of the housing markets, including the potential for mortgage rates to rise, continuing elevated levels of delinquencies exacerbated by unemployment and the large number of underwater borrowers, and the associated potential for a substantial increase in the number of foreclosure sales.

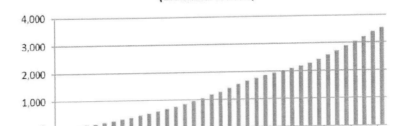

Cumulative Total Modifications Completed
(thousands of loans)

■ Completed (Proprietary) ■ Completed HAMP

Source: Making Home Affordable and HOPE NOW
HOPE NOW has collected data on Completed (Proprietary) Modifications since 2007. Data for Completed HAMP loans began in September 2009.

Figure 6-E.

Further, it is important to keep in mind that HAMP is only one of many Administration housing efforts that target these challenges: the Administration has also provided substantial support for the housing markets through investment in Fannie Mae and Freddie Mac to help keep mortgage rates affordable; purchase of agency mortgage-backed securities; refinancing opportunities that have allowed more than four million borrowers to refinance since the launch of the Making Home Affordable Program (MHA); and an initiative to provide support and financing to state and local Housing Finance Agencies (HFAs). These HFAs provide, in turn, tens of thousands of affordable mortgages to first time homebuyers and help develop tens of thousands of affordable rental units for working families, including those displaced by the housing crisis and foreclosures.

Second Lien Modification Program

A few months after launching HAMP, Treasury rolled out its first major expansion of the program: on August 13, 2009, Treasury published guidance introducing the Second Lien Modification Program (referred to as 2MP). Under 2MP, when a borrower's first lien is modified under HAMP and the servicer of the second lien is a 2MP participant, that servicer must offer to modify the borrower's second lien according to a defined protocol, which provides for a lump sum payment from Treasury in exchange for full extinguishment of the second lien, or a reduced lump sum payment from Treasury in exchange for a partial extinguishment and modification of the borrower's remaining second lien. Although 2MP was initially met with reluctance from servicers and investors who did not want to recognize losses on their second lien portfolios, Treasury has signed up several of the largest second lien servicers for 2MP this year. Servicers participating in the 2MP program service a majority of outstanding second liens.

Home Affordable Foreclosure Alternatives Program

Any modification program seeking to avoid preventable foreclosures has limits, HAMP included. HAMP does not, nor was it ever intended to, address every delinquent loan. Borrowers not qualifying for HAMP may benefit from an alternative that helps the borrower transition to more affordable housing and avoid the substantial costs of a foreclosure. On November 30, 2009, the Administration announced the Home Affordable Foreclosure Alternatives (HAFA) Program, pursuant to which Treasury provides incentives for short sales and deeds-in-lieu of foreclosure for circumstances in which borrowers are unable or unwilling to complete the HAMP modification process. Borrowers are eligible for relocation assistance of $1,500 and servicers receive a $1,000 incentive for completing a short sale or deed-in-lieu of foreclosure. In addition, investors are paid up to $1,000 for allowing short sale proceeds to be distributed to subordinate lien holders.

F. The Second Phase of HAMP

During the fall of 2009, in addition to the challenges articulated above, HAMP faced other challenges. Some servicers fell short of commitments they had made to Treasury to clear out their backlogs of loans in aged trial modifications. Participation in 2MP was lower than Treasury had hoped. The evolution of the economic landscape since early 2009 had directed attention toward two problems the program's broad framework had not specifically targeted: unemployment and negative equity. During 2009, employment had deteriorated severely, and while home prices had begun to show signs of stabilizing by late 2009, analysts projected a protracted period of recovery before prices returned to their pre-crisis levels. Unemployment and negative equity appeared to be the main potential causes of defaults going forward. In response, Treasury began designing a new phase of HAMP, with input from various constituencies.

In March 2010, the Obama Administration announced enhancements to HAMP aimed at the unemployment and negative equity problems, including providing temporary mortgage assistance to many unemployed homeowners, encouraging servicers to write down mortgage debt as part of a HAMP modification (the Principal Reduction Alternative, or PRA), allowing more borrowers to qualify for modifications through HAMP, and helping additional borrowers move to more affordable housing when modification is not possible.

Unemployment Program

The Unemployment Program (UP) requires servicers to grant qualified unemployed borrowers a forbearance period during which their mortgage payments are temporarily reduced for a minimum of three months, and up to six months for some borrowers, while they look for a new job. HAMP servicers are required to offer UP to any unemployed homeowner whose HAMP-eligible loan has not been previously modified under HAMP if the homeowner has been receiving unemployment benefits for three months on the date of the request. If a homeowner does not find a job before the temporary assistance period is over or finds a job with a reduced income, the homeowner will be evaluated for a permanent HAMP modification or may be eligible for HAMP's alternatives to the foreclosure program. Servicers are prohibited from initiating a foreclosure action or conducting a foreclosure sale while the borrower is being evaluated for UP, after a foreclosure plan notice is mailed, during the UP forbearance or extension, and while the borrower is being evaluated for or participating in HAMP or HAFA following the UP forbearance period. Servicers are reimbursed by TARP for any costs associated with UP, and there will be no cost to government or taxpayers from the forbearance plans.

Principal Reduction Alternative

Under PRA, servicers are required to evaluate the benefit of principal reduction and are encouraged to offer principal reduction whenever the NPV result of a HAMP modification using PRA is greater than the NPV result without considering principal reduction. The principal reduction and the incentives based on the dollar value of the principal reduced will be earned by the borrower and investor based on a pay-for -success structure. Under the contract with each servicer, Treasury cannot compel a servicer to select PRA over the standard HAMP modification even if the NPV of PRA is greater than the NPV of regular HAMP.

Enhancements to Home Affordable Foreclosure Alternatives (HAFA)

Treasury also doubled relocation assistance payments to homeowners receiving foreclosure alternatives, and increased incentives to servicers and lenders, including incentives for extinguishment of subordinate liens, to encourage more short sales and other alternatives to foreclosure.

FHA Short Refinance

In March 2010, the Obama Administration announced adjustments to existing FHA programs that will permit lenders to provide additional refinancing options to homeowners who owe more than their homes are worth because of large declines in home prices in their local markets. This program, known as the FHA Short Refinance program, will provide more opportunities for qualifying mortgage loans to be restructured and refinanced into FHA-insured loans. The terms of this program include that the homeowner must be current on the existing first lien mortgage; the homeowner must occupy the home as a primary residence and have a qualifying credit score; the mortgage investor must reduce the amount owed on the original loan by at least 10 percent; the new FHA loan must have a balance less than the current value of the home; and total mortgage debt for the borrower after the refinancing, including both the first lien mortgage and any other junior liens, cannot be greater than 115 percent of the current value of the home giving home-owners a path to regain equity in their homes and affordable monthly payments. TARP funds will be made available up to $11 billion in the aggregate to provide additional coverage to lenders for a share of potential losses on these loans and to provide incentives to support the write-downs of second liens and encourage participation by servicers.

Housing Finance Agency Innovation Fund for the Hardest Hit Housing Markets

On February 19, 2010, the Administration announced the $1.5 billion Housing Finance Agency Innovation Fund for the Hardest Hit Housing Markets (HFA Hardest Hit Fund, or HHF) for state housing finance agencies in the nation's hardest hit housing markets to design innovative, locally targeted foreclosure prevention programs. This first round of the HFA Hardest Hit Fund was intended to help address the housing problems facing those states that have suffered an average home price drop of more than 20 percent from their respective peaks in the housing bubble. The states included in this first round of HHF were California, Florida, Arizona, Michigan, and Nevada. Funds were allocated to these states according to a formula based on severity of home price declines and unemployment. HFAs designed the state programs themselves, tailoring the housing assistance to their local needs. Treasury required that the programs comply with the requirements of EESA, such as seeking to prevent avoidable foreclosures. All of the funded program designs are posted online at http://www.FinancialStability.gov/roadtostability/hardesthitfund.html.

In March 2010, the Obama Administration announced an expansion of the HFA Hardest Hit Fund to target an additional five states with high shares of their populations living in local areas of concentrated economic distress. The second HHF included up to $600 million in funding for locally-tailored measures to help families stay in their homes or otherwise avoid foreclosure. The $600 million in funds is equivalent on a per person basis to the $1.5 billion awarded in the first HHF. While the first HHF targeted five states affected by home price declines greater than 20 percent, the second HHF targeted states with the highest concentration of their populations living in counties with unemployment rates greater than 12 percent, on average, over the months of 2009. (States that were allocated funds under the first HHF program were not eligible for the second HHF program.) The five states that received allocations based on this criterion were North Carolina, Ohio, Oregon, Rhode Island, and South Carolina.

On August 11, 2010, in recognition of the particular challenges faced by states with extraordinarily high unemployment, the Administration announced that Treasury will make an additional $2 billion of assistance available for HHF programs for homeowners struggling to make their mortgage payments due to unemployment. The 18 states and jurisdictions eligible for this additional funding had high sustained unemployment rates over the last 12 months (through June, 2010) that were at or above the national average. This includes nine of the original HHF states (California, Florida, Michigan, Nevada, North Carolina, Ohio, Oregon, Rhode Island and South Carolina), which can use the funding for an existing unemployment bridge program or to implement the model provided, as well as Alabama, the District of Columbia, Georgia, Illinois, Indiana, Kentucky, Mississippi, New Jersey and Tennessee. Each state will use the funds for targeted unemployment programs that provide temporary assistance to eligible homeowners to help them pay their mortgages while they seek re-employment or additional employment or undertake job training.

On September 29, 2010, the Administration announced that Treasury will make an additional $3.5 billion of assistance available for the states and jurisdictions participating in HHF to expand the reach of their programs to help more struggling homeowners. Funds will be allocated to these 18 states and the District of Columbia based on population size.

G. Accomplishments

HAMP has achieved three critical goals:

- It has provided immediate relief to many struggling homeowners;
- It has used taxpayer resources efficiently; and
- It has transformed the way the entire mortgage servicing industry operates.

Eighteen months into the program, HAMP has helped more than 1.3 million homeowners by reducing their monthly mortgage payments to more affordable levels. This includes more than 460,000 homeowners whose mortgage terms have been modified permanently. These homeowners have experienced a 36 percent median reduction in their mortgage payments— more than $500 per month—amounting to a total, program-wide savings of nearly $3.2 billion. In short, hundreds of thousands of American families have been able to avoid foreclosure and keep their homes because of HAMP.

"HAMP serve[d] as a catalyst ... a mobilizing event to push servicers to take broader actions at a more rapid pace," and noted that "it pushed other investors, including Fannie and Freddie, to move in a direction of programmatic home loan modifications."
-Wells Fargo Home Mortgage Co-President Michael Heid (testimony before Congress)[17]

"One of the significant advantages of HAMP has been the establishment of standards. And in particular, the debt-to-income ratio that was used, even on our proprietary programs prior to HAMP, was higher than 31 percent."
- Bank of America Home Loan President Barbara DeSoer (testimony before Congress)[18]

In the year following initiation of HAMP, home retention strategies changed dramatically. In the first quarter of 2009, nearly half of mortgage modifications increased borrowers' monthly payments or left their payments unchanged. By the second quarter of 2010, 90 percent of mortgage modifications lowered payments for the borrower. This change means borrowers are receiving better solutions. Modifications with payment reductions perform materially better than modifications that increase payments or leave them unchanged. Moreover, even holding the percentage payment reduction constant, modifications appear to have improved since 2008. For modifications made in 2008, 15.8 percent of modifications that received a 20 percent payment reduction were 60 days or more delinquent three months into the modification. For the 2010 vintage, that delinquency rate has fallen almost in half, to 8.2 percent. The OCC's Mortgage Metrics Report from 2010:Q2 attributes the improvement in mortgage performance to "servicer emphasis on repayment sustainability and the borrower's ability to repay the debt."

Early indications suggest that the re default rate for permanent HAMP modifications is significantly lower than for historical private-sector modifications—a result of the program's focus on properly aligning incentives and achieving greater affordability. For HAMP modifications made in the fourth quarter of 2009, OCC records show that 7.9 percent of loans were delinquent three months into the modification and just 10.8 percent were delinquent six months into the modification. The comparable delinquency rates for non-HAMP modifications made in the same quarter were 12.1 percent and 22.4 percent, respectively. For modifications made in the first quarter of 2010, the delinquency rates for HAMP and non-HAMP modifications are similar – 10.5 percent and 11.6 percent delinquent at three months, respectively. Convergence between the HAMP and non-HAMP re-default rates going forward may suggest that the industry is adopting the HAMP modification standard.

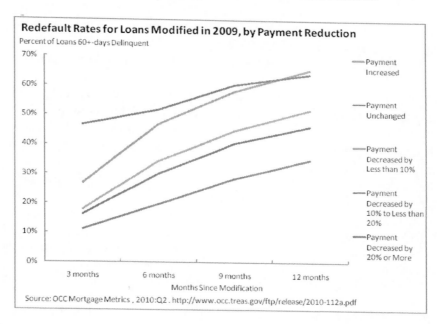

Figure 6-F.

Borrowers who do not ultimately qualify for HAMP modifications often receive alternative forms of assistance. Approximately one-half of homeowners who apply for HAMP modifications but do not qualify have received some form of private-sector modification. Less than ten percent have lost their homes through foreclosure. Industry representatives testifying at foreclosure prevention hearings before the Committee on Oversight and Government Reform United States House of Representatives on June 24, 2010 indicated that many of their private-sector modifications are intended to assist borrowers who are not eligible for HAMP.

HAMP uses taxpayer resources efficiently. HAMP's "payfor-- success" design utilizes a trial period to ensure that taxpayer-funded incentives are used only to support borrowers who are committed to staying in their homes and making monthly payments, and the investor retains the risk of the borrower re-defaulting into foreclosure. No taxpayer funds are paid to a servicer or an investor until a borrower has made three modified mortgage payments on time and in full. The majority of payments are made over a five-year period only if the borrower continues to fulfill this responsibility. These safeguards ensure that spending is limited to high-quality modifications. Comprehensive public reporting provides an additional layer of accountability, assuring that servicers fulfill their obligation to contact and help at -risk borrowers in exchange for taxpayer-funded incentives.

There is a worthwhile point to be made about who should "count" as being helped by administration housing programs. The Administration originally projected that HAMP would offer help to three to four million families through the end of 2012, expecting most of these to families to act on the offer of help and to receive a permanent modification. From one perspective counting borrowers who get a HAMP permanent modification or a FHA Short Refinance loan is overinclusive, - because some of the families will re-default and end up in foreclosure in any event, although these programs will increase the odds that they can prevent foreclosure and receive valuable temporary relief (up to $6,000 per year) as long as they remain current.

The "count" is also underinclusive, -because measures to reduce foreclosures help to stabilize housing markets and avoid community-wide costs of foreclosure. The measure is also under-inclusive because every person who is in a temporary modification is getting a significant benefit – the family has several months to remain in the home with a reduced payment and to try to remedy the situation and avoid foreclosure. It is under inclusive because homeowners able to take advantage of HAFA will receive significant help transitioning more quickly and less traumatically to new housing they can afford than they would if they suffered foreclosure. Lastly, it is under-inclusive because many of the unemployed homeowners who receive a temporary forbearance through UP are likely to become re-employed and resume mortgage payments – without the unemployment forbearance program those homeowners might have gone to foreclosure. This is especially important in the case of FHA Short Refinance, which could help to avert a wave of foreclosures due to strategic default, and HHF, which helps states provide targeted assistance to combat deteriorating conditions in local markets. As noted above, HAMP has transformed the way the mortgage servicing industry treats borrowers in distress. Because of HAMP, servicers have developed constructive private-sector options.

Finally, the measure does not include all of the new mortgages provided to families at reasonable cost because of FHA and government interventions with Fannie Mae and Freddie Mac. In many cases, these mortgages have provided financing to help families purchase foreclosed homes and become homeowners, often for the first time since housing has become so much more affordable as a result of the crisis.

H. Transparency and Accountability

To protect taxpayers and ensure that every TARP dollar is directed toward promoting financial stability, Treasury established rigorous accountability and transparency measures for all of its programs, including HAMP and the other housing programs, as more fully described later in this chapter. In addition to these public reports, Treasury has worked to maximize the transparency of the housing program to borrowers and ensure that servicers are held accountable. Every borrower is entitled to a clear explanation if he or she is determined to be ineligible for a HAMP modification. Treasury has established denial codes that require servicers to report the reason for modification denials in writing to Treasury. Servicers are required to use those denial codes as a uniform basis for sending letters to borrowers who are evaluated for HAMP but denied a modification. In those letters, borrowers will be provided with a phone number to contact their servicers as well as the phone number of the HOPE hotline, which has counselors who are trained to work with borrowers to help them understand reasons they may have been denied modifications and explain other modification or foreclosure prevention options that may be available to them.

Transparency of the NPV model a -key component of the eligibility test for HAMP is - also important. Treasury increased public access to the NPV white paper, which explains the methodology used in the NPV model. To ensure accuracy and reliability, Freddie Mac, Treasury's compliance agent, conducts periodic audits of servicers' implementation of the model. If servicers' models do not meet Treasury's NPV specifications, Freddie Mac will require the servicers to discontinue use of their own implementation of the model and revert back to the NPV application available from Treasury through the MHA Servicer Portal. As required by the Dodd-Frank Act, Treasury is preparing to establish a web portal that borrowers can access to run a NPV analysis using input data regarding their own mortgages, and to provide to borrowers who are turned down for a HAMP modification the input data used in evaluating the application.

All servicers voluntarily participating in HAMP have contractually agreed to follow the HAMP program guidelines, which require the servicer to offer a HAMP modification to all eligible borrowers and to have systems that can process all HAMP-eligible loans. Servicers are subject to periodic, on-site compliance reviews performed by Treasury's compliance agent, Making Home Affordable-Compliance (MHA-C), a separate, independent division of Freddie Mac, to ensure that servicers satisfy their obligations under HAMP requirements in order to provide a well-controlled program that assists as many deserving homeowners as possible to retain their homes while taking reasonable steps to prevent fraud, waste and abuse. Treasury works closely with MHA-C to design and refine the compliance program and conducts quality assessments of the activities performed by MHA-C. Following these reviews, MHAC-provides Treasury with assessments of each servicer's compliance with HAMP requirements. If appropriate, Treasury will implement remedies for non-compliance. These remedies may include withholding or reducing incentive payments to servicers, requiring repayments of prior incentive payments made to servicers with respect to affected loans, or requiring additional servicer oversight.

I. Looking Ahead for Housing

Since EESA was enacted, the housing market has remained distressed, and although there are promising signs of stabilization, the nature of that distress has changed. In late 2008 and 2009, the nation's housing market was in broad decline, as a result of the subprime mortgage collapse and the effects of the financial crisis and the severe recession. However, in the middle of 2009, house price declines started to show signs of stabilization in much of the country. Home prices leveled off after 30 straight months of decline.

Despite these nascent signs of stabilization at the national level, home prices have continued to decline and foreclosures have continued to rise in certain areas of the country as the nature of the stress in the housing market has evolved from defaults generated by poorly-underwritten loans, such as subprime, AltA -and option ARM mortgages, to concentrated unemployment, negative equity, excess housing inventory, and rising foreclosures in certain areas of the country, which act as a drag on housing prices and economic recovery in those communities. Negative equity and high unemployment tend to be concentrated in the same regions and appear to exacerbate one another; low equity levels give unemployed borrowers little opportunity to escape their mortgages except through foreclosure or short sale.

As described above, the Administration has responded by expanding the initial version of HAMP that was first announced in February 2009, which was designed to modify conventional first lien loans. HAMP has since been modified to include unemployment programs, second lien relief, foreclosure alternatives (such as short sales and deeds-in-lieu of foreclosure) and principal reduction programs. Recognizing that the housing market conditions vary widely by locality, and are especially stressed by continued unemployment, the Administration has quickly rolled out the HFA Hardest Hit Fund for those states most affected by these issues. In addition, to combat negative equity and improve affordability, Treasury has partnered with FHA in expanding refinance opportunities through the FHA Short Refinance program.

Because they are relatively recent expansions, these additions to HAMP, and of HHF and the FHA Short Refinance program, have not yet begun to penetrate the housing market. Nevertheless, these programs will allow Federal assistance to reach more distressed homeowners and provide additional stability to the housing market going forward. Servicers that participate in HAMP can continue to make modifications through the end of 2012. HHF permits participating HFAs to provide support through their programs until as late as 2017, depending on available funding. And the FHA Short Refinance program is expected to permit homeowners to refinance their mortgage loans and reduce their overall mortgage debt through the end of 2012.

Furthermore, in much the same way that HAMP's first lien modification program has provided a national blueprint for mortgage modifications, these new programs will continue to shape the mortgage servicing industry and act as a catalyst for industry standardization of short sale, refinance and principal reduction programs. The interplay of all these programs will provide a much more flexible response to continued changes in the housing market over the next two years. Rather than ending, TARP's positive effects on the housing market are expected to expand over time.

J. Summary Description of Housing Programs

1. Making Home Affordable Program (MHA)

a. Home Affordable Modification Program (HAMP)

The Home Affordable Modification Program (HAMP) is the largest program within MHA. HAMP provides eligible homeowners the opportunity to reduce their monthly mortgage payments to 31 percent of their gross (pretax)-income.

To qualify for HAMP, a borrower must:

- Own a one-to four-unit home that is a primary residence;
- Have received a mortgage on or before January 1, 2009;
- Have a mortgage payment (including principal, interest, taxes, insurance, and homeowners association dues) that is more than 31 percent of the homeowner's gross monthly income; and
- Owe not more than $729,750 on a first mortgage for a one–unit property (there are higher limits for two– to four– unit properties).

To create an affordable payment, a participating servicer applies a series of modification steps in the following order: rate reduction to as low as two percent; term extension up to 40 years; and principal deferral (or forbearance, at the servicer's option). The modified interest rate is fixed for a minimum of five years. Beginning in year six, the rate may increase no more than one percentage point per year until it reaches the Freddie Mac Primary Mortgage Market Survey rate (essentially the market interest rate) at the time the permanent modification agreement was prepared.

Before a mortgage is permanently modified, the homeowner must make the new, reduced monthly mortgage payment on time and in full during a trial period of three or four months. Homeowners who make payments on permanently modified loans on time accrue an incentive of $1,000 per year to reduce the amount of principal they owe up a maximum of $5,000.

b. Second Lien Modification Program (2MP)

Under the Second Lien Modification Program (2MP), an additional component of MHA, Treasury provides incentives for second-lien holders to modify or extinguish a second-lien mortgage when a modification has been initiated on the first lien mortgage for the same property under HAMP. Under 2MP, when a borrower's first lien is modified under HAMP and the servicer of the second lien is a 2MP participant, that servicer must offer to modify the borrower's second lien according to a defined protocol, which provides for a lump sum payment from Treasury in exchange for full extinguishment of the second lien, or a reduced lump sum payment from Treasury in exchange for a partial extinguishment and modification of the borrower's remaining second lien.

c. Home Affordable Foreclosure Alternatives (HAFA) Program

Under the Home Affordable Foreclosure Alternatives (HAFA) Program, an additional component of MHA, Treasury provides incentives for short sales and deeds-in-lieu of foreclosure for circumstances in which borrowers are unable or unwilling to complete the HAMP modification process. Borrowers are eligible for relocation assistance of $1,500 and servicers receive a $1,000 incentive for completing a short sale or deed-in-lieu of foreclosure. In addition, investors are paid up to $1,000 for allowing short sale proceeds to be distributed to subordinate lien holders.

d. The Unemployment Program (UP)

The Unemployment Program (UP), an additional component of MHA, requires participating servicers to grant qualified unemployed borrowers a forbearance period during which their mortgage payments are temporarily reduced for a minimum of three months, and up to six months for some borrowers, while they look for new jobs. If a homeowner does not find a job before the temporary assistance period is over or finds a job with a reduced income, the homeowner will be evaluated for a permanent HAMP modification or may be eligible for certain alternatives to the modification program under MHA.

e. Principal Reduction Alternative (PRA)

Under the Principal Reduction Alternative (PRA), an additional component of MHA, servicers are required to evaluate the benefit of principal reduction and are encouraged to offer principal reduction whenever the NPV result of a HAMP modification using PRA is greater than the NPV result without considering principal reduction. Incentives are paid based on the dollar value of the principal reduced.

2. Housing Finance Agency Innovation Fund for the Hardest Hit Housing Markets (HFA Hardest Hit Fund, or HHF)

The Housing Finance Agency Innovation Fund for the Hardest Hit Housing Markets (HFA Hardest Hit Fund, or HHF) allows state housing finance agencies (HFAs) in the nation's hardest hit housing markets to design innovative, locally targeted foreclosure prevention programs. Five of these states (Arizona, California, Florida, Michigan and Nevada) have had average home price declines greater than 20 percent since the housing market downturn, accounting for the majority of "underwater" mortgages in the country. The remaining fourteen states and jurisdictions (Alabama, Georgia, Illinois, Indiana, Kentucky, Mississippi, New Jersey, North Carolina, Ohio, Oregon, Rhode Island, South Carolina, Tennessee and Washington, DC) have concentrated areas of economic distress due to unemployment or had an unemployment rate at or above the national average for the past year.

HFAs designed the state programs themselves, tailoring the housing assistance to their local needs. Treasury required that the programs comply with the requirements of EESA, such as seeking to prevent avoidable foreclosures. All of the funded program designs are posted online at http://www.FinancialStability.gov/roadtostability/hardesthitfund.html.

3. *Support for the FHA Short Refinance Program*

In March 2010, the Administration announced adjustments to existing FHA programs that will permit lenders to provide additional refinancing options to homeowners who owe more than their homes are worth because of large declines in home prices in their local markets. This program, known as the FHA Short Refinance program, will provide more opportunities for qualifying mortgage loans to be restructured and refinanced into FHA-insured loans.

Among other requirements:

- The homeowner must be current on the existing first lien mortgage;
- The homeowner must occupy the home as a primary residence and have a qualifying credit score;
- The mortgage investor must reduce the amount owed on the original loan by at least ten percent;
- The new FHA loan must have a balance less than the current value of the home; and
- Total mortgage debt for the borrower after the refinancing, including both the first lien mortgage and any other junior liens, cannot be greater than 115 percent of the current value of the home – giving homeowners a path to regain equity in their homes and an affordable monthly payment.

TARP funds will be made available up to $11 billion in the aggregate to provide additional coverage to lenders for a share of potential losses on these loans and to provide incentives to support the write -downs of second liens and encourage participation by servicers.

7. EXECUTIVE COMPENSATION

Treasury Implemented the Executive Compensation Restrictions Required by the Laws That Created the Troubled Asset Relief Program

EESA set standards for executive compensation and corporate governance for recipients of financial assistance under the TARP. These executive compensation standards were then expanded under ARRA and Treasury's Interim Final Rule on executive compensation published on June 15, 2009. This rule created the Office of the Special Master for TARP Executive Compensation, and Kenneth R. Feinberg was appointed as Special Master in June 2009.

1. *Restrictions on exceptional assistance recipients and other recipients of TARP funds*

EESA, as amended by ARRA imposed restrictions on executive compensation for all recipients of financial assistance under TARP. The requirements include the following:

- Limits on bonuses and retention awards for the top executives;
- Prohibition on "golden parachutes" for the top executives;

- Limits on compensation to exclude incentives on senior executives to take unnecessary and excessive risks that threaten a firm's value;
- Prohibition on compensation plans that encourage manipulation of reported earnings to enhance the compensation of employees, and a "clawback" provision to permit recovery of certain payments based on earnings statements or other criteria that are later found to be materially inaccurate;
- Establishment of a company-wide policy regarding excessive or luxury expenditures;
- Establishment of a compensation committee composed entirely of independent directors; and
- A requirement for an annual, non-binding "say on pay" shareholder vote regarding compensation required to be disclosed under SEC rules.

Treasury also promulgated rules to implement these provisions that added additional requirements. These included a prohibition on paying "tax gross-ups" to top executives (which are designed to reduce or eliminate the tax burden on an executive relating to compensation arrangements) and a requirement to disclose certain executive perquisites.

Treasury's rules also created the Office of the Special Master, and gave to the Special Master the responsibility to review and approve the compensation of top executives at firms that received "exceptional assistance". These firms were AIG, Bank of America, Citigroup, General Motors, Chrysler, Ally Financial (formerly GMAC) and Chrysler Financial. The rule required the Special Master to review the individual pay packages of the top 25 most highly compensated employees at each firm and to review the compensation structures for the next 26-100 employees. The rule also outlined certain principles that the Special Master must follow in making his decisions.

The Special Master conducted extensive reviews of executive compensation at these companies for the 2009 and 2010 calendar years and imposed requirements based on the following key principles:

- For the top 25 individual pay packages: to (i) limit cash salary, (ii) pay incentives in long -term restricted stock, (iii) limit perquisites and "other" compensation, and (iv) limit executive pension and retirement programs; and
- For the next 26-100 employees' compensation structures: to (i) restrict shortterm-cash compensation, (ii) tie incentive compensation to real achievement, (iii) make sure compensation structures have a long-term focus, and (iv) align pay practices with shareholder and taxpayer interests.

The review and approval by the Special Master has led to significant reductions in compensation at these firms. This was to ensure that executive pay for the top 100 employees at the firms that received exceptional assistance is in line with long-term value creation and financial stability. For the five firms that were still exceptional assistance recipients for 2010 determinations, a large majority – 84 percent – of top 25 executives covered by the 2009 determinations remained with the companies through the 2010 determinations. The cash and overall compensation of most executives new to the top 25, who mostly filled slots created by employee departures prior to the 2009 determinations, was reduced substantially from historical levels.

Kenneth R. Feinberg observed in his Final Report that of "the seven [exceptional assistance] firms initially subject to the Office's jurisdiction, two have completed repayment to the taxpayers and three more have begun to do so—in one case fully returning the "exceptional" assistance . . . Four firms remain in the program, but I am encouraged by their record of retaining top employees and adding outside talent, and hopeful for their eventual repayment."

-"Final Report of Special Master for Executive Compensation Kenneth R. Feinberg",
September 10, 2010.

ARRA also required the Secretary to conduct a Look Back Review of bonuses, retention awards, and other compensation paid to each TARP recipient's Top 25 before the introduction of the additional requirements, to determine if any payments were inconsistent with the purpose of EESA or TARP, or otherwise inconsistent with the public interest. The Office of the Special Master carried out the Look Back Review and published its findings in July 2010. The Special Master did not determine that any reviewed payment was inconsistent with the law or the public interest. However, this outcome does not express a conclusion that these payments were appropriate or advisable, particularly in light of the circumstances facing the financial system generally, and some institutions specifically, in late 2008 and early 2009. Therefore, the Special Master proposed that all TARP recipients adopt a prospective compensation policy (a "brake" policy) that would provide companies the authority to alter pending payments to executives in the event of a financial crisis.

2. TARP Helped Curb The Influence Of Excessive Compensation At TARP Recipients, And In Doing So, Helped Lay The Ground Work For Corporate Governance Reform

After two years, the executive compensation landscape has changed significantly. While the Office of the Special Master focused on its responsibilities under TARP, a much broader policy initiative was moving forward. These efforts are critical steps to address compensation issues that contributed to the financial crisis, and significant progress has been made to date.

- In September 2009, G-20 leaders confirmed that compensation practices in the financial sector both reflected and encouraged excessive risk-taking, and endorsed standards intended to align compensation practices with long-term value creation and financial stability. These standards are being implemented worldwide.
- In the United States, the Federal Reserve and other federal banking regulators issued guiding principles on how incentive compensation at banks should be designed to protect safety and soundness, and committed to ensuring that banks adopt these principles. The SEC enhanced existing compensation disclosure requirements. The Dodd-Frank Act law requires public companies to give shareholders a "say on pay" vote and strengthens compensation committees' independence.

Kenneth R. Feinberg observed that there is a "profound difference in perspective on executive pay practices between some financial institutions and many of the taxpayers whose dollars rescued our economy and financial system. To our great benefit, the Treasury rules that created the Office of the Special Master anticipated the range of difficulties we would encounter, and provided authority to confront them as well as principles for doing so."

-"Final Report of Special Master for Executive Compensation Kenneth R. Feinberg",
September 10, 2010.

3. *Final Report of the Special Master for Executive Compensation*

In September 2010, after fourteen months of service, Kenneth R. Feinberg resigned as Special Master for TARP Executive Compensation and issued the "Final Report of Special Master for Executive Compensation Kenneth R. Feinberg" (Final Report). The Final Report summarizes the work of the Office of the Special Master for TARP Executive Compensation during Mr. Feinberg's tenure as Special Master and includes an overview of the compensation determinations issued for the 2009 and 2010 calendar years. The report also reviews, among other things, the processes (collection of data and analysis) and standards of review used for the determinations.

The 517-page report and exhibits, which include copies of all determination letters, can be found at http://www.FinancialStability.gov/docs/Exhibits.pdf and http://www.FinancialStability.gv/docs/Final%20Report%20of%20Kenneth%20Feinberg%20   -%20FINAL.PDF.

8. U.S. GOVERNMENT AS SHAREHOLDER

The U.S. Government is a reluctant shareholder in private companies and has no interest in owning companies over the long term. This unusual role is an unfortunate consequence of the financial crisis and the recession.

The Obama Administration has stated that core principles will guide Treasury's management of financial interests in private firms. One such principle is that the United States government will not interfere with or exert control over day-to-day company operations. Among other consequences, such involvement might actually reduce the value of the taxpayer's investments and impede the successful transition of the firms to the private sector.

In certain cases, Treasury has sought to pursue strong upfront conditions at the time of investment into a company, such as changes to the board of directors and management, to ensure that TARP funds were deployed in a way that promotes economic growth and financial stability and protects taxpayer value. Thereafter, Treasury has taken a commercial approach to its investments. Treasury does not participate in the day-to-day management of any company in which it has an investment nor is any Treasury employee a director or officer of any such company

Treasury's investments have generally been in the form of nonvoting - preferred stock. For example, the preferred shares that Treasury holds in financial institutions under the Capital Purchase Program do not have voting rights except in certain limited circumstances, such as amendments to the charter of the company, or in the event dividends are not paid for several quarters, in which case Treasury has the right to elect two directors to the board.

In a few cases, Treasury has acquired common stock. These include General Motors, Ally Financial (formerly GMAC), Citigroup and Chrysler, and a few small banks.

In the cases where Treasury has acquired voting rights, it has announced that it will follow the following principles in exercising its voting rights: (1) Treasury intends to exercise its right to vote only on certain matters consisting of the election or removal of directors; certain major corporate transactions such as mergers, sales of substantial amounts of assets, and dissolution; issuances of equity securities where shareholders are entitled to vote; and amendments to the charter or bylaws; and (2) on all other matters, Treasury will either abstain from voting or vote its shares in the same proportion (for, against or abstain) as all other shares of the company's stock are voted.

In the case of AIG, the U.S. Treasury is currently the beneficiary of a trust created by the Federal Reserve Bank of New York (FRBNY). That trust owns shares having 79.8 percent of the voting rights of the common stock. The FRBNY has appointed three independent trustees who have the power to vote and dispose of the stock with prior approval of FRBNY and after consultation with Treasury. The trust agreement provides that the trustees cannot be employees of Treasury or the FRBNY. The trust exists for the benefit of the U.S. Treasury, but the Department of the Treasury does not control the trust and it cannot direct the trustees. Treasury also directly owns preferred stock in AIG which does not have voting rights except in certain limited circumstances (such as amendments to the charter). Treasury has the right to appoint directors because AIG failed to pay dividends for four quarters on the preferred stock held by Treasury. Upon consummation of the proposed restructuring plan announced on September 30, 2010, Treasury will receive common shares in exchange for its preferred stock and the trust will be dissolved. As a result, the Treasury will own approximately 92 percent of the common stock of AIG.

9. ACCOUNTABILITY AND TRANSPARENCY

The Department of the Treasury is committed to transparency and accountability in all of its programs and policies, including all programs established under EESA. To protect taxpayers and ensure that every dollar is directed toward promoting financial stability, Treasury established comprehensive accountability and transparency measures.

A. Comprehensive Measures

Treasury publishes hundreds of reports other information about TARP so that the public knows how the money was spent, who received it and on what terms. This includes all contracts governing any investment or expenditure of TARP funds, and more than 275 reports over two years. All of these reports and information are posted on our website, www.FinancialStability.gov, including:

- Lists of all the institutions participating in TARP programs, and all of the investments Treasury has made;
- All investment contracts defining the terms of those investments within five to ten business days of a transaction's closing;
- All contracts with Treasury service providers involved with TARP programs;
- A report of each transaction (such as an investment in or repayment from a bank) within two business days of completing the transaction;
- Monthly reports of dividend and interest received, which allow the American people to see and evaluate the investment income they are receiving from these investments;

- Monthly reports to Congress, which present updates on our investments and programs in a clear, concise manner, and answer basic questions that many Americans have, such as how TARP funds are invested;
- Monthly reports detailing the progress of modifications under the Making Home Affordable program;
- All program guidelines, within two business days of any program launch; and
- A monthly lending survey, and an annual use of capital survey, which contains detailed information on the lending and other activities of banks that have received TARP funds to help the public understand what banks are doing with their TARP funds.

Please see "Section 10-Additional Resources" for links to the reports described above and other information related to TARP programs.

B. Audited Financial Statements

Treasury prepares separate financial statements for TARP on an annual basis. The initial Agency Financial Report for the year ended September 30, 2009 is available at www.FinancialStability.gov, and the second Agency Financial Report for the year ending September 30, 2010 will be released in November.

In its first year of operations, TARP's financial statements received an unqualified ("clean") audit opinion from the Government Accountability Office, and a separate report on internal control over financial reporting found no material weaknesses-- unprecedented achievements for a startup-operation with an extraordinary emergency mission. As a result of these efforts, the Treasury office responsible for implementing TARP-- the Office of Financial Stability received-- a Certificate of Excellence in Accountability Reporting (CEAR) from the Association of Government Accountants.

C. Oversight by Four Separate Agencies

Congress also established four additional avenues of oversight for TARP:

- The Financial Stability Oversight Board, established by EESA §104;
- Specific responsibilities for the Government Accountability Office as set out in EESA §116;
- The Special Inspector General for TARP, established by EESA §121; and
- The Congressional Oversight Panel, established by EESA §125.

Treasury has productive working relationships with all of these bodies, and cooperates with each oversight agency's effort to produce periodic audits and reports that focus on the many aspects of TARP. Individually and collectively, the oversight bodies' audits and reports have made and continue to make important contributions to the development, strengthening, and transparency of TARP programs.

D. Congressional Hearings and Testimony

Treasury officials have testified in numerous Congressional hearings since TARP was created. Copies of the written testimony are prepared for those hearings and are available at www.FinancialStability.gov/latest/pressreleases.html.

10. ADDITIONAL RESOURCES

A. Glossary

2MP-Second Lien Modification Program: 2MP offers homeowners a way to lower payments on their second mortgage.

AAA or Aaa: The highest rating given to bonds by bond rating agencies.

ABS-Asset Backed Security: A financial instrument representing an interest in a pool of other assets, typically consumer loans. Most ABS are collateralized by credit card receivables, auto loans, student loans, mortgage loans, or other loan and lease obligations.

ABX – Asset Backed Securities Index: A measure of the performance of a group of credit default swaps on ABS home equity loans, that serves as an indicator of investor sentiment regarding the performance of subprime mortgage holdings.

AGP Asset-Guarantee Program: A TARP program under which Treasury, together with the Federal Reserve and the FDIC, agreed to share losses on certain pools of assets held by systemically significant financial institutions that faced a high risk of losing market confidence due in large part to a portfolio of distressed or illiquid assets.

AIFP-Automotive Industry Financing Program: A TARP program under which Treasury provided loans or equity investments in order to avoid a disorderly bankruptcy of one or more auto companies that would have posed a systemic risk to the country's financial system..

AIG – American International Group, Inc.

Alt-A: A category of mortgages which have a risk potential that is greater than prime but less than subprime.

ARRA-American Recovery and Reinvestment Act of 2009: An act that contained, among other things, an economic stimulus package and amendments to EESA that require the Secretary to allow QFIs to repay TARP assistance at any time, subject to regulatory approval.

ASSP-Auto Supplier Support Program : A TARP program pursuant to which Treasury provided loans to ensure that auto suppliers receive compensation for their services and products, regardless of the condition of the auto companies that purchase their products.

AWCP-Auto Warranty Commitment Program: A TARP program pursuant to which Treasury provided loans to protect warranties on new vehicles purchased from General Motors and Chrysler during their restructuring periods.

BHC Bank-Holding Company: A company that controls a bank. Typically, a company controls a bank through the ownership of 25 percent or more of its voting securities.

CAP-Capital Assistance Program: A TARP program, created in connection with the SCAP or stress test, in which Treasury offered assistance to financial institutions to ensure that they had adequate capital to absorb losses and to continue to lend even in a worse than expected economic downturn. No funds were provided under the program.

CBLI-Consumer and Business Lending Initiative: A series of programs created under TARP which included the TALF, the CDCI, and the SBA 7(a) Securities Purchase Program. These were designed to jump start the credit markets that provide financing to consumers and businesses and otherwise support small banks.

CBO – Congressional Budget Office.

CDCI-Community Development Capital Initiative: A TARP program that provides low-cost capital to CDFIs to encourage lending to small businesses and help facilitate the flow of credit to individuals in underserved communities.

CDFI-Community Development Financial Institution: A financial institution that focuses on providing financial services to low -and moderate -income, minority and other underserved communities, and is certified by the CDFI Fund, an office within Treasury that promotes economic revitalization and community development.

CDO-Collateralized Debt Obligation: A financial instrument that entitles the holder to a portion of the cash flows generated by a portfolio of assets, which may include bonds, loans, mortgage-backed securities, or other CDOs.

CDX–Credit Default Swap Index: A measure of the performance of a group of credit default swaps.

CMBS-Commercial Mortgage-Backed Securities: A financial instrument representing an interest in a commercial real estate mortgage or a group of commercial real estate mortgages.

CMBX–Commercial Mortgage Backed Securities Index: A measure of the performance of a basket of credit default swaps on commercial mortgage backed securities.

CPP-Capital Purchase Program: A TARP program pursuant to which Treasury invested in preferred equity securities and other securities issued by financial institutions..

Credit Default Swap – A contract between two parties pursuant to which one party agrees to make periodic payments in exchange for the counterparty's agreement to pay a sum of money upon the occurrence of a credit default or other event relating to a particular financial instrument.

Dodd-Frank Act-Dodd-Frank Wall Street Reform and Consumer Protection Act of 2010.

DTI-Debt-to-Income Ratio: A ratio of the debt of a person to the income of such person.

EESA-Emergency Economic Stabilization Act of 2008: The law that created the Troubled Asset Relief Program (TARP).

Fannie Mae-Federal National Mortgage Association.

FDIC-Federal Deposit Insurance Corporation.

FHA-Federal Housing Administration.

FHFA-Federal Housing Finance Agency.

FRBNY-Federal Reserve Bank of New York.

Freddie Mac-Federal Home Loan Mortgage Corporation.

GAO-Government Accountability Office.

GSE-Government Sponsored Enterprises: Private corporations created by the U.S. Government. Fannie Mae and Freddie Mac are GSEs.

HAFA-Home Affordable Foreclosure Alternatives Program: HAFA offers homeowners, their mortgage servicers, and investors an incentive for completing a short sale or deed-in-lieu of foreclosure.

HAMP-Home Affordable Modification Program: A TARP program Treasury established to help responsible but struggling homeowners reduce their mortgage payments to affordable levels and avoid foreclosure.

HERA-Housing and Economic Recovery Act of 2008.

HFA: A state or local **Housing Finance Agency.**

HFA Hardest Hit Fund (HHF)-The-Housing Finance Agency Innovation Fund for the Hardest Hit Housing Markets: A program Treasury established under TARP to allow HFAs in the nation's hardest hit housing markets to design innovative, locally targeted foreclosure prevention programs.

HFSTHA-Helping Families Save Their Homes Act of 2009.

HUD-U.S. Department of Housing and Urban Development.

IMF-International Monetary Fund.

IPO-Initial Public Offering.

Legacy Securities: CMBS and non-agency RMBS issued prior to 2009 that were originally rated AAA or an equivalent rating by two or more NRSROs without ratings enhancement and that are secured directly by actual mortgage loans, leases or other assets and not other securities.

LIBOR-London Interbank Offered Rate: The rate of interest at which banks borrow funds from other banks, in marketable size, in the London interbank market. LIBOR rates are disseminated by the British Bankers Association.

MHA-Making Home Affordable: A comprehensive plan to stabilize the U.S. housing market and help responsible, but struggling, homeowners reduce their monthly mortgage payments to more affordable levels and avoid foreclosure. HAMP is part of MHA.

MBS-Mortgage Backed Securities: A type of ABS representing an interest in a pool of similar mortgages bundled together by a financial institution.

NPV – Net Present Value: An NPV test is used to compare the net present value of cash flows from the mortgage if modified under HAMP and the net present value of the cash flows from the mortgage without modification.

NRSRO-Nationally Recognized Statistical Rating Organization: A credit rating agency which issues credit ratings that the U.S. Securities and Exchange Commission permits other financial firms to use for certain regulatory purposes.

Non-Agency Residential Mortgage-Backed Securities: RMBS that are not guaranteed or issued by Ginnie Mae, Freddie Mac, Fannie Mae, any other GSE or a U.S. federal government agency.

OFS-Office of Financial Stability, the office within Treasury that implements TARP.

PRA – Principal Reduction Alternative Program: A program that offers mortgage relief to eligible homeowners whose homes are worth significantly less than the remaining amounts owed under their first lien mortgage loans.

Preferred Stock: Equity ownership that usually pays a fixed dividend and gives the holder a claim on corporate earnings superior to common stock owners. Preferred stock also has priority in the distribution of assets in the case of liquidation of a bankrupt company.

PPIF–Public Private Investment Fund: An investment fund established to purchase Legacy Securities from financial institutions under PPIP.

PPIP–Public Private Investment Program: A TARP program designed to improve the health of financial institutions holding real estate-related assets. The program is designed to increase the flow of credit throughout the economy by Treasury partnering with private investors to purchase legacy securities from financial institutions.

PSPA-referred Stock Purchase Agreements: The preferred stock purchase agreements that were entered into by Treasury and the GSEs pursuant to HERA.

QFI-ualifying Financial Institution: Private and public U.S.-controlled banks, savings associations, bank holding companies, certain savings and loan holding companies, and mutual organizations.

RMBS-Residential Mortgage-Backed Securities: A financial instrument representing an interest in a group of residential real estate mortgages.

S-PPIP-The Legacy Securities Public Private Investment Program.

SBA–U.S. Small Business Administration.

SBA 7(a) Loan Guarantee Program: A SBA loan program pursuant to which the SBA guarantees a percentage of loans for small businesses that cannot otherwise obtain conventional loans at reasonable terms.

SBA 7(a) Securities Purchase Program: A TARP program under which Treasury purchases securities backed by the guaranteed portions of the SBA 7(a) loans.

SCAP–Supervisory Capital Assessment Program: An assessment of capital, sometimes referred to as the "stress test", conducted by federal banking supervisors to determine if the largest U.S. financial organizations had sufficient capital continue lending and absorb the potential losses that could result from a more severe decline in the economy than projected.

SEC: U.S. Securities and Exchange Commission.

Servicer: An entity that collects payments and maintains accounts regarding mortgage loans.

SIGTARP-The Special Inspector General for the Troubled Asset Relief Program.

SPV-Special Purpose Vehicle: An off-balance sheet legal entity that holds the transferred assets presumptively beyond the reach of the entities providing the assets (e.g., legally isolated).

Stress Test: See SCAP.

TIP-Targeted Investment Program: A TARP program that Treasury created to stabilize the financial system by making investments in institutions that are critical to the functioning of the financial system.

TALF-Term Asset-Backed Securities Loan Facility: A program under which the Federal Reserve Bank of New York made term non-recourse loans to buyers of AAA-rated Asset-Backed Securities in order to stimulate consumer and business lending by the issuers of those securities. Treasury used TARP funds to provide credit support for the TALF as part of its Consumer and Business Lending Initiative.

TARP-Troubled Asset Relief Program: The Troubled Asset Relief Program, which was established under EESA to stabilize the financial system and prevent a systemic collapse.

Tier 1 Capital or "core capital": A measure of a bank's assets and liabilities that includes primarily common equity (including retained earnings), limited types and amounts of preferred equity, certain minority interests, and limited types and amounts of trust preferred securities, but excludes goodwill, certain other intangibles and certain other assets. It is used by banking regulators as a measure of a bank's ability to sustain future losses and still meet depositor's demands.

Tier 1 Common (also known as Tangible Common Equity or TCE): A measure of a bank's assets and liabilities calculated by removing all non-common elements from Tier 1 Capital, e.g., preferred equity, minority interests, and trust preferred securities. It can be thought of as the amount that would be left over if the bank were dissolved and all creditors and higher levels of stock, such as preferred stock, were paid off. Tier 1 Common is the highest "quality" of capital in the sense of providing a buffer against loss by claimants on the bank. Tier 1 Common is used in calculating the Tier 1 Common Ratio which determines the percentage of a bank's total assets that is categorized as Tier 1 Common. The higher the percentage, the better capitalized the bank. Preferred stock is an example of capital that may be counted in Tier 1 Capital, but not in Tier 1 Common.

TruPs-Trust Preferred Security: A security that has both equity and debt characteristics, created by establishing a trust and issuing debt to it. A company may create a trust preferred security to realize tax benefits, since the trust is tax deductible.

UP–Unemployment Program: The Home Affordable Unemployment Program is a supplemental program to HAMP which provides assistance to unemployed borrowers.

Warrant: A financial instrument that represents the right, but not the obligation, to purchase a certain number of shares of common stock of a company at a fixed price.

Warrant Preferred or Warrant Sub Debt: For CPP investments in a privately-held company, an S -corporation, or certain mutual institutions, Treasury received warrants to purchase, at a nominal cost, additional preferred stock (these securities are referred to as "warrant preferreds") or subordinated debentures (these securities are referred to as "warrant sub debt") equivalent to five percent of the aggregate liquidation preference of the primary CPP investment.

B. Links to Further Information

Office of Financial Stability, U.S. Department of the Treasury

- Financial Stability website: http://www.FinancialStability.gov/
- Agency Financial Report for Fiscal Year 2009: http://www.ustreas.gov/press /releases/OSF%20AFR%2009.pdf

Warrant Sales

- Warrant Disposition Reports: http://www.FinancialStability.gov/latest/rep ortsanddocs.html
- Treasury Analysis of Warrant Auction Results (March 18, 2010): www.Treas.go v/offices/economicpolicy/reports/Auction --Analysis-3 18-- 2010.pdf

Public Private Investment Program Quarterly Reports:

- www.FinancialStability.gov/roadtostability/legacysecurities.html#reports

Housing Initiatives

- Monthly Servicer and Performance Report: www.FinancialStability.gov/latest/ reportsanddocs.html
- Making Home Affordable Website: www.MakingHomeAffordable.gov
- Home Affordable Modification Program website (includes Supplemental Directives and the MHA Handbook): www.HMPadmin.com
- Monthly Housing Scorecard from the U.S. Department of Housing and Urban Development (HUD): www.HUD.gov/scorecard

Automotive Company Programs:

- Executive Office of the President, "A Look Back at GM, Chrysler and the American Auto Industry" (April 21, 2010): http://www.whitehouse.gov/sites/default/files/rss_ viewer/one_year_later_autos_report.pdf

Supervisory Capital Assistance Program and Capital Assistance Program

- SCAP White Paper: http://www.FederalReserve.gov/bankinforeg/ bcreg200904 24a1.pdf

Office of the Special Master for TARP Executive Compensation

- www.FinancialStability.gov/about/executivecompensation.html
- Final Report of the Special Master for TARP Executive Compensation Kenneth R. Feinberg: http://www.FinancialStability.gov/about/executivecompensation.html

End Notes

[1] The amount outstanding may be adjusted as further repayments are received and committed but undisbursed amounts for investments are made.

[2] Blinder and Zandi, "How the Great Recession Was Brought to an End," July 27, 2010.

[3] In 2008, these banks represented more than half of all bank assets.

[4] The contract terms include a number of incentives to encourage banks to replace TARP investments with private capital. These terms include a provision to increase the dividend rate over time, a restriction on the bank from paying dividends to its common shareholders and a restriction on repurchasing shares until the bank repays the TARP preferred stock.

[5] Data excludes the institutions that have entered bankruptcy or receivership at the time the quarterly payment was due.

[6] Reflections on the TALF and the Federal Reserve's Role as Liquidity Provider; http://www.newyorkfed.org/markets/talf.html.

[7] The "legacy securities PPIP" was announced in conjunction with a "legacy loan PPIP" to be implemented by the FDIC. The combined size of the both programs was initially contemplated to be $100 billion.

[8] The next Public Private Investment Program Quarterly Report, available at www.FinancialStability.gov/roadtostability/legacysecurities.html#reports, will have information through September 30, 2010.

[9] The National Information Center is a repository of financial data and institution characteristics collected by the Federal Reserve System.

[10] The ABX is a liquid, tradable tool developed by Markit, which allows investors to take positions in a standardized basket of subprime non-agency RMBS reference obligations via credit default swap contracts. The CMBX is a liquid, tradable tool developed by Markit, which allows investors to take positions in a standardized basket of CMBS reference obligations via credit default swap contracts. Such indices have become widely used benchmarks for the performance of (i) subprime non-agency RMBS and (ii) CMBS, respectively.

[11] Based on data from SBA.gov as of July 31, 2010.

[12] Colson Online Factor Database, www.colsonservices.com

[13] UBS Investment Research, "US Auto Supplier Survey Q2 2010" (July 8, 2010).

[14] The price of AIG common stock, as of Friday, October 1, 2010, was $38.86.

[15] See, for example, Secretary Geithner's Testimony before the House Committee on Oversight and Government Reform (January 27, 2010), available at: http://www.treas.gov/press/releases/tg514.htm; Written Testimony of Jim Millstein, Chief Restructuring Officer, U.S. Department of the Treasury, before the Congressional Oversight Panel (May 26, 2010), available at: http://cop.senate.gov/documents/testimony-052610-millstein.pdf; Federal Reserve Board Chairman Ben S. Bernanke's Testimony before the House Committee on Financial Services (March 24, 2009), available at: http://www.federalreserve.gov/newsevents/testimony/bernanke20090324a.htm; Scott G. Alvarez's Testimony before the Congressional Oversight Panel (May 26, 2010), available at: http://www.federalreserve.gov/newsevents/testimony/alvarez20100526a.htm; and Thomas C. Baxter's Testimony before the House Committee on Oversight and Reform (January 27, 2010), available at: http://www.newyorkfed.org/newsevents/speeches/2010/bax100127.html.

[16] At the time, the CDOs had a fair market value of about $29.6 billion and a par value of approximately $62 billion.

[17] Hearings on Foreclosure Prevention Part II: "Are Loan Servicers Honoring Their Commitments to Help Preserve Homeownership?" before the Committee on Oversight and Government Reform United States House of Representatives (June 24, 2010) (statement of Michael J. Heid, Co-President of Wells Fargo Home Mortgage).

[18] Hearings on Foreclosure Prevention Part II (statement of Barbara DeSoer, President of Bank of American Home Loans).

In: Reflections on the Troubled Asset Relief Program (TARP)   ISBN: 978-1-61209-519-6
Editor: Donna C. Hayworth   © 2011 Nova Science Publishers, Inc.

Chapter 2

Opportunities Exist to Apply Lessons Learned from the Capital Purchase Program to Similarly Designed Programs and to Improve the Repayment Process

United States Government Accountability Office

Why GAO Did This Study

Congress created the Troubled Asset Relief Program (TARP) to restore liquidity and stability in the financial system. The Department of the Treasury (Treasury), among other actions, established the Capital Purchase Program (CPP) as its primary initiative to accomplish these goals by making capital investments in eligible financial institutions. This chapter examines (1) the characteristics of financial institutions that received CPP funding and (2) how Treasury implemented CPP with the assistance of federal bank regulators. GAO analyzed data obtained from Treasury case files, reviewed program documents, and interviewed officials from Treasury and federal bank regulators.

What GAO Recommends

If Treasury administers programs containing elements similar to those of CPP, Treasury should implement a process for monitoring all applicants that regulators recommend for withdrawal to ensure that similar applicants are treated equitably. To improve monitoring of regulators' decisions on CPP repayments, Treasury should periodically collect and review information on the analysis supporting regulators' decisions and provide feedback for regulators' consideration on the extent to which they are evaluating similar institutions consistently. Treasury agreed to consider our recommendations. We also received technical comments from the Federal Reserve, FDIC, OCC, and Treasury and incorporated them as appropriate.

WHAT GAO FOUND

Institutions that received capital under CPP were diverse and generally exceeded eligibility guidelines, and while few institutions have failed, concerns remain about the growing numbers of institutions facing difficulties in paying dividend and interest payments to Treasury. Institutions that participated in CPP included roughly equal numbers of public and private firms of all sizes that were located throughout the country (see figure on next page). About half of CPP institutions that we reviewed were small—that is, had less than $500 million in risk-weighted assets. However, 25 of the largest firms received almost 90 percent of all CPP funds, and 9 of those comprised almost 70 percent of all funds. Approved institutions had similar overall examination ratings from their regulators and generally were rated as satisfactory. For example, almost all of the institutions we reviewed had an overall examination rating that was satisfactory or better. Many of the examination ratings were over 1 year old, but Treasury and regulatory officials said they took various actions to mitigate any limitations related to older examination results, including using preliminary ratings from ongoing bank examinations. Financial performance ratios that Treasury and regulators also used to evaluate CPP applicants—such as risk-based capital and nonperforming loan ratios— varied by institution but typically were well within guidelines as defined by Treasury and regulatory capital standards. Institutions generally were well above the minimum levels of regulatory capital. However, we identified 66 institutions—12 percent of the firms we reviewed—that exhibited weaker financial conditions relative to those of other approved institutions, and Treasury or regulators raised concerns about the viability of a few of these institutions. For almost all of these weaker firms, Treasury or regulators identified factors— such as management quality or substantial capital levels—that mitigated the weaknesses and provided additional support for the approval of the CPP investment. Four CPP institutions have failed, but the number of firms exhibiting signs of financial difficulty—such as missing their dividend or interest payments—has increased over time. Specifically, the number of institutions that have not made a scheduled dividend or interest payment has increased from 8 for payments due in February 2009 to 123 for payments due in August 2010. Over this period, a total of 144 institutions did not make at least one payment by the end of the reporting period in which they were due, for a total of 413 missed payments. As of August 31, 2010, 79 institutions had missed three or more payments and 24 had missed five or more. Through August 31, 2010, the total amount of missed dividend and interest payments was $235 million, although some institutions made their payments after the end of the reporting period.

The process Treasury established to invest in financial institutions included internal control procedures for approved applicants that enhanced consistency, but regulators' recommendations for application withdrawals and investment repayments received less oversight. Treasury relied on individual bank regulators to recommend applicants that it would consider for CPP investments and provided regulators with limited formal guidance on the factors to consider in evaluating the applicants. Because of the limited nature of Treasury's guidance, regulators used discretion and judgment in their assessments, which created the potential for inconsistency across regulators. Applicants that regulators recommended for approval received additional reviews as they moved through Treasury's process. For some, this included a review by a council of regulators and all recommended applicants were reviewed by Treasury. These reviews promoted a more consistent evaluation of recommendations made by different regulators. However, regulators recommended that some applicants withdraw their applications and these institutions may not have benefited from the additional reviews if they withdrew their applications before reaching the council or Treasury. Furthermore, the regional offices of some regulators could—and did—recommend that applicants withdraw without centralized review within the agency. Because Treasury did not monitor which institutions regulators excluded from its program, or the reasons for their decisions, it could not fully ensure that regulators treated similar applicants consistently. Limited oversight of withdrawal recommendations also may pose challenges to any future Treasury program that may follow the CPP model, such as the Small Business Lending Fund—an initiative to increase credit for small businesses through capital investments in certain financial institutions. Unless Treasury makes changes from the CPP model to include monitoring of withdrawal recommendations, such new programs may share the same increased risk of participants not being treated equitably. Treasury is required by statute to allow recipients to repay, subject to consultation with the federal banking regulators, but as with withdrawal recommendations, Treasury does not monitor or collect information or analysis supporting the regulators' decisions. Regulators said that they evaluate repayment requests based on their supervisory guidelines for capital reductions. Also, in the absence of monitoring by Treasury, regulators have developed generally similar guidelines for evaluating repayment requests and established processes for coordinating repayment decisions that involve multiple regulators. However, without collecting information on or monitoring different regulators' repayment decisions, Treasury has no basis for determining whether regulators evaluate similar institutions consistently and cannot provide feedback to regulators on the consistency of their decision making.

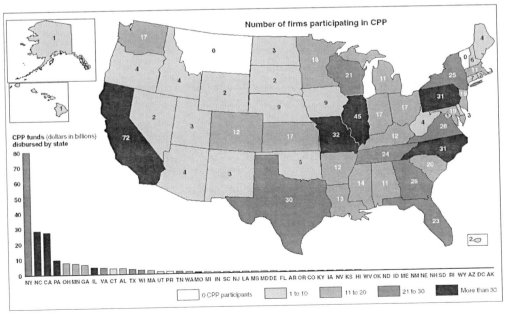

Sources: GAO analysis of OFS data: Map Resources (map).

Number of Participants and Amount of CPP Investments, by State, December 29, 2009

ABBREVIATIONS

ALLL   allowance for loan and lease losses
ARRA   American Recovery and Reinvestment Act of 2009
CAMELS   capital, asset quality, management, earnings, liquidity, and sensitivity
                  to market risk
CDCI   Community Development Capital Initiative
CPP   Capital Purchase Program
CRA   Community Reinvestment Act
EESA   Emergency Economic Stabilization Act of 2008
NCUA   National Credit Union Administration
OCC   Office of the Comptroller of the Currency
OFS   Office of Financial Stability
OREO   other real estate owned
OTS   Office of Thrift Supervision
PFR   primary federal regulator
QFI   qualified financial institution
RWA   risk-weighted assets
SBLF   Small Business Lending Fund
SCAP   Supervisory Capital Assessment Program
SIGTARP   Office of the Special Inspector General for TARP
TARP   Troubled Asset Relief Program

October 4, 2010

Congressional Committees

From October 2008 through December 2009, the U.S. Department of the Treasury (Treasury) invested over $200 billion in over 700 financial institutions as part of government efforts to stabilize U.S. financial markets and the economy.[1] These investments were made through the Capital Purchase Program (CPP), which was the initial and largest initiative under the Troubled Asset Relief Program (TARP).[2] Specifically, Treasury's authority under TARP enabled it to buy or guarantee up to almost $700 billion of the "troubled assets" that were deemed to be at the heart of the crisis, including mortgages and mortgage-based securities, and any other financial instrument Treasury determined it needed to purchase to help stabilize the financial system, including equities.[3] Treasury created CPP in October 2008 to provide capital to viable financial institutions through the purchase of preferred shares and subordinated debt. In return for its investments, Treasury would receive dividend or interest payments and warrants.[4] The program was closed to new investments on December 31, 2009, after Treasury had invested a total of $205 billion in 707 financial institutions over the life of the program. Since then, Treasury has continued to oversee its investments and collect dividend and interest payments. Some participants have repurchased their preferred shares or subordinated debt and left the program with the approval of their primary bank regulators.

Treasury has stated that it used CPP investments to strengthen financial institutions' capital levels rather than the purchases of troubled mortgage-backed securities and whole loans as initially envisioned under TARP because it saw these investments as a more effective mechanism to stabilize financial markets, encourage interbank lending, and increase confidence in lenders and investors. Treasury envisioned that the strengthened capital positions of viable financial institutions would enhance confidence in the institutions themselves and the financial system overall and increase the institutions' capacity to undertake new lending and support the economy. Financial institutions interested in receiving CPP investments sent their applications directly to their primary federal banking regulators, which did the initial evaluations. Institutions were evaluated to determine their long-term strength and viability, and weaker institutions were encouraged by their regulators to withdraw their applications. The regulators provided Treasury's Office of Financial Stability (OFS) with recommendations approving or denying applications. OFS made the final decisions.

This chapter is based upon our continuing analysis and monitoring of Treasury's process for implementing the Emergency Economic Stabilization Act of 2008, (EESA), which provided GAO with broad oversight authorities for actions taken under TARP and requires that we report at least every 60 days on TARP activities and performance.[5] To fulfill our statutorily mandated responsibilities, we have been monitoring and providing updates on TARP programs, including CPP, in several reports. This chapter expands on the previous work.[6] Its objectives are to (1) describe the characteristics of financial institutions that received CPP funding, and (2) assess how Treasury, with the assistance of federal bank regulators, implemented CPP.

To meet the report's objectives, we reviewed Treasury's case files for CPP institutions that were funded through April 30, 2009, and other supporting documentation such as records of meetings and transaction reports. We collected and analyzed information from the case files, including data on the characteristics of institutions that participated in CPP, such as risk-weighted assets, examination ratings, and selected financial ratios.[7] We also gathered information on the process that Treasury and regulators used to evaluate CPP applications. We reviewed program documents and interviewed officials from OFS who were responsible for processing applications and repayment requests to obtain their views on CPP implementation. Additionally, we interviewed officials from the four federal banking regulators—the Federal Deposit Insurance Corporation (FDIC), the Office of the Comptroller of the Currency (OCC), the Board of Governors of the Federal Reserve System (Federal Reserve), and the Office of Thrift Supervision (OTS)—to obtain information on their process for reviewing CPP applications and repayment requests. Further, we collected and reviewed program documents from the bank regulators, including their policies and procedures, guidance documents, and analysis summaries. Finally, we reviewed relevant laws (e.g., EESA) as well as relevant reports by GAO, the Office of the Special Inspector General for TARP (SIGTARP), the FDIC Office of Inspector General, and the Federal Reserve Office of Inspector General. This chapter is part of our coordinated work with SIGTARP and the inspectors general of the federal banking agencies to oversee TARP and CPP. The offices of the inspectors general of FDIC, Federal Reserve, and Treasury and SIGTARP have all completed work or have work under way at their respective agencies reviewing CPP's implementation. In coordination with the other oversight agencies and offices and to avoid duplication, we primarily focused our audit work (including our review of agency case files) on the phases of the CPP process from the point at which the regulators transmitted their recommendations to Treasury.

We conducted this performance audit from May 2009 to September 2010 in accordance with generally accepted government auditing standards. Those standards require that we plan and perform the audit to obtain sufficient, appropriate evidence to provide a reasonable basis for our findings and conclusions based on our audit objectives. We believe that the evidence obtained provides a reasonable basis for our findings and conclusions based on our audit objectives.

BACKGROUND

CPP was the primary initiative under TARP for stabilizing the financial markets and banking system. Treasury created the program in October 2008 to stabilize the financial system by providing capital on a voluntary basis to qualifying regulated financial institutions through the purchase of senior preferred shares and subordinated debt.[8] On October 14, 2008, Treasury allocated $250 billion of the $700 billion in overall TARP funds for CPP but adjusted its allocation to $218 billion in March 2009 to reflect lower estimated funding needs based on actual participation and the expectation that institutions would repay their investments. The program was closed to new investments on December 31, 2009, and, in total, Treasury invested $205 billion in 707 financial institutions over the life of the program. Through June 30, 2010, 83 institutions had repaid about $147 billion in CPP investments, including 76 institutions that repaid their investments in full.

Under CPP, qualified financial institutions were eligible to receive an investment of between 1 and 3 percent of their risk-weighted assets, up to a maximum of $25 billion.[9] In exchange for the investment, Treasury generally received shares of senior preferred stock that were due to pay dividends at a rate of 5 percent annually for the first 5 years and 9 percent annually thereafter.[10] In addition to the dividend payments, EESA required the inclusion of warrants to purchase shares of common stock or preferred stock, or a senior debt instrument to give taxpayers additional protection against losses and an additional potential return on the investments. Institutions are allowed to repay CPP investments with the approval of their primary federal bank regulators and afterward to repurchase warrants at fair market value.

While this was Treasury's program, the federal bank regulators played a key role in the CPP application and approval process. The federal banking agencies that were responsible for receiving and reviewing CPP applications and recommending approval or denial were the

- **Federal Reserve**, which supervises and regulates banks authorized to do business under state charters and that are members of the Federal Reserve System, as well as bank and financial holding companies;[11]
- **FDIC**, which provides primary federal oversight of any state-chartered banks insured by FDIC that are not members of the Federal Reserve System;
- **OCC**, which is responsible for chartering, regulating, and supervising commercial banks with national charters; and
- **OTS**, which charters federal savings associations (thrifts) and regulates and supervises federal and state thrifts and savings and loan holding companies.[12]

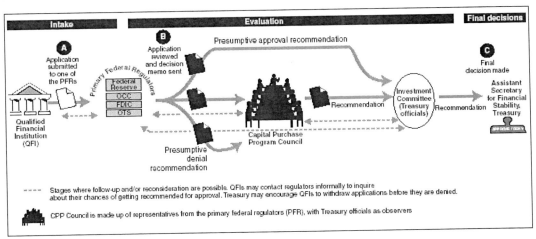

Sources: GAO analysis; Tre asury; Art Explosion (images).

Note: If the applicant was a bank holding company, an application was submitted to both the applicant's holding company regulator and the regulator of the largest insured depository institution controlled by the applicant.

Figure 1. Process for Accepting and Approving CPP Applications

Treasury, in consultation with the federal banking regulators, developed a standardized framework for processing applications and disbursing CPP funds. Treasury encouraged financial institutions that were considering applying to CPP to consult with their primary federal bank regulators.[13] The bank regulators also had an extensive role in reviewing the applications of financial institutions applying for CPP and making recommendations to Treasury. Eligibility for CPP funds was based on the regulator's assessment of the applicant's strength and viability, as measured by factors such as examination ratings, financial performance ratios, and other mitigating factors, without taking into account the potential impact of TARP funds. Institutions deemed to be the strongest, such as those with the highest examination ratings, received presumptive approval from the banking regulators, and their applications were forwarded to Treasury. Institutions with lower examination ratings or other concerns that required further review were referred to the interagency CPP Council, which was composed of representatives from the four banking regulators, with Treasury officials as observers. The CPP Council evaluated and voted on the applicants, and applications from institutions that received "approval" recommendations from a majority of the regulatory representatives were forwarded to Treasury. Treasury provided guidance to regulators and the CPP Council to use in assessing applicants that permitted consideration of factors such as signed merger agreements or confirmed investments of private capital, among other things, to offset low examination ratings or other weak attributes. Finally, institutions that the banking regulators determined to be the weakest and ineligible for a CPP investment, such as those with the lowest examination ratings, were to receive a presumptive denial recommendation. Figure 1 provides an overview of the process for assessing and approving CPP applications.

The banking regulator or the CPP Council sent approval recommendations to Treasury's Investment Committee, which comprised three to five senior Treasury officials, including OFS's chief investment officer (who served as the committee chair) and the assistant secretaries for financial markets, economic policy, financial institutions, and financial stability at Treasury. After receiving recommended applications from regulators or the CPP Council, OFS reviewed documentation supporting the regulators' recommendations but often collected additional information from regulators and the council before submitting applications to the Investment Committee. The Investment Committee could also request additional analysis or information in order to clear any concerns before deciding on an applicant's eligibility. After completing its review, the Investment Committee made recommendations to the Assistant Secretary for Financial Stability for final approval. Once the Investment Committee recommended preliminary approval, Treasury and the approved institution initiated the closing process to complete the legal aspects of the investment and disburse the CPP funds.

At the time of the program's announced establishment, nine major financial institutions were initially included in CPP.[14] While these institutions did not follow the application process that was ultimately developed, Treasury included these institutions because federal banking regulators and Treasury considered them to be essential to the operation of the financial system, which at the time had effectively ceased to function. At the time, these nine institutions held about 55 percent of U.S. banking assets and provided a variety of services, including retail and wholesale banking, investment banking, and custodial and processing services. According to Treasury officials, the nine financial institutions agreed to participate in CPP in part to signal the importance of the program to the stability of the financial system. Initially, Treasury approved $125 billion in capital purchases for these institutions and completed the transactions with eight of them on October 28, 2008, for a total of $115 billion. The remaining $10 billion was disbursed after the merger of Bank of America Corporation and Merrill Lynch & Co., Inc., was completed in January 2009.

CPP Institutions Were Diverse and with Some Exceptions Met CPP Guidelines, but More Institutions Are Showing Signs of Financial Difficulties

The institutions that received CPP capital investments varied in terms of ownership type, location, and size. The 707 institutions that received CPP investments were split almost evenly between publicly held and privately held institutions, with slightly more private firms.[15] They included state-chartered and national banks and U.S. bank holding companies located in 48 states, the District of Columbia, and Puerto Rico (see figure 2). Most states had fewer than 20 CPP firms, but 13 states had 20 or more. California had the most, with 72, followed by Illinois (45), Missouri (32), North Carolina (31), and Pennsylvania (31). Montana and Vermont were the only 2 states that did not have institutions that participated in CPP.

The total amount of CPP funds disbursed to institutions also varied by state. The amount of CPP funds invested in institutions in most states was less than $500 million, but institutions in 17 states received more than $1 billion each. Institutions in states that serve as financial services centers such as New York and North Carolina received the most CPP funds.[16] The median amount of CPP funds invested in institutions by state was $464 million.

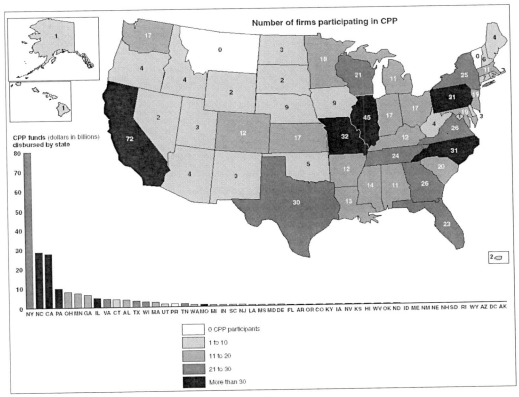

Source: GAO analysis of OFS data: Map Resources (map.

Figure 2. Number of Participants and Amount of CPP Investments by State as of December 31, 2009

The size of CPP institutions also varied widely. The risk-weighted assets of firms we reviewed that were funded through April 30, 2009, ranged from $10 million to $1.4 trillion.[17] However, most of the institutions were relatively small. For example, about half of the firms that we reviewed had risk-weighted assets of less than $500 million, and almost 70 percent had less than $1 billion. Only 30 percent were medium to large institutions (more than $1 billion in risk-weighted assets). Because the investment amount was tied to the firm's risk-weighted assets, the amount that firms received ranged widely, from about $300,000 to $25 billion. The average investment amount for all of the 707 CPP participants was $290 million, although half of the institutions received less than $11 million. The 25 largest institutions received almost 90 percent of the total amount of CPP investments, and 9 of these firms received almost 70 percent of the funds.

Regulatory Examinations Found That the Financial Condition of Most CPP Institutions Was At Least Satisfactory

The characteristics Treasury and regulators used to evaluate applicants indicated that approved institutions had bank or thrift examination ratings that generally were satisfactory, or within CPP guidelines.[18] Treasury and regulators used various measures of institutional strength and financial condition to evaluate applicants. These included supervisory examination ratings and financial performance ratios assessing an applicant's capital adequacy and asset quality.[19] While some examination results were more than a year old, regulatory officials told us that they had taken steps to mitigate the effect of these older ratings, such as collecting updated information.

Examination Ratings

Almost all of the 567 institutions we reviewed had overall examination ratings for their largest bank or thrift that were satisfactory or better (see figure 3).[20] The CAMELS ratings range from 1 to 5, with 1 indicating a firm that is sound in every respect, 2 denoting an institution that is fundamentally sound, and 3 or above indicating some degree of supervisory concern. Of the CPP firms that we reviewed, 82 percent had an overall rating of 2 from their most recent examination before applying to CPP, and an additional 11 percent had the strongest rating. Seven percent had an overall rating of 3 and no firms had a weaker rating. We also found relatively small differences in overall examination ratings for institutions by size or ownership type. For example, institutions that were above and below the median risk-weighted assets of $472 million both had average overall ratings of about 2. Also, public and private firms both had average overall examination ratings of about 2.

Bank or thrift examination ratings for individual components—such as asset quality and liquidity—exhibited similar trends. In particular, each of the individual components had an average rating of around 2. Institutions tended to have weaker ratings for the earnings component, which had an average of 2.2, than for the other components, which averaged between 1.8 and 1.9. Public and private institutions exhibited similar results for the average component ratings, although private institutions tended to have stronger ratings on all components except for earnings and sensitivity to market risk. Differences in average ratings by bank size also were small. For example, smaller institutions had stronger average ratings for the capital and asset quality components, but larger institutions had stronger average ratings for earnings and sensitivity to market risk.

Holding companies receiving CPP investments typically also had satisfactory or better examination ratings. The Federal Reserve uses its own rating system when evaluating bank holding companies.[21] Almost 80 percent of holding companies receiving CPP funds had an overall rating of 2 (among those with a rating), and an additional 14 percent had an overall rating of 1. The individual component ratings for holding companies (for example, for risk management, financial condition, and impact) also were comparable with overall ratings, with most institutions for which we could find a rating classified as satisfactory or better. Specifically, over 90 percent of the ratings for each of the components were 1 or 2, with most rated 2.

Many examination ratings were more than a year old, a fact that could limit the degree to which the ratings accurately reflect the institutions' financial condition, especially at a time when the economy was deteriorating rapidly. Specifically, about 25 percent of examination ratings were older than 1 year prior to the date of application, and 5 percent were more than 16 months old. On average, examination ratings were about 9 months older than the application date. Regulators used examination ratings as a key measure of an applicant's financial condition and viability, and the age of these ratings could affect how accurately they reflect the institutions' current state. For example, assets, liabilities, and operating performance generally are affected by the economic environment and depend on many factors, such as institutional risk profiles. Stressed market conditions such as those existing in the broad economy and financial markets during and before CPP implementation could be expected to have negative impacts on many of the applicants, making the age of examination ratings a critical factor in evaluating the institutions' viability. Further, some case decision files for CPP firms were missing examination dates. Specifically, 104 applicants' case decision files out of the 567 we reviewed lacked a date for the most recent examination results.

Treasury and regulatory officials told us that they took various actions to collect information on applicants' current condition and to mitigate any limitations of older examination results. Efforts to collect additional information on the financial condition of applicants included waiting for results of scheduled examinations or relying on preliminary CAMELS exam results, reviewing quarterly financial results such as recent information on asset quality, and sometimes conducting brief visits to assess applicants' condition. Officials from one regulator explained that communication with the agency's regional examiners and bank management on changes to the firm's condition was the most important means of allaying concerns about older examination results. However, officials from another regulator stated that they did use older examination ratings, depending on the institution's business model, lending environment, banking history, and current loan activity. For example, the officials said they would use older ratings if the institution was a small community bank with a history of conservative underwriting standards and was not lending in a volatile real estate market.

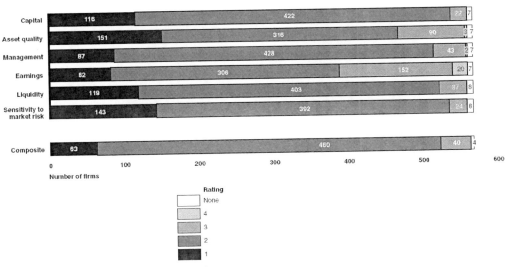

Source: GAO analysis of OFS documentation.
Note: The dates of CAMELS examination ratings span from December 2006 to December 2008. Dates were missing for 104 of the institutions that we reviewed. Institutions were identified as having no rating if we did not find the information in our review of Treasury's case files. This does not necessarily indicate that the institution had no examination rating. Some newly chartered institutions (de novos) did not have examination ratings completed at the time of the application.

Figure 3. CAMELS Overall and Component Ratings Used to Evaluate CPP Institutions Funded through April 30, 2009

As with the examination ratings, almost all of the institutions we reviewed had a rating for compliance with the Community Reinvestment Act (CRA) of satisfactory or better.[22] Over 80 percent of firms received a satisfactory rating and almost 20 percent had an outstanding rating. Only two institutions had an unsatisfactory rating. Average CRA ratings also were similar across institution types and sizes.

Performance Ratios

Performance ratios for the CPP firms we reviewed varied but typically were well within CPP guidelines. In assessing CPP applicants, Treasury and regulators focused on a variety of ratios based on regulatory capital levels, and institutions generally were well above the minimum required levels for these ratios.[23] Regulators generally used performance ratio information from regulatory filings for the second or third quarters of 2008. Two of these ratios are based on a key type of regulatory capital known as Tier 1, which includes the core capital elements that are considered the most reliable and stable, primarily common stock and certain types of preferred stock. Specifically, for the Tier 1 risk-based capital ratio, banks or thrifts and holding companies had average ratios that were more than double the regulatory minimum of 4 percent with only one firm below that minimum level. Further, only two institutions were below 6.5 percent (see figure 4).[24] Although almost all firms had Tier 1 risk-based capital ratios that exceeded the minimum level, the ratios ranged widely, from 3 percent to 43 percent.[25] Similarly, banks or thrifts and holding companies had average Tier 1 leverage ratios that were more than double the required 4 percent, and only 3 firms were below 4 percent.[26] The ratios also ranged widely, from 2 percent to 41 percent. Finally, for the total risk-based capital ratio, banks or thrifts and holding companies had average ratios of 12 percent, well above the 8 percent minimum, and only two firms were below 8 percent.[27] These ratios ranged from 4 percent to 44 percent.

Asset-based performance ratios for most CPP institutions also generally remained within Treasury's guidelines, although more firms did not meet the criteria for these ratios than did not meet the criteria for capital ratios. Treasury and the regulators established maximum guideline amounts for the three performance ratios relating to assets that they used to evaluate applicants. These ratios measure the concentration of troubled or risky assets as a share of capital and reserves—classified assets, nonperforming loans (including non-income-generating real estate, which is typically acquired through foreclosure), and construction and development loans. For each of these performance ratios, both the banks or thrifts and holding companies had average ratios that were less than half of the maximum guideline, well within the specified limits. For example, banks/thrifts and holding companies had average ratios of 25 and 32 percent, respectively, for classified assets, which had a maximum guideline of 100 percent. The substantial majority of banks or thrifts and holding companies also were well below the maximum guidelines for the asset ratios. For example, almost 90 percent of banks/thrifts and over 80 percent of holding companies had classified assets ratios below 50 percent. However, while only 3 firms missed the guidelines for any of the capital ratios, 38 banks/thrifts and holding companies missed the nonperforming loan ratio, 8 missed the construction and development loan ratio, and 1 missed the classified assets ratio.

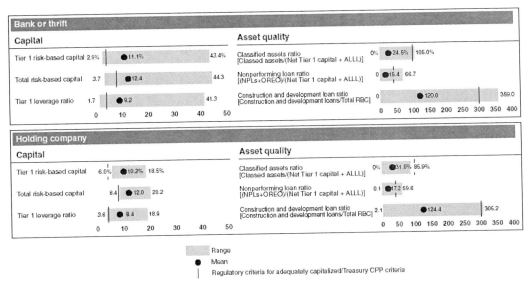

Source: GAO analysis of OFS documentation.

Note: The dates of performance ratios for all but one bank and one holding company were from 2008. The "allowance for loan and lease losses" (ALLL) is an account maintained by financial institutions to cover expected losses in their loan and lease portfolios. The "other real estate owned" (OREO) is an account used for examination and reporting purposes that primarily includes real estate owned by a financial institution as a result of foreclosure.

Figure 4. Bank or Thrift and Holding Company Performance Ratios Used to Evaluate CPP Institutions Funded through April 30, 2009

Treasury and Bank Regulators Took Steps to Help Ensure That CPP Applicants Met Guidelines for Viability

A small group of CPP participants exhibited weaker attributes relative to other approved institutions (see table 1). For most of these cases, Treasury or regulators described factors that mitigated the weaknesses and supported the applicant's viability. Specifically, we identified 66 CPP institutions—12 percent of the firms we reviewed—that either (1) did not meet the performance ratio guidelines used to evaluate applicants, (2) had an unsatisfactory overall bank or thrift examination rating, or (3) had a formal enforcement action involving safety and soundness concerns.[28] We use these attributes to identify these 66 firms as marginal institutions, although the presence of these attributes does not necessarily indicate that a firm was not viable or that it was ineligible for CPP participation.[29] However, they generally may indicate firms that either had weaker attributes than other approved firms or required closer evaluation by Treasury and regulators. Nineteen of the institutions met multiple criteria, including those that missed more than one performance ratio for the largest bank/thrift or holding company. The most common criteria for the firms identified as marginal was an unsatisfactory overall examination rating or an unsatisfactory nonperforming loan ratio. A far smaller number of firms exceeded the construction and development loan ratio or had experienced a formal enforcement action related to safety and soundness concerns. One bank and two holding companies missed the capital or classified assets ratios.

Table 1. Number of Institutions Participating in CPP That Exhibited Weak Characteristics Prior to Approval

Characteristic	Number of institutions exhibiting the characteristic
Overall CAMELS bank examination rating of 3, 4, or 5	40
Active, formal safety-and-soundness-related enforcement action	5
Tier 1 risk-based capital ratio less than 4 percent	1
Total risk-based capital ratio less than 8 percent	1
Tier 1 leverage ratio less than 4 percent	3
Classified assets ratio greater than 100 percen[ta]	1
Nonperforming loan ratio greater than 40 percent[b]	38
Construction and development loans/total risk-based capital ratio greater than 300 percent	8
Total institutions exhibiting characteristics	**66[c]**

Source: GAO analysis of OFS documentation.

[a]Classified assets / (net Tier 1 capital + ALLL).

[b](Nonperforming loans + OREO) / (Net Tier 1 capital + ALLL).

[c]Total does not add because 19 firms exhibited multiple characteristics.

In their evaluations of CPP applicants, Treasury and regulators documented their reasons for approving institutions with marginal characteristics. They typically identified three types of mitigating factors that supported institutions' overall viability: (1) the quality of management and business practices; (2) the sufficiency of capital and liquidity; and (3) performance trends, including asset quality. The most frequently cited attributes related to management quality and capital sufficiency.

High-quality management and business practices. In evaluating marginal applicants, regulators frequently considered the experience and competency of the applicants' senior management team. Officials from one bank regulator said that they might be less skeptical of an applicant's prospects if they believed it had high-quality management. For example, they used their knowledge of institutions and the quality of their management to mitigate economic concerns for banks in the geographic areas most severely affected by the housing market decline. Commonly identified strengths included the willingness and ability of management to respond quickly to problems and concerns that regulators identified such as poor asset quality or insufficient capital levels. The evaluations of several marginal applicants described management actions to aggressively address asset quality problems as an indication of an institution's ability to resolve its weaknesses. Regulators also had a positive view of firms whose boards of directors implemented management changes such as replacing key executives or hiring more experienced staff in areas such as credit administration. Finally, regulators evaluated the quality of risk management and lending practices in determining management strength.

Capital and liquidity. Regulators often reviewed the applicant's capital and liquidity when evaluating whether an institution's weaknesses might affect its viability. In particular, regulators and Treasury considered the sufficiency of capital to absorb losses from bad assets and the ability to raise private capital. As instructed by Treasury guidance, regulators evaluated an institution's capital levels prior to the addition of any CPP investment. Although an institution might have high levels of nonperforming loans or other problem assets, regulators' concerns about viability might be eased if it also had a substantial amount of capital available to offset related losses. Likewise, capital from private sources could shore up an institution's capital buffers and provide a signal to the market that it could access similar sources if necessary.

When evaluating the sufficiency of a marginal applicant's capital, regulators also assessed the amount of capital relative to the firm's risk profile, the quality of the capital, and the firm's dependence on volatile funding sources. Institutions with a riskier business model that included, for instance, extending high-risk loans or investing in high-risk assets generally would require higher amounts of capital as reserves against losses. Conversely, an institution with a less risky strategy or asset base might need somewhat less capital to be considered viable. Regulators reviewed the quality of a firm's capital because some forms of capital, such as common shareholder's equity, can absorb losses more easily than other types, such as subordinated debt or preferred shares, which may have restrictions or limits on their ability to take losses.[30] Finally, regulators considered the nature of a firm's funding sources. They viewed firms that financed their lending and other operations with stable funding sources, such as core deposit accounts or long-term debt, as less risky than firms that obtained financing through brokered deposits or wholesale funding, which could be more costly or might need to be replaced more frequently.

Performance trends. Regulators also examined recent trends in performance when evaluating marginal applicants. For example, regulators considered strong or improving trends in asset quality, earnings, and capital levels, among others, as potentially favorable indicators of viability. These trends included reductions in nonperforming and classified assets, consistent positive earnings, reductions in commercial real estate concentrations, and higher net interest margins and return on assets. In some cases, regulators identified improvements in banks' performance through preliminary examination ratings. Officials from one bank regulator stated that the agency refrained from making recommendations until it had recent and complete examination data. For example, if an examination was scheduled for an applicant that had raised regulatory concerns or questions, the agency would wait for the updated results before completing its review and making a recommendation to Treasury.

Some Firms Were Approved despite Questions about Their Ongoing Viability

Regulators and Treasury raised specific questions about the viability of a small number of institutions that ultimately were approved and received their CPP investments between December 19, 2008, and March 27, 2009. Most of the questions about viability involved poor asset quality, such as nonperforming loans or bad investments, and lending that was highly concentrated in specific product types, such as commercial real estate (see table 2). For these institutions, various mitigating factors were used to provide support for the firm's ultimate approval. For example, regulators and Treasury identified the addition of private capital, strong capital ratios, diversification of lending portfolios, and updated examination results as mitigating factors in approving the institutions. One of these institutions had weaker characteristics than the others, and regulators and Treasury appeared to have more significant concerns about its viability. Ultimately, regulators and the CPP Council recommended approval of this institution based, in part, on criteria in Section 103 of EESA, which requires Treasury to consider providing assistance to financial institutions having certain attributes such as serving low- and moderate-income populations and having assets less than $1 billion.

Table 2. Mitigating Factors for Viability Concerns Identified by Regulators or Treasury

Eligibility or viability concerns	Mitigating factors
<ul><li>Very high commercial real estate concentration</li><li>High construction and development loan concentration</li><li>State of bank's lending market</li><li>Poor performance ratios</li><li>Nonperforming loans</li><li>Precarious financial position</li><li>Elimination of capital by investment losses</li><li>Continual subpar management ratings</li><li>Questionable viability without CPP funds</li><li>Unsatisfactory management responsiveness</li><li>High commercial real estate exposure</li><li>Potential impairment in mortgage servicing assets</li><li>Viability of business plan given the current industry turmoil</li><li>Overall credit quality</li><li>Viability questionable without additional capital</li><li>Ability to improve operating performance</li><li>Proportion of non-owner-occupied commercial real estate</li></ul>	<ul><li>Preliminary examination results</li><li>Relative strength of local market area</li><li>Management strong and conservative</li><li>Strong capital position</li><li>Bank committed to raising additional capital</li><li>Private capital investment</li><li>Aggressive in recognizing losses</li><li>Relatively strong capital ratios</li><li>Fannie Mae and Freddie Mac investment losses</li><li>Favorable capital treatment</li><li>Bank profitable with strong capital</li><li>Commercial real estate portfolio diversified by product type</li><li>Condition due to investment rather than loan losses</li><li>Conservative underwriting standards</li><li>Low construction and development loans</li><li>Special consideration based on provisions in statute</li><li>Approval conditioned upon planned issuance of additional equity capital</li><li>Improved effectiveness of servicing rights hedging program</li><li>Recent examination rating of composite 2</li><li>Strong loan review and approval procedures</li><li>Low ratios of classified and nonperforming loans</li></ul>

Source: GAO analysis of OFS documentation.

A Growing Number of CPP Firms, Including Many That Had Identified Weaknesses, Have Exhibited Signs of Financial Difficulty

Through July 2010, 4 CPP institutions had failed, but an increasing number of CPP firms have missed their scheduled dividend or interest payments, requested to have their investments restructured by Treasury, or appeared on FDIC's list of problem banks.[31] First, the number of institutions missing the dividend or interest payments due on their CPP investments has increased steadily, rising from 8 in February 2009 to 123 in August 2010, or 20 percent of existing CPP participants.[32] Between February 2009 and August 2010, 144 institutions did not pay at least one dividend or interest payment by the end of the reporting period in which they were due, for a total of 413 missed payments.[33] As of August 31, 2010, 79 institutions had missed three or more payments and 24 had missed five or more. Through August 31, 2010, the total amount of missed dividend and interest payments was $235 million, although some institutions made their payments after the scheduled payment date. Institutions are required to pay dividends only if they declare dividends, although unpaid cumulative dividends accrue and the institution must pay the accrued dividends before making dividend payments to other types of shareholders in the future, such as holders of common stock. Federal and state bank regulators also may prevent their supervised institutions from paying dividends to preserve their capital and promote their safety and soundness. According to the standard terms of CPP, after participants have missed six dividend payments—consecutive or not—Treasury can exercise its right to appoint two members to the board of directors for that institution. In May 2010, the first CPP institution missed six dividend payments, but as of August 2010, Treasury had not exercised its right to appoint members to its board of directors. An additional seven institutions missed their sixth dividend payment in August 2010. Treasury officials told us that they are developing a process for establishing a pool of potential directors that Treasury could appoint on the boards of institutions that missed at least six dividend payments. They added that these potential directors will not be Treasury employees and would be appointed to represent the interests of all shareholders, not just Treasury. Treasury officials expect that any appointments will focus on banks with CPP investments of $25 million or greater, but Treasury has not ruled out making appointments for institutions with smaller CPP investments. We will continue to monitor and report on Treasury's progress in making these appointments in future reports.

Although none of the 4 institutions that have failed as of July 31, 2010, were identified as marginal cases, 39 percent of the 66 approved institutions with marginal characteristics have missed at least one CPP dividend payment, compared with 20 percent of CPP participants overall. Through August 2010, 26 of the 144 institutions that had missed at least one dividend payment were institutions identified as marginal. Of these 26 marginal approvals, 20 have missed at least two payments, and 14 have missed at least four. Several of the marginal approvals also have received formal enforcement actions since participating in CPP. As of April, regulators filed formal actions against nine of the marginal approvals, including four cease-and-desist orders and four written agreements.[34] Seven of these institutions also missed at least one dividend payment. However, none of the approvals identified as marginal had filed for bankruptcy or were placed in FDIC receivership as of July 31, 2010.[35]

Second, since June 2009, at least 16 institutions have formally requested that Treasury restructure their CPP investments, and most of the institutions have made their requests in recent months.[36] Specifically, as of July, 9 of the 11 requests received this year were received since April. Treasury officials said that institutions have pursued a restructuring primarily to improve the quality of their capital and attract additional capital from other investors. Treasury has completed six of the requested restructurings and entered into agreements with 2 additional institutions that made requests. According to officials, Treasury considers multiple factors in determining whether to restructure a CPP investment. These factors include the effect of the proposed capital restructuring on the institution's Tier 1 and common equity capital and the overall economic impact on the U.S. government's investment. The terms of the restructuring agreements most frequently involve Treasury exchanging its CPP preferred shares for either mandatory convertible preferred shares—which automatically convert to common shares if certain conditions such as the completion of a capital raising plan are met—or trust preferred securities—which are issued by a separate legal entity established by the CPP institution.

Finally, the number of CPP institutions on FDIC's list of problem banks has increased. At December 31, 2009, there were 47 CPP firms on the problem list. This number had grown to 71 firms by March 31, 2010, and to 78 at June 30, 2010. The FDIC tracks banks that it designates as problem institutions based on their composite examination ratings. Institutions designated as problem banks have financial, operational, or managerial weaknesses that threaten their continued viability and include firms with either a 4 or 5 composite rating.

WHILE TREASURY'S PROCESSES INCLUDED MULTIPLE REVIEWS OF APPROVED CPP APPLICANTS, CERTAIN OPERATIONAL CONTROL WEAKNESSES OFFER LESSONS LEARNED FOR SIMILARLY DESIGNED PROGRAMS

Reviews of regulators' approval recommendations helped ensure consistent evaluations and mitigate risk from Treasury's limited guidance for assessing applicants' viability. Reviews of regulators' recommendations to fund institutions are an important part of CPP's internal control activities aimed at providing reasonable assurance that the program is performing as intended and accomplishing its goals.[37] The process that Treasury and regulators implemented established centralized control mechanisms to help ensure consistency in the evaluations of approved applicants. For example, regulators established their own processes for evaluating applicants, but they generally had similar structures including initial contact and review by regional offices followed by additional centralized review at the headquarters office for approved institutions. FDIC, OTS, and the Federal Reserve conducted initial evaluations and prepared the case decision memos at regional offices (or Reserve Banks in the case of the Federal Reserve), while the regulators' headquarters (or Board of Governors) performed secondary reviews and verification. At OCC, district offices did the initial analysis of applicants and provided a recommendation to headquarters, which prepared the case decision memo using input from the district. All of the regulators also used review panels or officials at headquarters to review the analyses and recommendations before submission to the CPP Council or Treasury.

Applicants recommended for approval by regulators also received further evaluation at the CPP Council or Treasury. Regulators sent to the CPP Council applications that they had approved but that had certain characteristics identified by Treasury as warranting further review by the council. These characteristics included indications of relative weakness, such as unsatisfactory examination ratings and performance ratios. At the council, representatives from all four federal bank regulators discussed the viability of applicants and voted on recommending them to Treasury for approval. As Treasury officials explained, the CPP Council was the deliberative forum for addressing concerns about marginal applicants whose eligibility for CPP was unclear. The council's charter describes its purpose as acting as an advisory body to Treasury for ensuring that CPP guidelines are applied effectively and consistently across bank regulators and applicants. By requiring the regulators to reach consensus when recommending applicants whose approval was not straightforward, the CPP Council helped ensure that the final outcome of applicants was informed by multiple bank regulators and generally promoted consistency in decision making.

After regulators or the CPP Council submitted a recommendation to Treasury, the applicant received a final round of review by Treasury's CPP analysts and the Investment Committee. CPP analysts conducted their own reviews of applicants and the case files forwarded from the regulators, including the case decision memos. They collected additional information for their reviews from regulators' data systems and publicly available sources and also gathered information from regulators to clarify the analysis in the case files. According to Treasury officials, the CPP analysts were experienced bank examiners serving on detail from each of the bank regulators except OCC. Treasury officials explained that CPP analysts did not make decisions about preliminary approvals or preliminary disapprovals. Only the Investment Committee made those decisions.

In the final review stage, the Investment Committee evaluated all of the applicants forwarded by regulators or the CPP Council. On the basis of its review of the regulators' recommendations and analysis and additional information collected by Treasury CPP analysts, the Investment Committee recommended preliminary approval or denial to applicants, subject to the final decision of the Assistant Secretary for Financial Stability. By reviewing and issuing a preliminary decision on all forwarded applicants, the Investment Committee represented another important control, much like the CPP Council. Unlike the CPP Council, however, the Investment Committee deliberated on all applicants referred by regulators rather than just those meeting certain marginal criteria.

The reviews by the CPP Council, analysts at OFS, and the Investment Committee were important steps to limit the risk of inconsistent evaluations by different regulators. This risk stemmed from the limited guidance that Treasury provided to regulators concerning the application review process. Specifically, the formal written guidance that Treasury initially provided to regulators consisted of broad high-level guidance, which was supplemented with other informal guidance to address specific concerns.[38] The written guidance provided by Treasury established the institution's strength and overall viability as the baseline criteria for the eligibility recommendation.[39] Regulators said that while the guidance was useful in providing a broad framework or starting point for their reviews, they could not determine an applicant's viability using Treasury's written guidance alone. Officials from several regulators said that they also relied on regulatory experience and judgment when evaluating CPP applicants and making recommendations to Treasury. Treasury officials told us that they believed they were not in a position to provide more specific guidance to regulators on how to evaluate the viability of the institutions they oversaw. Treasury officials further explained that with many different kinds of institutions and unique considerations, regulators needed to make viability decisions on an individual basis.

A 2009 audit by the Federal Reserve's Inspector General (Fed IG) assessing the Federal Reserve's process and controls for reviewing CPP applications similarly found that Treasury provided limited guidance in the early stages of the program regarding how to determine applicants' viability.[40] As a result, the Federal Reserve and other regulators developed their own procedures for analyzing CPP applications. The report also found that formal, detailed, and documented procedures would have provided the Federal Reserve with additional assurance that CPP applications would be analyzed consistently and completely. However, the multiple layers of reviews involving the regulators, the CPP Council, and Treasury staff helped compensate for the risk of inconsistent evaluation of applicants that received recommendations for CPP investments. The Fed IG recommended that the Federal Reserve incorporate lessons learned from the CPP application review process to its process for reviewing repurchase requests. The Federal Reserve generally agreed with the report's findings and recommendations.

Treasury and the Regulators' Documentation of Approval Decisions Improved as the Program Matured

As Treasury fully implemented its CPP process, it and the regulators compiled documentation of the analysis supporting their decisions to approve program applicants. For example, regulators consistently used a case decision memo to provide Treasury with standard documentation of their review and recommendations of CPP applicants. This document contained basic descriptive and evaluative information on all applicants forwarded by regulators, including identification numbers, examination and compliance ratings, recent and post-investment performance ratios, and a summary of the primary regulator's evaluation and recommendation. Although the case decision memo contained standard types of information, the amount and detail of the information that regulators included in the form evolved over time. According to regulators and Treasury, they engaged in an iterative process whereby regulators included additional information after receiving feedback from Treasury on what they should describe about their assessment of an applicant's viability. For example, regulators said that often Treasury wanted more detailed explanations for more difficult viability decisions. According to bank regulatory officials, other changes included additional discussion of specific factors relevant to the viability determination, such as information on identified weaknesses and enforcement actions, analysis of external factors such as economic and geographic influences, and consideration of nonbank parts of holding companies. Treasury officials explained that as CPP staff learned about the types of information the Investment Committee wanted to see, they would communicate it to the regulators for inclusion in case decision memos.

Our review of CPP case files indicated that some case decision memos were incomplete and missing important information, but typically only for applicants approved early in the program. For instance, several case decision memos contained only one or two general statements supporting viability, largely for the initial CPP firms.[41] Eventually, the case decision memos included several paragraphs, and some contained multiple pages, with detailed descriptions of the applicant's condition and viability assessment. Most of the cases in which the regulator did not explain its support for an applicant's viability occurred in the first month of the program. Some case decision memos lacked other important information, although these memos also tended to be from early in the program. For example, multiple case decision memos were missing either an overall examination rating, all of the component examination ratings, or a performance ratio related to capital levels. Most or all of those were approved prior to December 2008. Further, 104 of 567 case files we reviewed lacked examination ratings dates, and almost all of these firms were approved before the end of December 2008. Missing CRA dates, which occurred in 214 cases, exhibited a similar pattern.

For applications that regulators sent to Treasury with an approval recommendation, Treasury staff used a "team analysis" form to document their review before submitting the applications to the Investment Committee for its consideration. According to Treasury officials, the team analysis evolved over time as CPP staff became more experienced and different examiners made their own modifications to the form. For example, as the CPP team grew in size, additional fields were added to document multiple levels of review by other examiners. As with the case decision memos, the consistency of information in the team analysis improved with time. For instance, team analysis documents did not include calculations of allowable investment amounts for almost 60 files that we reviewed that Treasury had approved by the end of December 2008. Finally, a small number of case files did not contain an award letter, but all of those approvals had also occurred before the end of December 2008.

Treasury and regulators compiled meeting minutes for the CPP Council and Investment Committee, although they did not fully document some early Investment Committee meetings. The minutes described discussions of policy and guidance related to TARP and CPP and also the review and approval decisions for individual applicants. However, records do not exist for four meetings of the Investment Committee that occurred between October 23, 2008, and November 12, 2008. According to Treasury, no minutes exist for those meetings. We did not find any missing meeting minutes for the CPP Council, although at the early meetings, regulators did not collect the initials of voting members to document their recommendations to approve or disapprove applicants they reviewed. Within several weeks however, regulators began using the CPP Council review decision sheets to document council members' votes in addition to the meeting minutes.

Treasury's Implementation Process Limited Its Ability to Oversee Regulators' Recommendations for Applicant Withdrawals

Although the multiple layers of review for approved institutions enhanced the consistency of the decision process, applicants that withdrew from consideration in response to a request from their regulator received no review by Treasury or other regulators. To avoid a formal denial, regulators recommended that applicants withdraw when they were unable to recommend approval or believed that Treasury was unlikely to approve the institution. Some regulators said that they also encouraged institutions not to formally submit applications if approval appeared unlikely. Applicants could insist that the regulator forward their application to the CPP Council and ultimately to the Investment Committee for further consideration even if the regulator had recommended withdrawal. However, Treasury officials said that they did not approve any applicants that received a disapproval recommendation from their regulator or the CPP Council. Regulators also could recommend that applicants withdraw after the CPP Council or Investment Committee decided not to recommend approval of their application. One regulator stated that all the applicants it suggested withdraw did so rather than receive a formal denial. Treasury officials also said that institutions receiving a withdrawal recommendation generally withdrew and that no formal denials were issued.

Almost half of all applicants withdrew from CPP consideration before regulators forwarded their applications to the CPP Council or Treasury. Regulators had recommended withdrawal in about half of these cases where information was available. Over the life of the program, regulators received almost 3,000 CPP applications, about half of which they sent to the CPP Council or directly to Treasury (see table 3). The remaining applicants withdrew either voluntarily or after receiving a recommendation to withdraw from their regulator. Three of the regulators—OCC, OTS, and the Federal Reserve—indicated that about half of their combined withdrawals were the result of their recommendations. FDIC, which was the primary regulator for most of the applicants, did not collect information on the reasons for applicants' withdrawals.[42] According to Treasury officials, those applicants that chose to withdraw voluntarily did so for various reasons, including uncertainty over future program requirements and increased confidence in the financial condition of banks. In addition to institutions that withdrew after applying for CPP, Treasury officials and officials from a regulator indicated that some firms decided not to formally apply after discussing their potential application with their regulator. However, regulators did not collect information on the number of firms deciding not to apply after having these discussions.

Although applications recommended for approval received multiple reviews and were coordinated among regulators and Treasury, each regulator made its own decision on withdrawal recommendations. Most regulators conducted initial reviews of applicants at their regional offices, and staff at these offices had independent authority to recommend withdrawal for certain cases. Regulatory officials said that regional staff (including examiners and more senior officials) made initial assessments of applicants' viability using Treasury guidelines and would recommend withdrawal for weak firms with the lowest examination ratings that were unlikely to be approved.[43] Applicants that received withdrawal recommendations might have had weak characteristics relative to those of other firms and might have received a denial from Treasury. But following regulators' suggestions to withdraw before referral to the CPP Council or Treasury, or to not apply, ensured that they would not receive the centralized reviews that could have mitigated any inconsistencies in their initial evaluations. Further, while regulators had panels or senior officials at their headquarters offices providing central review of approved applicants, most of the regulators allowed their regional offices to recommend withdrawal for weaker applicants or encourage such applicants not to apply, thereby limiting the benefit of that control mechanism. Allowing regional offices to recommend withdrawal without any centralized review may increase the risk of inconsistency within as well as across regulators. In its report on the processing of CPP applications, the FDIC Office of Inspector General found that one of FDIC's regional offices suggested that three institutions withdraw from consideration that were well capitalized and technically met Treasury guidelines.[44] Regional FDIC management cited poor bank management as the primary concern in recommending that the institutions withdraw. The report concluded that the use of discretion by regional offices in recommending that applicants withdraw increased the risk of inconsistency. The report made two recommendations to enhance controls over the process for evaluating applications: (1) forwarding applications recommended for approval that do not meet one or more of Treasury's criteria to the CPP Council for additional review and (2) requiring headquarters review of institutions recommended for withdrawal when the institutions technically meet Treasury's criteria. In commenting on the report, FDIC concurred with the recommendations.

Treasury did not collect information on applicants that had received withdrawal recommendations from their regulators or on the reasons for these decisions. According to Treasury officials, Treasury did not receive, request, or review information on applicants that regulators recommended to withdraw and thus could not monitor the types of institutions that regulators were restricting from the program or the reasons for their decisions. The officials said that Treasury did not collect or review information on withdrawal recommendations in part to minimize the potential for external parties to influence the decision-making process. However, such considerations did not prevent Treasury from reviewing information on applicants that regulators recommended for approval, and concerns about external influence could also be addressed directly through additional control procedures rather than by limiting the ability to collect information on withdrawal recommendations. The lack of additional review outside of the individual regulator or oversight of withdrawal requests by Treasury presents the risk that applicants may not have been evaluated in a consistent fashion across regulators. As the agency responsible for implementing CPP, it is equally beneficial for Treasury to understand the reasons that regulators recommended applicants withdraw from the program as it is for Treasury to understand the reasons regulators recommended approval. Collecting and reviewing information on withdrawal requests would have served as an important control mechanism and allowed Treasury to determine whether leaving certain applicants out of CPP was consistent with program goals. It also would have allowed Treasury to determine whether similar applicants were evaluated consistently across different regulators in terms of their decisions to recommend withdrawal.

Table 3. Withdrawals by CPP Applicants before Submission to CPP Council or Treasury as of December 31, 2009

Bank regulator	Total applications received	Voluntary withdrawal	Recommended withdrawal	Total applications sent to CPP Council or Treasury
FDIC	1,814	Not available	Not available	917
Federal Reserve	342	42	82	218
OCC	442	93	130	219
OTS	297	131	40	126
Total	2895	Not available	Not available	1,480

Sources: FDIC, Federal Reserve, OCC, and OTS.

Note: Of the total 1,480 applications sent to the CPP Council or Treasury, Treasury ultimately received 1,403 applications. These 1,403 applications resulted in 738 CPP transactions (for 707 institutions because some institutions submitted multiple applications), 658 withdrawals, and 7 applications that were not approved.

Treasury has indicated that it may use the CPP model for new programs to stimulate the economy and improve conditions in financial markets, and unless corrective actions are taken, such programs may share the same increased risk of similar participants not being treated consistently. Specifically, in February 2010, Treasury announced terms for a new TARP program—the Community Development Capital Initiative (CDCI)—to invest lower-cost capital in Community Development Financial Institutions that lend to small businesses. According to Treasury and regulatory agency officials, Treasury modeled its implementation of the CDCI program after the process it used for CPP, with federal bank regulators—in this case including the National Credit Union Administration (NCUA)—conducting the initial reviews and making recommendations. The CDCI program also uses a council of regulators to review marginal approvals, and an Investment Committee at Treasury reviews all applicants recommended by regulators for approval. As in the case of CPP, control mechanisms exist for reviewing approved applicants, but no equivalent reviews are done for applicants that receive withdrawal recommendations. Thus, the CDCI structure could raise similar concerns about a lack of control mechanisms to mitigate the risk of inconsistency in evaluations by different regulators. The deadline for financial institutions to apply to participate in the CDCI was April 30, 2010, and all disbursements or exchanges of CPP securities for CDCI securities must be completed by September 30, 2010.

The Small Business Jobs Act of 2010, enacted on September 27, 2010, established a new Treasury program—the Small Business Lending Fund (SBLF)—to invest up to $30 billion in small institutions to increase small business lending.[45] Treasury may choose to model the new program's implementation on the CPP process, as it did with the CDCI. Treasury is required to consult with the bank regulators to determine whether an institution may receive a capital investment, and Treasury officials have indicated that they would likely rely on regulators to determine applicants' eligibility. Unless Treasury also takes steps to coordinate and monitor withdrawal requests by regulators, the disparity that existed in CPP between the control mechanisms for approved applicants and those receiving withdrawal recommendations may persist in this new program, potentially resulting in similar applicants being treated differently.

Treasury Does Not Monitor Regulators' Decisions to Approve or Deny CPP Repayments

Treasury relies on decisions from federal bank regulators concerning whether to allow CPP firms to repay their investments, but as with withdrawal recommendations, it does not monitor or collect information on regulators' decisions. The CPP institution submits a repayment request to its primary federal regulator and Treasury (see figure 5). Bank regulatory officials explained that their agencies use existing supervisory procedures generally applicable to capital reductions as a basis for reviewing CPP repurchase requests and that they approach the decision from the perspective of achieving regulatory rather than CPP goals. Following their review, regulators provide a brief e-mail notification to Treasury indicating whether they object or do not object to allowing an institution to repay its CPP investment. Treasury, in turn, communicates the regulators' decisions to the CPP firms.

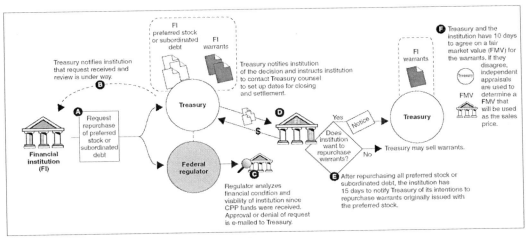

Sources: GAO (analysis); Art Explosion (images).

Figure 5. Investment Repayment Process for CPP

Table 4. Repayment Requests as of August 2010

Status of repayment request	Federal Reserve	FDIC	OCC	OTS	Total
Requests received	95	2	1	11	109
Recommended for approval	78	2	1	10	91
Not recommended for approval	17[a]	0	0	1[b]	18

Sources: Federal Reserve, FDIC, OCC, OTS

[a]Includes requests with a decision pending.

[b]Decision pending.

As of August 2010, 109 institutions had formally requested that they be allowed to repay their CPP investments, and regulators had approved over 80 percent of the requests (see table 4). According to Treasury officials, there have been no instances where Treasury has raised concerns about a regulator's decision. Officials at the Federal Reserve—which is responsible for reviewing most CPP repayment requests because requests for bank holding companies go to the holding company regulator—explained that they had not denied any requests but had asked institutions to wait or to raise additional capital. In these cases, institutions typically had experienced significant deterioration since the CPP investment, raising concerns about the adequacy of their capital levels.

Under the original terms of CPP, Treasury prohibited institutions from repaying their funds within 3 years unless the firm had completed a qualified equity offering to replace a minimum amount of the capital.[46] However, the American Recovery and Reinvestment Act of 2009 (ARRA) included provisions modifying the terms of CPP repayments. These provisions require that Treasury allow any institution to repay its CPP investment subject only to consultation with the appropriate federal bank regulator without considering whether the institution has replaced such funds from any other source or applying any waiting period.[47] Treasury officials indicated that, as a result of these restrictions, they did not provide guidance or criteria to regulators. The officials explained that even before the ARRA provisions limited Treasury's role, the standard CPP contract terms allowed institutions to repay the funds at their discretion—subject to regulatory approval—as long as they completed a qualified equity offering or the 3-year time frame had passed. The officials said that the contract terms themselves helped ensure that CPP goals were achieved.

While the decision to allow repayment ultimately lies with the bank regulators, Treasury is not statutorily prohibited from reviewing their decision-making process and collecting information or providing feedback about the regulators' decisions. The two regulators responsible for most repayment requests prepare a case decision memo to document their analysis that is similar to the memo they used to document their evaluations of CPP applicants, but Treasury and agency officials said that Treasury does not request or review the memo or other analyses supporting regulators' decisions. One regulator indicated that it would provide Treasury with a brief explanation of the basis for its decisions to deny repayment requests and a brief discussion of the supervisory concerns raised by the proposed repayment. But Treasury officials stated that they did not review any information on the basis for regulators' decisions to approve or deny repayment requests. Without collecting or monitoring such information, Treasury has no basis for considering whether decisions about similar institutions are being made consistently and thus whether CPP firms are being treated equitably. Furthermore, absent information on why regulators made repayment decisions, Treasury cannot provide feedback to regulators on the consistency of regulators' decision making for similar institutions as part of its consultation role.

Regulators Independently Developed Similar Guidelines for Evaluating Repurchase Requests and Processes for Coordinating Their Decisions without Treasury Guidance

Regulators have independently developed similar guidelines for evaluating repurchase requests and also established processes for coordinating decisions that involved multiple regulators, and Treasury officials stated that they did not provide input to these guidelines or processes. Regulators said that, in general, they considered the same types of factors when evaluating repayment requests that they considered when reviewing CPP applications. According to the officials, regulators follow existing regulatory requirements for capital reductions—including the repayment of CPP funds—that apply to all of their supervised institutions. In addition to following existing supervisory procedures, officials from the different banking agencies indicated that they also considered a broad set of similar factors, including the following:

- the institution's continued viability without CPP funds;
- the adequacy of the institution's capital and ability to maintain appropriate capital levels over the subsequent 1 to 2 years, even assuming worsening economic conditions;
- the level and composition of capital and liquidity;
- earnings and asset quality; and
- any major changes in financial condition or viability that had occurred since the institution received CPP funds.

Although regulators said that they considered similar factors in their evaluations, without reviewing any information or analysis supporting regulators' recommendations, Treasury cannot be sure that regulators are using these guidelines consistently for all repayment requests.

In addition to setting out guidelines for standard repayment requests, the Federal Reserve established a supplemental process to evaluate repayment requests by the 19 largest bank holding companies that participated in the Supervisory Capital Assessment Program (SCAP).[48] As we reported in our June 2009 review of Treasury's implementation of TARP, the Federal Reserve required any SCAP institution seeking to repay CPP capital to demonstrate that it could access the long-term debt markets without reliance on debt guarantees by FDIC and public equity markets in addition to other factors.[49] As of September 16, 2010, four bank holding companies that participated in SCAP had not repurchased their CPP investment and one had not repaid funds from TARP's Automotive Industry Financing Program.[50]

Bank regulators said that they also shared their repayment process documents with each other to enhance the consistency of their evaluations and recommendations. For example, the Federal Reserve designed a repayment case decision memo that documents the review of repayment requests and the factors considered in making the decision and shared it with other regulators to promote consistency in their reviews. Officials from OTS explained that they used the Federal Reserve's repurchase case decision memo as the framework for their document while adding certain elements specific to thrifts such as confirmation that FDIC concurrence was received for thrift holding companies with state bank subsidiaries regulated by FDIC. Bank regulatory officials also stated that bank regulators discussed the repayment process during their weekly conference calls on CPP-related topics. OCC also prepares a memo to document its review of repurchase requests that differs from the form used by the Federal Reserve and OTS; however, it contains similar elements such as an explanation of the analysis and the basis for the decision. Finally, FDIC officials said that they followed existing procedures for capital retirement applications from FDIC-supervised institutions that included safety and soundness considerations.

Bank regulators also established processes for coordinating repayment decisions for CPP firms with a holding company and subsidiary bank supervised by different regulators. For example, Federal Reserve officials said that if a holding company it supervised that had a subsidiary bank under another regulator requested to repay CPP funds, the agency would consult with the subsidiary's regulator before making a final decision. The officials stated that if the regulator of the subsidiary bank objected to the Federal Reserve's preliminary decision, the regulators would try to reach a consensus. However, as regulator of the holding company that received the CPP investment, the Federal Reserve has the ultimate responsibility for making the decision as it is considered the primary federal regulator in such cases. According to Federal Reserve officials, when OTS is the primary regulator of a subsidiary thrift, it provides a repayment case decision memo to the Federal Reserve for it to consider as it evaluates the repayment request. OCC also provides the Federal Reserve with its analysis of any subsidiary bank for which it is the primary regulator, and FDIC identifies certain individuals who provide their recommendation and are available to discuss the decision. OTS performs a similar coordination role for CPP repayment requests that involve thrift holding companies with nonthrift financial subsidiaries. However, if Treasury does not collect information on or monitor the processes regulators use to make their repayment decisions,

Treasury cannot provide any feedback to regulators on the extent to which they are coordinating their decisions.

CONCLUSIONS

Approved CPP applicants generally had similar examination ratings and other strength characteristics that exceeded guidelines. However, a smaller group of firms had weaker characteristics and were approved after consideration of mitigating factors by regulators and Treasury. The ability to approve institutions after consideration of mitigating factors illustrates the importance of including controls in the review and selection process to provide reasonable assurance of the achievement of program goals and consistent decision making.

While Treasury established such controls for applicants that regulators recommended for approval, Treasury's process was inconsistent in the control mechanisms that existed for applicants that regulators recommended to withdraw from program consideration. These institutions did not benefit from the multiple levels of review that Treasury and regulators applied to approved applicants. For example, regulators could decide independently which applicants they would recommend to withdraw and may have considered mitigating factors differently. Treasury did not collect information on these firms or the reasons for regulators' decisions. Without mechanisms such as those that exist for approved applicants to control for the risk of inconsistent evaluations across different regulators, Treasury cannot have reasonable assurance that all similar applicants were treated consistently or that some potentially eligible firms did not end up withdrawing after following the advice of their regulator. Treasury officials explained their desire to conduct adequate due diligence on all applicants recommended for approval, but as Treasury is the agency responsible for implementing CPP, understanding the reasons that regulators recommended applicants withdraw would have been equally beneficial for Treasury. Collecting and reviewing information on withdrawal requests would allow Treasury to determine whether applicants that were left out of CPP were evaluated consistently across different regulators and conformed to Treasury's goals for the program.

Although Treasury is no longer making investments in financial institutions through CPP, it may continue to use the process as a model for similar programs as it has for the CDCI program. One such program is the SBLF, which Congress authorized in September 2010. SBLF contains elements similar to those of CPP and requires Treasury to administer the program with bank regulators. Unless Treasury makes changes to the CPP model to include monitoring and reviews of withdrawal recommendations, these new programs may share the same increased risk of similar participants not being treated consistently that existed in CPP.

As with the approval process, agencies are expected to establish control mechanisms to provide reasonable assurance that program goals are being achieved. Treasury has not established mechanisms to monitor, review, or coordinate regulators' decisions on repayment requests because, in its view, it lacks the authority to do so and is limited to carrying out regulators' decisions regarding the institution making the request. However, Treasury is not precluded from providing feedback to help ensure that regulators are treating similar institutions consistently when considering their repayment requests. Although regulators said that they consider similar factors when evaluating CPP firms' repayment requests, without collecting information on how and why regulators made their decisions, Treasury cannot verify the degree to which regulators' decisions on requests to exit CPP actually were based on such factors.

RECOMMENDATIONS FOR EXECUTIVE ACTION

If Treasury administers programs containing elements similar to those of CPP, such as the SBLF, we recommend that Treasury apply lessons learned from the implementation of CPP and enhance procedural controls for addressing the risk of inconsistency in regulators' decisions on withdrawals. Specifically, we recommend that the Secretary of the Treasury direct the program office responsible for implementing SBLF to establish a process for collecting information from bank regulators on all applicants that withdraw from consideration in response to a regulator's recommendation, including the reasons behind the recommendation. We also recommend that the program office evaluate the information to identify trends or patterns that may indicate whether similar applicants were treated inconsistently across different regulators and take action, if necessary, to help ensure a more consistent treatment.

As part of its consultation with regulators on their decisions to allow institutions to repay their CPP investments to Treasury, and to improve monitoring of these decisions, we recommend that the Secretary of the Treasury direct OFS to periodically collect and review certain information from the bank regulators on the analysis and conclusions supporting their decisions on CPP repayment requests and provide feedback for the regulators' consideration on the extent to which regulators are evaluating similar institutions consistently.

List of Committees

The Honorable Daniel K. Inouye
Chairman
The Honorable Thad Cochran
Vice Chairman
Committee on Appropriations
United States Senate

The Honorable Christopher J. Dodd
Chairman
The Honorable Richard C. Shelby
Ranking Member
Committee on Banking, Housing, and Urban Affairs
United States Senate

The Honorable Kent Conrad
Chairman
The Honorable Judd Gregg

Ranking Member
Committee on the Budget
United States Senate

The Honorable Max Baucus
Chairman
The Honorable Charles E. Grassley
Ranking Member
Committee on Finance
United States Senate

The Honorable David R. Obey
Chairman
The Honorable Jerry Lewis
Ranking Member
Committee on Appropriations
House of Representatives

The Honorable John M. Spratt, Jr.
Chairman
The Honorable Paul Ryan
Ranking Member
Committee on the Budget
House of Representatives

The Honorable Barney Frank
Chairman
The Honorable Spencer Bachus
Ranking Member
Committee on Financial Services
House of Representatives

The Honorable Sander M. Levin
Acting Chairman
The Honorable Dave Camp
Ranking Member
Committee on Ways and Means
House of Representatives

APPENDIX I. OBJECTIVES, SCOPE, AND METHODOLOGY

The objectives of our report were to (1) describe the characteristics of financial institutions that received funding under the Capital Purchase Program (CPP), and (2) assess how the Department of the Treasury (Treasury), with the assistance of federal bank regulators, implemented CPP.

To describe the characteristics of financial institutions that received CPP funding, we reviewed and analyzed information from Treasury case files on all of the 567 institutions that received CPP investments through April 30, 2009.[51] We gathered information from the case files using a data collection survey that recorded our responses in a database. Multiple analysts reviewed the collected information, and we performed data quality control checks to verify its accuracy. We used the database to analyze the characteristics of CPP applicants including their supervisory examination ratings, financial performance ratios, and regulators' assessments of their viability, among other things. We spoke with Treasury and regulatory officials about their processes for evaluating applicants, in particular about actions they took to collect up-to-date information on firms' financial condition. We also collected and analyzed information from the records of the CPP Council and Investment Committee meetings to understand how the committees evaluated and recommended approval of CPP applicants. Additionally, we collected limited updated information on all CPP institutions approved through December 31, 2009—for example, their location, primary federal regulator, ownership type, and CPP investment amount—from Treasury's Office of Financial Stability (OFS) and from publicly available reports on OFS's Web site to present characteristics for all approved institutions. To describe how Treasury and regulators assessed firms with weaker characteristics, we collected information on the reasons regulators approved these firms and the concerns regulators raised about their eligibility from case files and records of committee meetings. To describe enforcement actions that regulators took against these institutions, we reviewed publicly available documents on formal enforcement actions from federal bank regulators' Web sites. We also collected information on CPP firms that missed their dividend or interest payments or restructured their CPP investments from OFS and publicly available reports on its Web site. Finally, we collected information from the Federal Deposit Insurance Corporation (FDIC) on the number of CPP firms added to its list of problem banks.

To assess how Treasury implemented CPP with the assistance of federal bank regulators, we reviewed Treasury's policies, procedures, and guidance related to CPP, including nonpublic documents and publicly available material from the OFS Web site. We met with OFS officials to discuss how they evaluated applications and repayment requests and coordinated with regulators to decide on these applications and requests. We interviewed officials from FDIC, the Office of the Comptroller of the Currency (OCC), Office of Thrift Supervision (OTS), and the Board of Governors of the Federal Reserve System (Federal Reserve) to obtain information on their processes for reviewing and providing recommendations on CPP applications and repayment requests. We also discussed the guidance and communication they received from Treasury and their methods of formulating their CPP procedures. Additionally, we collected and analyzed program documents from the bank regulators, including policies and procedures, guidance documents, and summaries of their evaluations of applications and repayment requests. We also gathered data from regulators on applicants that withdrew from CPP consideration—including the reason for withdrawing—and on the number of repayment requests and their outcomes. We reviewed relevant laws, such as the Emergency Economic Stabilization Act of 2008 and the American Recovery and Reinvestment Act of 2009, to determine the impact of statutory changes to Treasury's authority. To assess how Treasury and regulators documented their decisions to approve CPP applicants, we analyzed information from case files and CPP Council and

Investment Committee meeting minutes to identify how consistently Treasury and regulators included relevant records of their reviews and decision-making processes. We also discussed with Treasury and regulatory officials the key forms they used to document their decisions and the evolution of these forms over time. To assess Treasury programs that were modeled after CPP, we collected and reviewed publicly available documents from Treasury and interviewed Treasury officials to discuss the nature of these programs—including the Community Development Capital Initiative (CDCI) and Small Business Lending Fund (SBLF)—and plans for implementing them. Finally, we met with the Federal Reserve's Office of Inspector General to learn about its work examining the Federal Reserve's CPP process and reviewed its report and other reports by GAO, the Special Inspector General for the Troubled Asset Relief Program (SIGTARP), and the FDIC Office of Inspector General.

This chapter is part of our coordinated work with SIGTARP and the inspectors general of the federal banking agencies to oversee TARP and CPP. The offices of the inspectors general of FDIC, Federal Reserve, and Treasury and SIGTARP have all completed work or have work under way reviewing CPP's implementation at their respective agencies. In coordination with the other oversight agencies and offices and to avoid duplication, we primarily focused our audit work (including our review of agency case files) on the phases of the CPP process from the point at which the regulators transmitted their recommendations to Treasury.

We conducted this performance audit from May 2009 to September 2010 in accordance with generally accepted government auditing standards. Those standards require that we plan and perform the audit to obtain sufficient, appropriate evidence to provide a reasonable basis for our findings and conclusions based on our audit objectives. We believe that the evidence obtained provides a reasonable basis for our findings and conclusions based on our audit objectives.

APPENDIX II. INFORMATION ON PROCESSING TIMES FOR THE CAPITAL PURCHASE PROGRAM

In general, the time frame for the Department of the Treasury and regulators to complete the evaluation and funding process for Capital Purchase Program applicants increased based on three factors. First, smaller institutions had longer processing time frames than larger firms. The average number of days between a firm's application date and the completion of the CPP investment increased steadily based on the firm's size as measured by its risk-weighted assets. The smallest 25 percent of firms we reviewed had an average processing time of 100 days followed by 83 days for the next largest 25 percent of firms. The two largest quartiles of firms had average processing times of 72 days and 53 days respectively. Also, it took longer to complete the investment for smaller firms, as the average time between preliminary approval and disbursement increased as the institution size decreased. Second, private institutions took longer for Treasury and regulators to process than public firms. The average and median processing time frames from application through disbursement of funds was about 6 weeks longer for private firms than for public firms. As with the trend for smaller institutions, private institutions had longer average time frames between preliminary approval and disbursement. Third, when Treasury returned an application to regulators for additional review, it took an average of about 2 weeks to receive a response from regulators. On average, Treasury preliminarily approved these applicants after an additional 3 days of review.

Firms that applied earlier had shorter average processing times—from application to disbursement—than firms that applied in later months. The average time from application through disbursement was 70 days for firms that applied in October, 82 days for firms that applied in November, and 89 for those that applied in December. Also, public firms tended to apply earlier than private firms and larger firms tended to apply earlier than smaller firms. For example, 62 percent of firms that applied in October were public, while 93 percent of firms that applied in December were private—a trend that largely resulted from the later release of program term sheets for the privately held banks. Likewise, 61 percent of firms that applied in October were the largest firms and 84 percent of firms that applied in December were the smallest firms. Because larger firms and public firms also had shorter average processing time frames than smaller and private firms, this may explain why firms that applied earlier had shorter processing times than those that applied later in the program.

The overall process for most firms, from when they applied to when they received their CPP funds, took 2 1/2 months. There were many interim steps within this broad process that can shorten or lengthen the overall time frame. For example, in our June 2009 report on the status of Treasury's implementation of the Troubled Asset Relief Program, we reported that the average processing days from application to submission to Treasury varied among the different regulators from 28 days to 57 days.[52] Also, Treasury preliminarily approved most firms within 5 weeks from application. The Investment Committee approved most firms the same day it reviewed them; however, it generally took longer to approve firms with the lowest examination ratings, resulting in a longer average review time frame. As previously mentioned, firms that Treasury returned to regulators for additional review took longer to receive Treasury's preliminary approval, and these firms tended to be those with lower examination ratings. Once Treasury preliminarily approved an applicant, it took an average of 33 days to complete the investment. As with the trends for the overall processing time frames, the final investment closing and disbursement took longer for smaller institutions and private institutions.

APPENDIX III. COMMENTS FROM THE DEPARTMENT OF THE TREASURY'S OFFICE OF FINANCIAL STABILITY

DEPARTMENT OF THE TREASURY
WASHINGTON, D.C. 20220

ASSISTANT SECRETARY

September 17, 2010

Thomas J. McCool
Director, Center for Economics
Applied Research and Methods
U.S. Government Accountability Office
441 G Street, N.W.
Washington, D.C. 20548

Dear Mr. McCool:

The Department of the Treasury (Treasury) appreciates the opportunity to review the GAO's latest draft report on Treasury's Troubled Asset Relief Program (TARP), titled *Opportunities to Apply Lessons Learned from the Capital Purchase Program to Similarly Designed Programs and to Improve the Repayment Process* (Draft Report). Much in the Draft Report, the product of a 15-month review by a talented and professional GAO staff, is likely to be beneficial if any future programs are modeled after the Capital Purchase Program (CPP).

The GAO's recommendations are that Treasury should monitor and evaluate the actions of the federal banking regulators with respect to CPP funding and repayment. First, the GAO recommends that Treasury monitor decisions made by federal banking regulators not to recommend an institution for funding in order to ensure that similar applicants are treated equitably. The goal of insuring consistent treatment is one with which no one would disagree. We also believe that the independent judgment of the federal banking regulators was of great value to the CPP process and would be of great value in any similar program in the future. The system that was used to evaluate and approve CPP applications balanced these objectives. In particular, we believe that having certain applications reviewed by a council of all four regulators, the meetings of which Treasury attended as a nonvoting member, served to help ensure consistency. The use of standardized applications and further review by a Treasury investment committee also helped achieve consistency. As you know, we have followed a similar approval process for the Community Development Capital Initiative. Nevertheless, we are happy to consider the GAO's suggestion should there be a similar program in the future. Ensuring that there are regular discussions among the regulators regarding their standards, which could be done at "council" meetings or otherwise, could be another way to address the GAO's concern.

The second recommendation is that Treasury should monitor and evaluate the regulators' decisions on CPP repayments. This recommendation also raises the issues of how to balance the goals of consistency and respecting the independence of the regulators. As you know, the Emergency Economic Stabilization Act of 2008 was amended to override contractual provisions in the CPP contracts which required Treasury's consent before an institution could repay unless certain standards were met. Instead, the law provides that Treasury shall permit a TARP recipient to repay "subject to consultation with the appropriate Federal banking agency." The law explicitly provides that this right to repay is "without regard to whether the financial institution has replaced such funds from any other source or to any waiting period". In light of this change in the law, Treasury cannot dictate standards for repayment. However, Treasury helped facilitate meetings among the regulators in the spring of 2009 at which they discussed what would be the standards for permitting TARP recipients to repay.

The recommendation that Treasury "collect information" on regulators decisions and "provide feedback on the extent to which regulators are evaluating similar institutions consistently" must be considered in this context. Among the benefits of having the appropriate regulator perform such assessments are that the relevant examiners are the most familiar with the institutions and are free to make the decisions in an independent manner. Moreover, Treasury does not receive confidential supervisory information about CPP recipients on a regular basis, which would limit any information collection contemplated by the GAO.

Nevertheless, we recognize the value of the objective you propose, and we will consider ways to address that objective in a manner consistent with the law, the principles of regulatory independence, and the need to treat supervisory information confidentially.

We look forward to continuing to work with you and your team as we continue our efforts to stabilize our financial system.

Sincerely,

Herbert M. Allison, Jr.
Assistant Secretary for Financial Stability

2

End Notes

[1] Other government efforts to stabilize the financial system included Treasury's Targeted Investment Program, the Federal Deposit Insurance Corporation's Temporary Liquidity Guarantee Program and the Board of Governors of the Federal Reserve System's Term Asset-Backed Securities Loan Facility and emergency lending

programs such as the Commercial Paper Funding Facility, the Primary Dealer Credit Facility, and the Term Securities Lending Facility.

[2] As authorized by the Emergency Economic Stabilization Act of 2008 (EESA), Pub. L. No. 110-343, 122 Stat. 3765 (2008), codified at 12 U.S.C. §§ 5201 et seq. EESA was signed into law on October 3, 2008 to help stem the worst financial crisis since the 1930s. EESA established the Office of Financial Stability within Treasury and provided it with broad, flexible authorities to buy or guarantee troubled mortgage-related assets or any other financial instruments necessary to stabilize the financial markets.

[3] Section 3(9) of the act, 12 U.S.C. § 5202(9). The act requires that the appropriate committees of Congress be notified in writing that the Secretary of the Treasury, after consultation with the Federal Reserve Chairman, has determined that it is necessary to purchase other financial instruments to promote financial market stability.

[4] A warrant is an option to buy shares of common stock or preferred stock at a predetermined price on or before a specified date.

[5] Section 116 of EESA, 122 Stat. at 3783 (codified at U.S.C. § 5226).

[6] See GAO, *Troubled Asset Relief Program: Additional Actions Needed to Better Ensure Integrity, Accountability, and Transparency*, GAO-09-161 (Washington, D.C.: Dec. 2, 2008); *Troubled Asset Relief Program: Status of Efforts to Address Transparency and Accountability Issues*, GAO-09-296 (Washington, D.C.: Jan. 30, 2009); *Troubled Asset Relief Program: March 2009 Status of Efforts to Address Transparency and Accountability Issues,* GAO-09-504 (Washington, D.C.: Mar. 31, 2009); *Troubled Asset Relief Program: June 2009 Status of Efforts to Address Transparency and Accountability Issues*, GAO-09-658 (Washington, D.C.: Jun. 17, 2009); and *Troubled Asset Relief Program: One Year Later, Actions Are Needed to Address Remaining Transparency and Accountability Challenges,* GAO-10-16 (Washington, D.C.: Oct. 8, 2009).

[7] Risk-weighted assets are the total assets and off-balance-sheet items held by an institution that are weighted for risk according to the federal banking agencies' regulatory capital standards.

[8] For purposes of CPP, qualifying financial institutions generally include stand-alone U.S.-controlled banks and savings associations, as well as bank holding companies and most savings and loan holding companies.

[9] In May 2009, Treasury increased the maximum amount of CPP funding that small financial institutions (qualifying financial institutions with total assets less than $500 million) may receive from 3 percent of risk-weighted assets to 5 percent of risk-weighted assets.

[10] For certain types of institutions known as S corporations, Treasury received subordinated debt rather than preferred shares to preserve these institutions' special tax status.

[11] Bank holding companies are entities that own or control one or more U.S. commercial banks. Financial holding companies are a subset of bank holding companies that may engage in a wider range of activities.

[12] The Dodd-Frank Wall Street Reform and Consumer Protection Act, Pub. L. No. 111-203, Title III, 124 Stat. 1376, 1520 (2010), includes provisions to abolish OTS and allocate its functions among the Federal Reserve, OCC, and FDIC.

[13] The primary federal regulator is generally the regulator overseeing the lead bank of the institution. Where the institution is owned by a bank holding company, the primary federal regulator also consults with the Federal Reserve.

[14] The nine major financial institutions were Bank of America Corporation; Citigroup, Inc.; JPMorgan Chase & Co.; Wells Fargo & Company; Morgan Stanley; The Goldman Sachs Group, Inc.; The Bank of New York Mellon Corporation; State Street Corporation; and Merrill Lynch & Co., Inc.

[15] Under CPP program guidelines, a public institution is a company (1) whose securities are traded on a national securities exchange and (2) that is required to file, under the federal securities laws, periodic reports such as the annual and quarterly reports with either the Securities and Exchange Commission or a primary federal bank regulator. A privately held institution is a company that does not meet the definition of a public institution. Institutions traded in over-the-counter markets had the option to participate under the terms for private institutions.

[16] The top 5 states receiving the most CPP investments were New York ($80,194,291,000), North Carolina ($28,695,010,000), California ($27,667,578,000), Pennsylvania ($9,848,886,000), and Ohio ($7,840,580,000). The states receiving the least amount of CPP investments were Alaska ($4,781,000), the District of Columbia ($6,000,000), Arizona ($8,047,000), Wyoming ($8,100,000), and Rhode Island ($31,065,000).

[17] The dates of the risk-weighted assets were from 2008, although dates were not available for 161 of the 567 firms we reviewed.

[18] FDIC was the primary regulator for most of the institutions that participated in CPP—424 firms, or 60 percent of those we reviewed. The Federal Reserve was the primary regulator for 112 firms, or 16 percent; OCC was the primary regulator for 116, or 16 percent; and OTS for 55, or 8 percent.

[19] The federal banking agencies assign a supervisory rating when they conduct examinations of a bank or thrift's safety and soundness. The numerical ratings range from 1 to 5, with 1 being the strongest and 5 the weakest. The ratings—referred to as CAMELS—assess six components of an institution's financial health: capital, asset quality, management, earnings, liquidity, and sensitivity to market risk. Treasury instructed regulators to consider CAMELS ratings, among other indicators, in making approval recommendations. Treasury and

regulators also identified six performance ratios for evaluating applicants. Three of the ratios related to regulatory capital levels—Tier 1 risk-based capital ratio, total risk-based capital ratio, and Tier 1 leverage ratio. The other three ratios measured certain classes of assets—including classified assets, nonperforming loans, and construction and development loans—as a share of capital and reserves.

[20] SunTrust Banks, Inc., and Bank of America Corporation each received two CPP investments in separate transactions. Therefore, the number of unique institutions receiving CPP investments through April 30, 2009 is 565.

[21] The Federal Reserve assigns each bank holding company a composite rating (C) based on an evaluation of its managerial and financial condition and an assessment of future potential risk to its subsidiary bank or thrift. The main components of the rating system represent risk management (R), financial condition (F), and potential impact (I) of the holding company and nonbank or nonthrift subsidiaries on the bank or thrift. Examiners assign ratings based on a 1-to-5 numeric scale. A 1 indicates the highest rating, strongest performance and practices, and least degree of supervisory concern; a 5 indicates the lowest rating, weakest performance, and highest degree of supervisory concern.

[22] Federal banking regulators also examine the institutions they supervise to determine their compliance with CRA. Congress enacted CRA in 1977 to encourage depository institutions to help meet the credit needs of the communities in which they operate, including low- and moderate-income neighborhoods. A CPP applicant's CRA rating is another factor that Treasury instructed the federal banking regulators to consider in making approval recommendations.

[23] The minimum amount of regulatory capital is the amount required by bank regulators for an institution to be considered adequately capitalized for purposes of prompt corrective action. Prompt corrective action is a supervisory framework for banks that links supervisory actions closely to a bank's capital ratios. Under prompt corrective action, institutions below this threshold are considered undercapitalized.

[24] The Tier 1 risk-based capital ratio is defined as Tier 1 capital as a share of risk-weighted assets (RWA). Tier 1 capital consists of core elements such as common stock, noncumulative perpetual preferred stock, and minority interests in consolidated subsidiaries. Risk-weighted assets are on- and off-balance sheet assets adjusted for their risk characteristics.

[25] Some of the CPP institutions we reviewed were newly chartered banks, referred to as de novo institutions. In their early years of operation, de novo banks may have high amounts of capital relative to their assets and low levels of nonperforming loans as they extend credit to new clients and grow their loan portfolios. One such bank that opened the same year it applied for CPP accounted for the highest regulatory capital ratios in each of the three categories (Tier 1 risk-based capital ratio, Tier 1 leverage ratio, and total risk-based capital ratio).

[26] The Tier 1 leverage ratio is defined as Tier 1 capital as a share of average total consolidated assets.

[27] The total risk-based capital ratio is defined as total capital as a share of risk-weighted assets. Total capital includes Tier 1 capital and Tier 2 capital, or supplementary capital.

[28] At the initiation of CPP, Treasury and regulators defined acceptable levels for the three performance ratios relating to asset quality (classified assets ratio, nonperforming loan and real estate-owned ratio, and construction and development loan ratio). The criteria for the three performance ratios relating to capital levels (Tier 1 risk-based capital ratio, total risk-based capital ratio, and the Tier 1 leverage ratio) are based on regulatory minimums for an institution to be considered adequately capitalized. For the leverage ratio, we used the minimum level that applies to most banks and bank holding companies (4 percent), although regulators applied a lower level to banks and bank holding companies with strong examination ratings. Banks with overall unsatisfactory examination ratings are those with a composite CAMELS rating weaker than 2. We reviewed enforcement actions available through regulators' Web sites to determine whether actions were formal or informal, active at the time of CPP approval, or related to compliance or safety and soundness.

[29] Treasury and regulatory officials said that they did not have absolute criteria for evaluating CPP applicants and did not make approval decisions solely on the basis of specific quantitative measurements. Treasury and regulatory officials explained that they also relied on their judgment and familiarity with the firms they supervised.

[30] For example, holders of subordinated debt have a claim on the firm's assets, and institutions issuing subordinated debt have an obligation to repay those funds, even though holders of the subordinated debt may have a lower priority for repayment than depositors or senior debt holders in the event of an insolvency or bank seizure. Institutions do not have an obligation to repay funds received from purchasers of their common stock or certain types of preferred stock.

[31] Under the CPP terms, institutions pay cumulative dividends on their preferred shares except for banks that are not subsidiaries of holding companies, which pay noncumulative dividends. Some other types of institutions, such as S corporations, received their CPP investment in the form of subordinated debt and pay Treasury interest rather than dividends.

[32] The following number of institutions missed their scheduled dividend or interest payments by due date: February 2009–8, May 2009–18, August 2009–34, November 2009–54, February 2010–79, May 2010–97, and August 2010—123.

[33] CPP dividend and interest payments are due on February 15, May 15, August 15 and November 15 of each year, or the first business day subsequent to those dates. The first CPP dividend and interest payments were due in February 2009, for a total of seven possible payments due through August 2010. The reporting period ends on the last day of the calendar month in which the dividend or interest payment is due. Some institutions made their dividend or interest payments after the end of the reporting period.

[34] One firm identified as a marginal approval has had two formal enforcement actions since receiving its CPP investment—one each from FDIC and the Federal Reserve.

[35] Four CPP institutions have filed for bankruptcy protection or had regulators place their banking subsidiary in receivership—UCBH Holdings Inc., CIT Group Inc., Pacific Coast National Bancorp, and Midwest Banc Holdings. However, none of these firms failed to meet the CPP program guidelines or other criteria used to identify institutions with weak characteristics.

[36] The information on restructured CPP investments does not include Citigroup, which exchanged its CPP shares for financial instruments that converted to common shares in September 2009. Treasury said that it does not include Citigroup because it received investments under several TARP programs in addition to CPP such as the Targeted Investment Program and it is monitored separately within Treasury.

[37] See GAO, *Standards for Internal Control in the Federal Government*, GAO/AIMD-00-21.3.1 (Washington, D.C.: Nov. 1, 1999).

[38] In addition to the limited formal guidance, Treasury subsequently provided regulators with informal and case-specific guidance using e-mails and conference calls. For example, Treasury held regular weekly conference calls with the bank regulators to discuss concerns about specific applicants and also broader process and policy issues such as commercial real estate exposures.

[39] The guidance identified other factors for consideration, such as the existence of a signed merger agreement involving the institution or a confirmed private equity investment. Finally, the guidance document defined three categories for regulators to use in classifying applicants that were based on examination ratings (such as the CAMELS ratings), the age of the ratings, and financial performance ratios (including capital and asset quality ratios).

[40] Board of Governors of the Federal Reserve System Office of Inspector General, *Audit of the Board's Processing of Applications for the Capital Purchase Program under the Troubled Asset Relief Program*, (Washington, D.C.: Sept. 30, 2009).

[41] For example, one memo stated only "Confirmed Category 1 institution. Recommend Approval." Others stated "Category 1 institution; approved under 12 USC 1823(c)(4) systemic risk exception."

[42] As part of its review of FDIC's processing of CPP applicants, FDIC's Office of Inspector General evaluated the reasons for application withdrawals that occurred as of December 10, 2008, and found that 42 percent had been suggested to withdraw by FDIC regional offices. The remainder withdrew voluntarily. See FDIC Office of Inspector General, *Controls Over the FDIC's Processing of Capital Purchase Program Applications from FDIC-Supervised Institutions*, EVAL-09-004 (Arlington, VA.: Mar. 20, 2009).

[43] We did not examine regulators' files on withdrawn applicants to identify actual instances of inconsistencies to avoid duplication of work conducted by SIGTARP and agency inspectors general that reviewed CPP implementation at their respective agencies.

[44] FDIC Office of Inspector General, *Controls Over the FDIC's Processing of Capital Purchase Program Applications from FDIC-Supervised Institutions.*

[45] Pub. L. No. 111-240, Title IV, Subtitle A, 124 Stat. 2504 (2010).

[46] A qualified equity offering is the sale and issuance of Tier 1 qualifying perpetual preferred stock, common stock, or a combination of such stock for cash. Under the original terms, CPP investments in the form of senior preferred shares could only be redeemed prior to 3 years from the date of investment with the proceeds of qualified equity offerings that resulted in aggregate gross proceeds to the financial institution of not less than 25 percent of the issue price of the senior preferred.

[47] Pub. L. No. 111-5, div. B, § 7001, 123 Stat. 115, 516 (2009). Section 7001 provides, in part, that "Subject to consultation with the appropriate Federal banking agency, if any…Treasury shall permit a TARP recipient to repay any assistance previously provided under the TARP to such financial institution, without regard to whether the financial institution has replaced the funds from any other source or to any waiting period."

[48] SCAP was an effort initiated in February 2009 by the Federal Reserve and other federal banking regulators to conduct a comprehensive simultaneous assessment of the capital held by the 19 largest bank holding companies. It was designed as a forward-looking exercise intended to help regulators gauge the extent of additional capital necessary to keep the institutions strongly capitalized and able to lend even if economic conditions were worse than had been expected.

[49] For more information, see GAO-09-658.

[50] The four CPP firms that participated in SCAP and had not repaid the capital as of September 16, 2010 were Fifth Third Bancorp, KeyCorp, Regions Financial Corporation, and SunTrust Banks, Inc. The fifth firm was GMAC, which received TARP funds through the Automotive Industry Financing Program, which Treasury established in December 2008 to help stabilize the U.S. automotive industry and avoid disruptions that would pose systemic risk to the nation's economy. Citigroup, Inc., exchanged its CPP shares for financial instruments

that converted to common shares in September 2009, and Treasury has begun the process of selling its shares of Citigroup, Inc., common stock.

[51] In total, Treasury invested in 707 financial institutions through December 31, 2009, when it closed CPP to new investments.

[52] See GAO-09-658.

In: Reflections on the Troubled Asset Relief Program (TARP)   ISBN: 978-1-61209-519-6
Editor: Donna C. Hayworth   © 2011 Nova Science Publishers, Inc.

Chapter 3

TROUBLED ASSET RELIEF PROGRAM (TARP): IMPLEMENTATION AND STATUS

Baird Webel

SUMMARY

The Troubled Asset Relief Program (TARP) was created by the Emergency Economic Stabilization Act (EESA; P.L. 110-343) in October 2008. EESA was passed by Congress and signed by President Bush to address an ongoing financial crisis that reached near-panic proportions in September 2008. EESA granted the Secretary of the Treasury authority to either purchase or insure up to $700 billion in troubled assets owned by financial institutions. This authority was granted for up to two years from the date of enactment and was very broad. In particular, the definitions of both "troubled asset" and "financial institution" allowed the Secretary wide leeway in deciding what assets might be purchased or guaranteed and what might qualify as a financial firm.

The financial crisis grew out of an unprecedented housing boom that turned into a housing bust. Much of past lending for housing was based on asset-backed securities, which used the repayment of housing loans as the basis for repaying these securities. As housing prices fell and mortgage defaults increased, these securities became illiquid and fell sharply in value, causing capital losses for financial firms. Uncertainty about future losses on illiquid and complex assets led to some firms having reduced access to private liquidity, with the loss in liquidity being in some cases catastrophic. September 2008 saw the government takeover of Fannie Mae and Freddie Mac, the bankruptcy of Lehman Brothers, and the near collapse of AIG, which was saved only by an $85 billion loan from the Federal Reserve. There was widespread suspicion in the financial markets as participants were unsure which firms might be holding so-called toxic assets that might now be worth much less than previously estimated, and thus might be unreliable counterparties in financial transactions.

As EESA was moving through Congress, most attention focused on the idea of the government purchasing mortgage-related toxic assets, thus removing the widespread uncertainty and suspicion. The initial TARP Capital Purchase Program, however, directly added capital onto banks' balance sheets through preferred share purchases, rather than removing assets that had become liabilities through purchasing mortgage-related assets. Several other TARP programs followed, including an asset guarantee program; programs designed to spur consumer and business lending; financial support for companies such as AIG, GM, and Chrysler; and programs to aid homeowners at risk of foreclosure. Eventually, the Public-Private Investment Program did result in the purchase of some mortgage-related assets from banks, but this has remained a relatively small part of TARP.

With the immediate crisis subsiding through 2009, congressional attention in financial services turned largely to consideration of broad regulatory changes. The resulting Dodd-Frank Wall Street Reform and Consumer Protection Act (P.L. 111-203) amended the TARP authority, including (1) reduction of the overall amount to $475 billion; (2) removal of the ability to reuse TARP funds that had been repaid; and (3) removal of the authority to create new TARP programs or initiatives. TARP authority to purchase new assets or enter new contracts is set to expire on October 3, 2010. Outlays under the existing contracts, however, may continue through the life of these contracts. Overall cost estimates for TARP have decreased significantly since the passage of EESA, with August 2010 estimates from the Congressional Budget Office foreseeing approximately $67 billion in losses for the government. Most of this loss is from aid to homeowners, AIG, and the automakers. The assistance to banks is generally showing a profit for the government.

INTRODUCTION

The Troubled Asset Relief Program (TARP) was created by the Emergency Economic Stabilization Act[1] (EESA) enacted on October 3, 2008. EESA was passed by Congress and signed by President Bush to address an ongoing financial crisis that reached near-panic proportions in September 2008.

Financial turmoil began in August 2007 when asset-backed securities, particularly those backed by subprime mortgages, suddenly became illiquid and fell sharply in value as an unprecedented housing boom turned to a housing bust. The Federal Reserve (Fed) stepped in with emergency measures to restore liquidity, temporarily calming markets. Losses in mortgage markets, however, continued and spilled into other markets. Financial firms eventually wrote down many of these losses, depleting their capital. Uncertainty about future losses on illiquid and complex assets led to some firms having reduced access to private liquidity, with the loss in liquidity being in some cases catastrophic.

September 2008 saw the government takeover of Fannie Mae and Freddie Mac, the bankruptcy of Lehman Brothers, and the near collapse of AIG, which was averted with an $85 billion loan from the Fed. There was widespread unwillingness to lend in the financial markets as participants were unsure which firms might be holding so-called toxic assets now worth much less than previously estimated, and thus might be unreliable counterparties in financial transactions.

EESA authorized the Secretary of the Treasury (hereafter "the Secretary") to either purchase or insure up to $700 billion in troubled assets owned by financial firms. This authority was granted for a maximum of two years from the date of enactment, expiring on October 3, 2010. The general concept was that by removing such assets from the financial system, confidence in counterparties could be restored and the system could resume functioning. This authority granted in EESA was very broad. In particular, the definitions of both "troubled assets" and "financial institutions" allowed the Secretary wide latitude in deciding what assets might be purchased or guaranteed and what might qualify as a financial institution.[2]

This chapter provides a brief outline of the programs created under TARP, recent changes made by Congress, and a summary of the current status and estimated costs of the program. It will be updated as warranted by market and legislative events.

TARP PROGRAMS

Treasury reacted quickly after the enactment of EESA, announcing the first TARP program on October 14, 2008. The initial **Capital Purchase Program** (CPP), however, did not purchase the mortgage-backed securities that were seen as toxic to the system, but instead purchased preferred shares in banks. The resulting addition of capital, it was hoped, would allow banks to overcome the effect of the toxic assets while the assets remained on bank balance sheets. Additional TARP programs included the following:

- **Targeted Investment Program:** This program provided for exceptional preferred share purchases and was used only for Citigroup and Bank of America.
- **Asset Guarantee Program:** Required by Section 102 of EESA, guarantees provided under this program were also part of the exceptional assistance to Citigroup and Bank of America.
- **Systemically Significant Failing Institution Program:** Preferred share purchases to supplement and supplant assistance to AIG previously provided by the Federal Reserve.[3]
- **Consumer and Business Lending Initiatives:** Three different attempts to increase lending and spur the economy. The Term Asset-Backed Securities Loan Facility (TALF) supported the asset-backed security market.[4] The Section 7a Securities Purchase Program supports the Small Business Administration's (SBA) Section 7a loan program through purchasing pooled SBA guaranteed securities. The Community Development Capital Initiative provides for lower dividend rates on preferred share purchases from banks that target their lending to small businesses.
- **Housing Assistance Programs:** These programs are unlike the other TARP programs in that they do not result in valuable assets or income in return for the TARP funding. The Home Affordable Modification Program (HAMP) pays mortgage servicers if they modify mortgages to reduce the financial burden on homeowners. The Hardest Hit Fund provides aid to state housing authority programs in states that have high unemployment rates and foreclosures.[5]
- **Public-Private Investment Program:** This program provides funds and guarantees for purchases of mortgage-related securities from bank balance sheets. Purchases and management of the securities is done by private investors who have provided capital to invest along with the TARP funds.

- **Automaker Industry Support:** This program provided loans to support General Motors (GM) and Chrysler. The program ultimately resulted in majority government ownership of GM (60.8%) and its financing arm, GMAC (56.3%), and minority government ownership of Chrysler (9.9%).[6]

TARP AND THE DODD-FRANK ACT[7]

Unlike EESA, which was a temporary response to the immediate financial crisis, the Dodd-Frank Wall Street Reform and Consumer Protection Act (the Dodd-Frank Act) was a broad bill that permanently changed many parts of the U.S. financial regulatory system. The act included a relatively short amendment to EESA in Title XIII, entitled the "Pay It Back Act." Section 1302 of Dodd-Frank made three primary changes to EESA:

- reducing the overall authorization to purchase from nearly $700 billion[8] to $475 billion;
- removing the implicit authority for the Secretary to reuse TARP funds when TARP assets are sold[9]; and
- limiting the authorities under the act to programs or initiatives initiated prior to June 25, 2010.

As of June 30, 2010, the Treasury reported that it planned to spend approximately $537 billion on the various programs, with $491 billion committed under signed contracts and $385 billion actually disbursed.[10] The July 21, 2010 enactment of the $475 billion limit in the Dodd-Frank Act thus required Treasury to reduce the amounts planned for TARP by more than $60 billion and the legal commitments under TARP by more than $16 billion. The Congressional Budget Office (CBO) scored the TARP changes in the Dodd-Frank Act as resulting in a decrease in direct spending of $11 billion in 2010.[11]

The TARP changes reported by Treasury[12] following the Dodd-Frank Act appear in **Table 1**.

Under the broad authorities granted by EESA, Treasury could unilaterally change the planned program allocations. Following the Dodd-Frank Act, this authority is limited to the difference between the total of Treasury's plans and the total of the signed contracts, approximately $21 billion as of July 31, 2010.

CURRENT STATUS AND FUTURE OF TARP

As detailed above, up until October 3, 2010, the Secretary has the authority to purchase or insure nearly any financial asset under the programs in place on June 25, 2010. After October 3, 2010, this authority expires. The legal contracts entered into under the previous authority, however, are still in force. Thus, TARP funds may still flow out from the Treasury after October 3, 2010. For example, the legally committed assistance for AIG totals $69.8 billion. Of this amount, $29.8 billion is in the form of an agreement for Treasury to purchase, at AIG's discretion, preferred shares until March 2014. As of August 30, 2010, only $7.54

billion in preferred shares had been purchased under this agreement, for a total of $47.54 billion in TARP funds for AIG.[13] AIG has not indicated a specific intent to draw additional amounts from TARP after October 3, 2010, but it would have the option to do so. The programs with the largest gap between legal commitments and the actual amount disbursed, and thus the largest potential to grow after October 3, 2010, are the aforementioned AIG assistance and the housing support programs. Table 2 presents the figures reported by the Treasury for planned, committed, and actually disbursed TARP funds.

Table 1. TARP Changes Following the Dodd-Frank Act ($ in billions)

TARP Program	Planned Allocation Prior to Dodd-Frank	Change Following Dodd-Frank	Planned Allocation July 31, 2010	Legal Commitments July 31, 2010
Capital Purchase Program	$204.9	$0.0	$204.9	$204.9
Targeted Investment Program	$40.0	$0.0	$40.0	$40
Asset Guarantee Program	$5.0	$0.0	$5.0	$5.0
AIG (Systemically Significant Failing Institutions)	$69.8	$0.0	$69.8	$69.8
Term Asset-Backed Securities Program	$20.0	-$15.7	$4.3	$4.3
SBA Section 7(a)	$1.0	-$0.6	$0.4	
Community Development Capital Initiative	$0.8	$0.0	$0.8	$1.0a
Small Business Lending Fund	$30	-$30.0b	$0.0	$0.0
Public Private Investment Program	$30.4	-$7.9	$22.4	$22.4
Automotive Industry Financing Program	$84.8	-$3.1	$81.8	$81.8
Housing/HAMP	$48.7	-$3.1	$45.6	$30.25
Total	**$535.5**	**-60.5**	**$475.0**	**$454**

Source: July 2010 TARP Monthly Report
Notes: Figures may not add due to rounding.
a. Treasury's reporting did not separate the legal commitments for the two programs.
b. The Administration proposed creating a similar fund outside of TARP. See CRS Report R4 1385, Small Business Legislation: H.R. 3854 and H.R. 5297, by Robert Jay Dilger, Oscar R. Gonzales, and Gary Guenther.

Table 2. Outlay of TARP Funds ($ in billions; as of August 30, 2010)

TARP Program	Planned Amount	Legally Committed Amount	Actual Disbursements
Capital Purchase Program	$204.89	$204.89	$204.89
Targeted Investment Program	$40.0	$40.0	$40.0
Asset Guarantee Program	$5.0	$0	$0
Consumer and Business Lending Initiative	$5.48	$5.37	$0.32
Public-Private Investment Program	$22.41	$22.41	$13.51
AIG	$69.84	$69.84	$47.54
Auto Industry Financing Program	$81.76	$81.76	$79.69
Housing Support	$45.63	$30.86	$0.44
Totals	**$475.0**	**$460.12**	**$386.4**

Source: August 2010 TARP Monthly Report
Note: Figures may not add due to rounding.

Although the total amount of assets held or insured under TARP was initially capped at $700 billion, and the program was widely reported as a "$700 billion bailout,"[14] the actual cost of TARP was never likely to approach $700 billion. Unlike most government programs, where funds are simply expended, TARP funds were generally used in ways that resulted in either the holding of assets by the government or in some form of income accruing to the government. The incoming receipts from TARP outlays have taken several forms, including

- funds from the sale of previously purchased assets;
- repayment of principal from loans;
- premium payments for insured assets;
- dividend and interest payments from assets and loans; and
- proceeds from the sale of warrants issued by companies who sold assets to TARP.

Table 3 summarizes these incoming revenues from TARP.

Table 3. Incoming TARP Funds ($ in billions; as of July 3 1, 2010)

TARP Program	Asset Sales/ Repayment of Loan Principal	Dividends, Interest, Premiums, and Warrant Proceeds	Unpaid Accrued Dividends and Interest[a]
Capital Purchase Program	$147.53b	$9.8 (dividends); $7.2 (warrants); $2.0 (Citigroup)	$0.14
Targeted Investment Program	$40	$3.0	$0
Asset Guarantee Program	none	$0.41	$0
Consumer and Business Lending Initiative	$0	$0	$0
Public-Private Investment Program	$0.37	$0.14	$0
AIG	$0	$0	$1.6
Auto Industry Financing Program	$11.20	$2.61	$0.34 (Chrysler)
Housing Support	$0	$0	$0
Totals	**$199.1**	**$25.2**	**$2.8**

Source: August 2010 TARP Monthly Report; August 2010 TARP Dividends and Interest Report; Chrysler 2010 2nd Quarter Financial Statement..

Notes: The CPP preferred shares in Citigroup were converted into common equity, which the Treasury has begun selling into the open market. Treasury splits the resulting receipts between repayment and income. Figures may not add due to rounding.

a. For both AIG and Chrysler, the unpaid dividends and interest have been converted into principal under contracts agreed to between the company and the Treasury. The unpaid Capital Purchase Program dividends are due to banks missing their scheduled dividend payments.

b. Some 707 banks received CPP funds. Of these, 80 banks have fully repaid and 9 have partially repaid; the bulk of the outstanding CPP funds are in relatively small financial institutions.

THE COSTS OF TARP

In arriving at an overall cost to the government of TARP, or any similar program, it is important to account for the difference in time between initial outlay of funds and the receipt of any income. Some TARP contracts run for five years or more and the difference in value between a dollar in 2008 and 2013, for example, could be significant. To compare dollar values over time, economists use present value calculations that reduce costs or income in the future relative to the present by a discount rate. Present value calculations can be very sensitive to the rate used if the amount of time involved is large. In preparing the budget cost estimates for TARP, the Administration and the CBO are directed by Section 123 of EESA to adjust their estimates by current market borrowing rates, as opposed to the borrowing rate paid by Treasury. Using market rates instead of government borrowing rates increases the net calculated cost of these investments, and is meant to better represent the true economic costs of the programs. **Table 4** presents a range of TARP cost estimates over the life of the program whereas **Table 5** summarizes the latest detailed estimates of TARP 's cost from CBO (March 2010; the August 2010 estimate contains only a total) and the Treasury (May 2010).

Table 4. Estimates of Overall TARP Costs ($ in billions)

Date/Agency	Amount
October 2008/CBO	"likely to be substantially less than $700 billion but is more likely than not to be greater than zero."
January 2009/CBO	$189
March 2009/CBO	$356
May 2009/Administration	$307.5
August 2009/Administration	$208
August 2009/CBO	$241
January 2010/CBO	$99
February 2010/Administration	$127
March 2010/CBO	$109
May 2010/Administration	$105.4
August 2010/CBO	$67

Source: CBO, Analysis of Dodd Substitute Amendment for H.R. 1424, October 1, 2008; OMB, Analytical Perspectives, FY2010 President's Budget, Table 702, May 2009; CBO, Budget and Economic Outlook, (January 2009, August 2009, January 2010, and August 2010); OMB, Analytical Perspectives, FY2011 President's Budget, Table 4-7; February 2010; CBO, Report on the Troubled Asset Relief Program—March 2010, March 17 2010; U.S. Treasury, Summary Tables of Trouble Asset Relief Program (TARP) Investments as of March 31, 2010, May 2010;

Table 5. Detailed Cost/Gain Estimates for TARP ($ in billions)

TARP Program	CBO (March 2010)[a]	Treasury (May 2010)
Capital Purchase Program	-$2	-$9.8
Targeted Investment Program	-$3	-$3.8
Asset Guarantee Program	-$3	-$3.1
Consumer and Business Lending Initiative	$1	$3.0
Public-Private Investment Program	$1	$0.5
AIG	$36	$45.2
Auto Industry Financing Program	$34	$24.6
Housing Support	$22	$48.8

Source: CBO, Report on the Troubled Asset Relief Program—March 2010, March 17 2010; U.S. Treasury, Summary Tables of Trouble Asset Relief Program (TARP) Investments as of March 31, 2010, May 2010.

Note: Negative numbers (-) indicate a gain for the program.

a. Since March 2010, CBO released a new estimate for total TARP spending that was lower than the March 2010 total, but did not provide details about which programs had changed in cost.

The cost estimates of TARP are very sensitive to financial markets and the state of the economy. The ultimate cost of the program will depend largely on recouping value from the financial assets held in TARP. The CPP bank preferred shares and warrants have turned out to be relativelyvaluable, thus CBO and the Treasury estimate that the CPP may show an overall profit as the increase in asset values outweigh any losses from defaults by banks in the CPP. In the cases, for example, of AIG or the automakers, however, both CBO and the Treasury estimate that the assets held by the government ultimately will not return enough to recoup the cash put into the companies. A significant test of the cost of the automaker intervention may occur shortly as General Motors has filed with the Securities and Exchange Commission to sell shares on the open market in an initial public offering (IPO). Although all the U.S. government shares may not be sold in this IPO, it will provide a relatively straightforward valuation of the share of GM held by the government. Sale of the government stakes in other companies, such as AIG and Chrysler, are likely to occur in the future. As the outlook for the economy has changed over time, the estimates of the overall cost of TARP have also fallen significantly.

End Notes

[1] P.L. 110-343, 12 USC 5311 et seq.

[2] The definition for financial institution gives examples, such as banks and credit unions, but specifically does not limit the definition to the types of firms named. The definition of troubled asset includes "any financial instrument" determined by the Secretary, in consultation with the Chairman of the Fed, the purchase of which would promote financial stability.

[3] For more detailed information on AIG, see CRS Report R40438, *Ongoing Government Assistance for American International Group (AIG)*, by Baird Webel.

[4] For more information see CRS Report RL34427, *Financial Turmoil: Federal Reserve Policy Responses*, by Marc Labonte.

[5] For more information see CRS Report R40210, Preserving Homeownership: *Foreclosure Prevention Initiatives*, by Katie Jones.

[6] For more information see CRS Report R41401, *General Motors' Initial Public Offering: Review of Issues and Implications for TARP*, by Bill Canis, Baird Webel, and Gary Shorter and CRS Report R41 154, *The U.S. Motor Vehicle Industry: A Review of Recent Domestic and International Developments,* by Bill Canis and Brent D. Yacobucci.

[7] P.L. 111-203, see CRS Report R41350, *The Dodd-Frank Wall Street Reform and Consumer Protection Act: Issues and Summary,* coordinated by Baird Webel.

[8] The initial $700 billion had been reduced by $1.26 billion in P.L. 111-22.

[9] Section 115(a)(3) of EESA limits the Secretary's authority to purchase or guarantee assets to $700 billion "outstanding at any one time." While the interpretation was never subject to determination by the courts, this language can be read to allow total purchase of assets beyond $700 billion if assets are sold before additional purchases are made. Section 1302 of Dodd-Frank removed the phrase "outstanding at any one time."

[10] U.S. Treasury, *Troubled Assets Relief Program (TARP) Monthly 105(a) Report – June 2010, July 12, 2010*, p. 5; hereafter referred to as "June 2010 TARP Monthly Report."

[11] Congressional Budget Office, *CBO Estimate of the Net Deficit Effects of H.R. 4173, the Dodd-Frank Wall Street Reform and Consumer Protection Act,* June 29, 2010.

[12] U.S. Treasury, *Troubled Assets Relief Program (TARP) Monthly 105(a) Report – July 2010,* August 10, 2010, pp.4- 6; hereafter referred to as "July 2010 TARP Monthly Report."

[13] U.S. Treasury, *Troubled Assets Relief Program (TARP) Monthly 105(a) Report – August 2010,* September 10, 2010, p. 5; hereafter referred to as "August 2010 TARP Monthly Report."

[14] See, for example, "7 Questions about the $700 Billion Bailout," *Time*, September 24, 2008, http://www.time.com/time/politics/article/0,8599,1843941,00.html and "Administration Is Seeking $700 Billion for Wall Street," *New York Times*, September 20, 2008, p. A1.

In: Reflections on the Troubled Asset Relief Program (TARP)   ISBN: 978-1-61209-519-6
Editor: Donna C. Hayworth   © 2011 Nova Science Publishers, Inc.

Chapter 4

BANK STRESS TEST OFFERS LESSONS AS REGULATORS TAKE FURTHER ACTIONS TO STRENGTHEN SUPERVISORY OVERSIGHT

United States Government Accountability Office

WHY GAO DID THIS STUDY

The Supervisory Capital Assessment Program (SCAP) was established under the Capital Assistance Program (CAP)—a component of the Troubled Asset Relief Program (TARP)—to assess whether the 19 largest U.S. bank holding companies (BHC) had enough capital to withstand a severe economic downturn. Led by the Board of Governors of the Federal Reserve System (Federal Reserve), federal bank regulators conducted a stress test to determine if these banks needed to raise additional capital, either privately or through CAP. This chapter (1) describes the SCAP process and participants' views of the process, (2) assesses SCAP's goals and results and BHCs' performance, and (3) identifies how regulators and the BHCs are applying lessons learned from SCAP. To do this work, GAO reviewed SCAP documents, analyzed financial data, and interviewed regulatory, industry, and BHC officials.

WHAT GAO RECOMMENDS

This chapter recommends that the Federal Reserve complete a final 2-year SCAP analysis, and apply lessons learned from SCAP to improve transparency of bank supervision, examiner guidance, risk identification and assessment, and regulatory coordination. The Federal Reserve agreed with our five recommendations and noted current actions that it has underway to address them. Treasury agreed with the report's findings.

WHAT GAO FOUND

The SCAP process appeared to have been mostly successful in promoting coordination, transparency, and capital adequacy. The process utilized an organizational structure that facilitated coordination and communication among regulatory staff from multiple disciplines and organizations and with the BHCs. Because SCAP was designed to help restore confidence in the banking industry, regulators took unusual steps to increase transparency by releasing details of their methodology and sensitive BHC-specific results. However, several participants criticized aspects of the SCAP process. For example, some supervisory and bank industry officials stated that the Federal Reserve was not transparent about the linkages between some of the test's assumptions and results. But most of the participants in SCAP agreed that despite these views, coordination and communication were effective and could serve as a model for future supervisory efforts. According to regulators, the process resulted in a methodology that yielded credible results. By design, the process helped to ensure that BHCs would be capitalized for a potentially more severe downturn in economic conditions from 2009 through 2010.

SCAP largely met its goals of increasing the level and quality of capital held by the 19 largest U.S. BHCs and, more broadly, strengthening market confidence in the banking system. The stress test identified 9 BHCs that met the capital requirements under the more adverse scenario and 10 that needed to raise additional capital. Nine of the 10 BHCs were able to raise capital in the private market, with the exception of GMAC LLC, which received additional capital from the U.S. Department of the Treasury (Treasury). The resulting capital adequacy of the 19 BHCs has generally exceeded SCAP's requirements, and two-thirds of the BHCs have either fully repaid or begun to repay their TARP investments. Officials from the BHCs, credit rating agencies, and federal banking agencies indicated that the Federal Reserve's public release of the stress test methodology and results in the spring of 2009 helped strengthen market confidence. During the first year of SCAP (2009), overall actual losses for these 19 BHCs have generally been below GAO's 1-year pro rata loss estimates under the more adverse economic scenario. Collectively, the BHCs experienced gains in their securities and trading and counterparty portfolios. However, some BHCs exceeded the GAO 1-year pro rata estimated 2009 losses in certain areas, such as consumer and commercial lending. Most notably, in 2009, GMAC LLC exceeded the loss estimates in multiple categories for the full 2-year SCAP period. More losses in the residential and commercial real estate markets and further deterioration in economic conditions could challenge the BHCs, even though they have been deemed to have adequate capital levels under SCAP.

SCAP provided a number of important lessons for regulators about the benefits of increased transparency, the need for regulators to strengthen bank supervision, the need for regulators and BHCs to improve their risk identification and assessment practices, and the need for regulators to improve coordination and communication. First, SCAP underscored the potential benefits that increased transparency about the financial health of the nation's largest BHCs can provide. Many experts have said that the lack of transparency about potential losses from certain assets contributed significantly to the instability in financial markets during the current crisis. But transparency in the banking supervisory process is a controversial issue. Some observers say that publicly disclosing sensitive bank information without a federal capital backstop could have unintended negative effects, such as runs on banks, that would disproportionately affect weaker banks. However, other observers believe that more transparency about banks' asset valuations and losses could help the public better understand the risk exposures of BHCs, increase market discipline, and improve the oversight of these institutions. A final analysis by the Federal Reserve of BHCs' performance during the full 2-year SCAP period can help in this regard. The Federal Reserve and other banking regulators could benefit from developing a plan to improve the transparency of bank supervision. Second, SCAP showed that more robust regulatory oversight of bank stress tests was necessary to better understand banks' capacity to withstand downturns in the economy. Regulators and BHC officials commented that internal bank stress tests prior to SCAP did not comprehensively stress their portfolios. The Federal Reserve is finalizing examiner guidance for assessing capital adequacy, including stress testing, but it has not established criteria for assessing the rigor of the BHCs' stress test assumptions. Without more robust guidance, ensuring that stress tests are being evaluated thoroughly and consistently is difficult. Third, the SCAP exercise highlighted opportunities to enhance both the process and data inputs for conducting future stress tests. The Federal Reserve has started to build a plan to enhance its risk identification and assessment infrastructure in response to the financial crisis, but further planning is needed to reflect recent changes under the Dodd-Frank Wall Street Reform and Consumer Protection Act of 2010. Finally, SCAP demonstrated the need for robust coordination and communication among regulators in examining complex institutions. While SCAP promoted coordination and communication, further efforts are needed to ensure the participation of relevant regulators in multiagency examinations of banks.

Table 1. Indicative Loss Rates Estimates and Actual SCAP BHCs and Banking Industry Average Loss Rates, December 31, 2009

Percentage				
	SCAP indicative loss rate estimates		2009 actual loss rates	
Loan category	Federal Reserve's more adverse 2-year loss rate[a]	GAO's more adverse 1- year pro rata loss rate[b]	SCAP BHCs average loss rate	Banking industry average loss rate[c]
First-lien mortgage	7-8.5%	3.5-4.25%	1.9%	1.7%
Second/junior lien mortgages	12-16	6-8	4.4	3.9
Commercial and industrial	5-8	2.5-4	2.5	2.3
Commercial real estate	9-12	4.5-6	2.3	2.4
Credit cards	18-20	9-10	10.1	10.2
Other consumer	8-12	4-6	4.1	4.4
Other loans	4-10	2-5	1.4	1.1

Sources: Federal Reserve SCAP results report and GAO analysis of SNLFinancial Y-9C regulatory data.

[a] Data as of December 31, 2010.

[b] GAO calculated the more adverse 1-year pro rata loss rate by dividing the SCAP more adverse 2-year loss rates by 2. A key limitation of this approach is that it assumes equal distribution of losses, revenues, expenses, and changes to reserves over time, although these items were unlikely to be distributed evenly over the 2-year period. Another important consideration is that actual results were not intended and should not be expected to align with the SCAP projections.

[c] Data are for BHCs with greater than $1 billion in total assets.

ABBREVIATIONS

ALLL	allowance for loan and lease losses
BHC	bank holding company BB&T
BB&T	Corporation
CAP	Capital Assistance Program
CES	common equivalent securities
CPP	Capital Purchase Program
DTA	deferred tax asset
EESA	Emergency Economic Stabilization Act of 2008
ESOP	Employee Stock Ownership Plan
FDIC	Federal Deposit Insurance Corporation
FSP	Financial Stability Plan
GDP	gross domestic product
GMAC	GMAC LLC
ICAAP	internal capital adequacy assessment process
OCC	Office of the Comptroller of the Currency
PPNR	preprovision net revenue
SCAP	Supervisory Capital Assessment Program
TARP	Troubled Asset Relief Program
TIP	Targeted Investment Program
Y-9C	Consolidated Financial Statements for Bank Holding Companies–FR Y-9C

September 29, 2010

Congressional Committees

The recent financial crisis seriously undermined confidence in the nation's financial system and institutions. In February 2009, to help restore confidence, the U.S. Department of the Treasury (Treasury) announced the Financial Stability Plan, which established the Supervisory Capital Assessment Program (SCAP).[1] SCAP, as implemented by the Board of Governors of the Federal Reserve System (Federal Reserve) and other federal banking regulators,[2] was to determine through a stress test whether the largest 19 U.S. bank holding companies (BHC)[3] had enough capital for the next 2 years (2009-2010) to support their lending activities and survive a second similar economic shock.[4] As of December 31, 2008, the largest 19 BHCs accounted for approximately 67 percent of the assets and more than 50 percent of loans in the U.S. banking system. BHCs that were found to need additional capital would be allowed, and were encouraged, to raise the funds privately, but if they could not, Treasury would provide capital infusions using funding available under the Troubled Asset Relief Program's (TARP) Capital Assistance Program (CAP).[5] However, Treasury made no investments under CAP and terminated the program in November 2009. When SCAP was first announced in February 2009, and again around the time the Federal Reserve released the results of the stress test in May 2009, some academics, market participants, and others raised concerns about the test, noting that the assumptions used in the more adverse economic scenario were not severe enough and that the test did not account for differences in institutions' business models.

As part of GAO's continued analysis and monitoring of Treasury's process for implementing the Emergency Economic Stabilization Act of 2008,[6] this chapter on the stress test expands on SCAP activities that we reported on in June 2009.[7] Specifically, this chapter (1) describes the process used to design and conduct the stress test and participants' views on the process, (2) describes the extent to which the stress test achieved its goals and compares its estimates with the BHCs' actual results, and (3) identifies the lessons regulators and BHCs learned from SCAP and examines how each are using those lessons to enhance their risk identification and assessment practices.

To meet the report's objectives, we reviewed the Federal Reserve's *The Supervisory Capital Assessment Program: Design and Implementation* (SCAP design and implementation document) dated April 24, 2009, and *The Supervisory Capital Assessment Program: Overview of Results* (SCAP results document) dated May 7, 2009. In addition to the publicly released BHC-level loss estimates, we analyzed the initial stress test results that the Federal Reserve provided to each BHC, the subsequent adjustments the Federal Reserve made to these results, and its reasons for making them. We also reviewed the BHCs' quarterly regulatory filings, such as the Federal Reserve's 2009 Consolidated Financial Statements for Bank Holding Companies—FR Y-9C (Y-9C); form 10-Qs and annual form 10-Ks; speeches, testimonies, and articles regarding SCAP and stress testing; and BHC presentations to shareholders and earnings reports. To more completely understand the execution of SCAP, we completed a literature search of stress tests that other entities have conducted, such as the Committee of European Banking Supervisors and the International Monetary Fund. We also reviewed the Congressional Oversight Panel's analysis of SCAP. In addition, we reviewed the capital plans of the 10 BHCs that were required to raise capital to satisfy their SCAP capital requirement. We collected and analyzed data on the BHCs' actual performance from a private financial database of public information and compared it with the 2-year SCAP estimates and with GAO's 1-year pro rata loss estimates for the more adverse scenario (pro rata loss estimate). GAO calculated the pro rata loss estimates by dividing the SCAP more adverse 2-year loss estimates by 2. This pro rata estimate methodology has some limitations, because losses, expenses, revenues, and changes to reserves are historically unevenly distributed and loss rates over a 2-year period in an uncertain economic environment can follow an inconsistent path. However, the Federal Reserve, the Office of the Comptroller of the Currency (OCC), credit rating agencies, an SNL Financial analyst, and all of the BHCs we interviewed that are tracking performance relative to SCAP estimates are also using the same methodology. We obtained Federal Reserve and BHCs comments on our performance comparison. Further, we interviewed regulatory and BHC officials to get their views on the SCAP stress test. Regulatory officials included bank examiners, economists, and attorneys from the Federal Reserve; the Federal Reserve district banks; the OCC; the Federal Deposit Insurance Corporation (FDIC); the Office of Thrift Supervision; and BHC senior officials, including chief financial officers and chief risk officers, who participated in the SCAP stress test and were responsible for coordinating and discussing the results with regulators. These officials represented several types of BHCs, including traditional, custodial, investment, auto finance, and credit card institutions. Finally, we met with credit rating agency officials to get their views on SCAP and understand their own stress testing practices for banks. For additional information on the scope and methodology for this engagement, see appendix I.

We conducted this performance audit from August 2009 to September 2010 in accordance with generally accepted government auditing standards. Those standards require that we plan and perform the audit to obtain sufficient, appropriate evidence to provide a reasonable basis for our findings and conclusions based on our audit objectives. We believe that the evidence obtained provides a reasonable basis for our findings and conclusions based on our audit objectives.

BACKGROUND

Despite efforts undertaken by TARP to bolster capital of the largest financial institutions, market conditions in the beginning of 2009 were deteriorating and public confidence in the ability of financial institutions to 1withstand losses and to continue lending were further declining. On February 10, 2009, Treasury announced the Financial Stability Plan, which outlined measures to address the financial crisis and restore confidence in the U.S. financial and housing markets. The goals of the plan were to (1) restart the flow of credit to consumers and businesses, (2) strengthen financial institutions, and (3) provide aid to homeowners and small businesses. Under SCAP, the stress test would assess the ability of the largest 19 BHCs to absorb losses if economic conditions deteriorated further in a hypothetical "more adverse" scenario, characterized by a sharper and more protracted decline in gross domestic product (GDP) growth,[8] a steeper drop in home prices, and a larger rise in the unemployment rate than in a baseline consensus scenario. BHCs that were found not to meet the SCAP capital buffer requirement under the "more adverse" scenario would need to provide a satisfactory capital plan to address any shortfall by raising funds, privately if possible. CAP, which was a key part of the plan, would provide backup capital to financial institutions unable to raise funds from private investors. Any of the 19 BHCs that participated in the stress test and had a capital shortfall could apply for capital from CAP immediately if necessary.[9] The timeline in figure 1 provides some highlights of key developments in the implementation of SCAP.

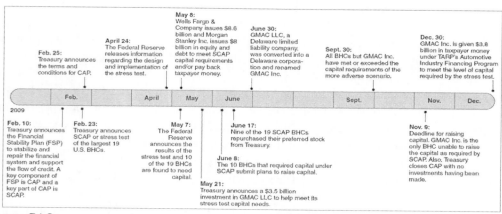

Source: GAO.

Note: On May 10, 2010, GMAC Inc. changed its name to Ally Financial Inc.

Figure 1. Timeline of Key Activities Regarding Implementation of SCAP, February 10, 2009, through December 31, 2009

In a joint statement issued on February 10, 2009, Treasury, along with the Federal Reserve, FDIC, and OCC (collectively referred to as the SCAP regulators), committed to design and implement the stress test. According to a Treasury official, the department generally did not participate in the design or implementation of SCAP, but was kept informed by the Federal Reserve during the stress test. The SCAP regulators developed economic assumptions to estimate the potential impact of further losses on BHCs' capital under two scenarios. The baseline scenario reflected the consensus view about the depth and duration of the recession, and the more adverse scenario reflected a plausible but deeper and longer recession than the consensus view. Regulators then calculated how much capital, if any, was required for each BHC to achieve the required SCAP buffer at the end of 2010 under the more adverse scenario.

The SCAP assessment examined tier 1 capital and tier 1 common capital, and the BHCs were required to raise capital to meet any identified capital shortfall (either tier 1 capital or tier 1 common capital). Tier 1 risk-based capital is considered core capital—the most stable and readily available for supporting a bank's operations and includes elements such as common stock and noncumulative perpetual preferred stock.[10] SCAP's focus on tier 1 common capital, a subset of tier 1 capital, reflects the recent regulatory push for BHCs to hold a higher quality of capital.[11] The focus on common equity reflected both the long held view by bank supervisors that common equity should be the dominant component of tier 1 capital and increased market scrutiny of common equity ratios, driven in part by deterioration in common equity during the financial crisis. Common equity offers protection to more senior parts of the capital structure because it is the first to absorb losses in the capital structure. Common equity also gives a BHC greater permanent loss absorption capacity and greater ability to conserve resources under stress by changing the amount and timing of dividends and other distributions.

To protect against risks, financial regulators set minimum standards for the capital that firms are to hold.[12] However, SCAP set a one-time minimum capital buffer target for BHCs to hold to protect against losses and preprovision net revenue (PPNR) that were worse than anticipated during the 2009 to 2010 period.[13] For the purposes of SCAP, the one-time target capital adequacy ratios are at least 6 percent of risk-weighted assets in tier 1 capital and at least 4 percent in tier 1 common capital projected as of December 31, 2010. For the purposes of the projection, the regulators assumed that BHCs would suffer the estimated losses and earned revenues in 2009 and 2010 in the more adverse scenario. SCAP regulators conducted the stress test strictly on the BHCs' assets as of December 31, 2008,[14] and—with the exception of off-balance sheet positions subject to Financial Accounting Statements No. 166 and 167, which assumed in the analysis to come on balance sheet as of January 1, 2010—did not take into account any changes in the composition of their balance sheets over the 2-year time frame.[15]

Stress testing is one of many risk management tools used by both BHCs and regulators. Complex financial institutions need management information systems that can help firms to identify, assess, and manage a full range of risks across the whole organization arising from both internal and external sources and from assets and obligations that are found both on and off the BHC's balance sheet. This approach is intended to help ensure that a firmwide approach to managing risk has been viewed as being crucial for responding to rapid and unanticipated changes in financial markets. Risk management also depends on an effective corporate governance system that addresses risk across the institution and also within specific areas, such as subprime mortgage lending.[16] The board of directors, senior management, audit committee, internal auditors, external auditors, and others play important roles in effectively operating a risk management system. The different roles of each of these groups represent critical checks and balances in the overall risk management system. However, the management information systems at many financial institutions have been called into question since the financial crisis began in 2007. Identified shortcomings, such as lack of firmwide stress testing, have led banking organizations and their regulators to reassess capital requirements, risk management practices, and other aspects of bank regulation and supervision.[17]

Stress testing has been used throughout the financial industry for more than 10 years, but has recently evolved as a risk management tool in response to the urgency of the financial crisis. The main evolution is towards the use of comprehensive firmwide stress testing as an integral and critical part of firms' internal capital adequacy assessment processes. In the case of SCAP, the intent of the stress test was to help ensure that the capital held by a BHC is sufficient to withstand a plausible adverse economic environment over the 2-year time frame ending December 31, 2010. The Basel Committee on Banking Supervision (Basel Committee) issued a document in May 2009 outlining several principles for sound stress testing practices and supervision.[18] The Basel Committee document endorses stress testing by banks as a part of their internal risk management to assess the following:

- **Credit risk.** The potential for financial losses resulting from the failure of a borrower or counterparty to perform on an obligation.
- **Market risk.** The potential for financial losses due to an increase or decrease in the value of an asset or liability resulting from broad price movements; for example, in interest rates, commodity prices, stock prices, or the relative value of currencies (foreign exchange).
- **Liquidity risk.** The potential for financial losses due to an institution's failure to meet its obligations because it cannot liquidate assets or obtain adequate funding.
- **Operational risk.** The potential for unexpected financial losses due to a wide variety of institutional factors including inadequate information systems, operational problems, breaches in internal controls, or fraud.
- **Legal risk.** The potential for financial losses due to breaches of law or regulation that may result in heavy penalties or other costs.
- **Compliance risk.** The potential for loss arising from violations of laws or regulations or nonconformance with internal policies or ethical standards.
- **Strategic risk.** The potential for loss arising from adverse business decisions or improper implementation of decisions.
- **Reputational risk.** The potential for loss arising from negative publicity regarding an institution's business practices.

SCAP PROCESS GENERALLY VIEWED AS PROMOTING COORDINATION, TRANSPARENCY, AND CAPITAL ADEQUACY

According to SCAP regulators and many market participants we interviewed, the process used to design and implement SCAP was effective in promoting coordination and transparency among the regulators and participating BHCs, but some SCAP participants we interviewed expressed concerns about the process. The majority of supervisory and bank industry officials we interviewed stated that they were satisfied with how SCAP was implemented, especially considering the stress test's unprecedented nature, limited time frame, and the uncertainty in the economy. SCAP established a process for (1) coordinating and communicating among the regulators and with the BHCs and (2) promoting transparency of the stress test to the public. In addition, according to regulators, the process resulted in a methodology that yielded credible results and by design helped to assure that the BHCs would be sufficiently capitalized to weather a more adverse economic downturn.

SCAP Process Included Coordination and Communication among the Federal Bank Regulators and with the BHCs

Robust coordination and communication are essential to programs like SCAP when bringing together regulatory staff from multiple agencies and disciplines to effectively analyze complex financial institutions and understand the interactions among multiple layers of risk. Moreover, supervisory guidance emphasizes the importance of coordination and communication among regulators to both effectively assess banks and conduct coordinated supervisory reviews across a group of peer institutions, referred to as "horizontal examinations."

The regulators implemented each phase of SCAP in a coordinated interagency fashion. Also, while some disagreed, most regulators and market participants we interviewed were satisfied with the level of coordination and communication. They also thought that the SCAP process could serve as a model for future supervisory efforts. The regulators executed the SCAP process in three broad phases:

- In the first phase, the Analytical Group, comprising interagency economists and supervisors, generated two sets of economic conditions—a baseline scenario and a more adverse scenario with a worse-than-expected economic outcome—and then used these scenarios to aid in estimating industrywide indicative loan loss rates. To develop these scenarios, the Analytical Group used three primary indicators of economic health: the U.S. GDP, housing prices in 10 key U.S. cities,[19] and the annual average U.S. unemployment rate.[20] The baseline scenario reflected the consensus view of the course for the economy as of February 2009, according to well-known professional economic forecasters.[21] The Federal Reserve developed the more adverse scenario from the baseline scenario by taking into account the historical accuracy of the forecasts for unemployment and the GDP and the uncertainty of the economic outlook at that time by professional forecasters. The Federal Reserve also used regulators' judgment about the appropriate severity of assumed additional stresses against which BHCs would be required to hold a capital buffer, given that the economy was already in a recession at the initiation of SCAP.

- In the second phase, several Supervisory Analytical and Advisory Teams—comprising interagency senior examiners, economists, accountants, lawyers, financial analysts, and other professionals from the SCAP regulators—collected, verified, and analyzed each BHC's estimates for losses, PPNR, and allowance for loan and lease losses (ALLL).[22] The teams also collected additional data to evaluate the BHC's estimates, and to allow supervisors to develop their own independent estimates of losses for loans, trading assets, counterparty credit risk, and securities and PPNR for each BHC.

- In the third phase, the Capital Assessment Group, comprising interagency staff, served as the informal decision-making body for SCAP. The Capital Assessment Group developed a framework for combing the Supervisory Analytical and Advisory Teams' estimates with other independent supervisory estimates of loan losses and resources available to absorb these losses.[23] They evaluated the estimates by comparing across BHCs and by aggregating over the 19 BHCs to check for consistency with the specified macroeconomic scenarios to calculate the amount, if any, of additional capital needed for each BHC to achieve the SCAP buffer target capital ratios as of December 31, 2010, in the more adverse economic environment. Lastly, the Capital Assessment Group set two deadlines: (1) June 8, 2009, for BHCs requiring capital to develop and submit a capital plan to the Federal Reserve on how they would meet their SCAP capital shortfall and (2) November 9, 2009, for these BHCs to raise the required capital.

A key component of this process was the involvement of multidisciplinary interagency teams that leveraged the skills and experiences of staff from different disciplines and agencies. The Federal Reserve, OCC, and FDIC had representatives on each SCAP team (the Analytical Group, Supervisory Analytical and Advisory Teams, and the Capital Assessment Group). For example, OCC officials said that they contributed to the development of quantitative models required for the implementation of SCAP and offered their own models for use in assessing the loss rates of certain portfolios. In addition, each of the SCAP regulators tapped expertise within their organization for specific disciplines, such as accounting, custodial banking, macroeconomics, commercial and industry loan loss modeling, and consumer risk modeling. According to the FDIC, the broad involvement of experts from across the agencies helped validate loss assumptions and also helped improve confidence in the results. Further, these officials noted that the SCAP process was enhanced because productive debate became a common event as team members from different regulatory agencies and disciplines brought their own perspectives and ideas to the process. For example, some SCAP staff argued for a more moderate treatment of securities in BHCs' available for sale portfolios, which would have been consistent with generally accepted accounting principles under a new change in accounting standards.[24] They maintained that the modified accounting standard for declines in market value (and discounting the impact of liquidity premia) that had been implemented after the stress test was announced and before the numbers had been finalized was in some ways more reflective of the realized credit loss expectations for the affected securities. After significant discussion, the regulators decided to allow for the accounting change in the baseline loss estimates, but not in the more adverse scenario estimates. They believed that under the more adverse scenario there was a heightened possibility of increased liquidity demands on banks and that many distressed securities would need to be liquidated at distressed levels. Consequently, for securities found to be other than temporarily impaired in the more adverse scenario, they assumed the firm would have to realize all unrealized losses (i.e., write down the value of the security to market value as of year end 2008).[25] Similarly, some staff argued against adopting other changes in accounting standards that were expected to impact BHCs' balance sheets, including their capital adequacy. Primary among these was the inclusion of previously off-balance sheet items.[26] As noted above, ultimately, the more conservative approach prevailed and the expected inclusion of these assets was addressed in SCAP.

To facilitate coordination, the Federal Reserve instituted a voting system to resolve any contentious issues, but in practice differences among regulators were generally resolved through consensus. When SCAP regulators met, the Federal Reserve led the discussions and solicited input from other regulators. For example, officials from OCC and FDIC both told us that they felt that they were adequately involved in tailoring the aggregate loss estimates to each BHC as part of the determination of each BHC's SCAP capital requirement. SCAP regulators were also involved in drafting the design and results documents, which were publicly released by the Federal Reserve.

Representatives from most of the BHCs were satisfied with the SCAP regulators' coordination and communication. Many of the BHC officials stated that they were generally impressed with the onsite SCAP teams and said that these teams improved the BHCs' coordination and communication with the regulators. BHC officials said that they usually received answers to their questions in a timely manner, either during conference calls held three times a week, through the distribution of answers to frequently asked questions, or from onsite SCAP examiners. Collecting and aggregating data were among the most difficult and time-consuming tasks for BHCs, but most of them stated that the nature of the SCAP's requests were clear. At the conclusion of SCAP, the regulators presented the results to each of the institutions showing the final numbers that they planned to publish.

Market Participants Generally Agreed that the SCAP Process Was Transparent

The SCAP process included steps to promote transparency, such as the release of key program information to SCAP BHCs and the public. According to SCAP regulators, BHCs, and credit rating agency officials we interviewed, the release of the results provided specific information on the financial health and viability of the 19 largest BHCs regarding their ability to withstand additional losses during a time of significant uncertainty. Many experts have said that the lack of transparency about potential losses from certain assets contributed significantly to the instability in financial markets during the current crisis. Such officials also stated that publicly releasing the methodology and results of the stress test helped strengthen market confidence. Further, many market observers have commented that the Federal Reserve's unprecedented disclosure of sensitive supervisory information for each BHC helped European bank regulators decide to publicly release detailed results of their own stress tests in July 2010.

Not all SCAP participants agreed that the SCAP process was fully transparent. For example, some participants questioned the transparency of certain assumptions used in developing the stress test. According to BHC officials and one regulator, the Federal Reserve could have shared more detailed information about SCAP loss assumptions and calculations with BHCs.[27] According to several BHC officials, the Federal Reserve did not fully explain the methodology for estimating losses but expected BHC officials to fully document and provide supporting data for all of their assumptions. Without knowing the details of the methodology, according to some BHC officials, they could not efficiently provide all relevant information to SCAP examiners.

SCAP Was Designed to Help Ensure That BHCs Were Adequately Capitalized under the More Adverse Economic Scenario

SCAP regulators aimed to ensure that SCAP sufficiently stressed BHCs' risk exposures and potential PPNR under the more adverse scenario. To accomplish this, the regulators made what they viewed to be conservative assumptions and decisions in the following areas. First, the regulators decided to stress only assets that were on the BHCs' balance sheets as of December 31, 2008, (i.e., a static approach) without accounting for new business activity. According to BHC officials, new loans were thought to have generally been of better quality than legacy loans because BHCs had significantly tightened their underwriting standards since the onset of the financial crisis.[28] As a result, BHCs would have been less likely to charge-off these loans within the SCAP time period ending December 31, 2010, resulting in the potential for greater reported revenue estimates for the period. By excluding earnings from new business, risk-weighted assets were understated, charge-off rates were overstated, and projected capital levels were understated.

Second, SCAP regulators generally did not allow the BHCs to cut expenses to address the anticipated drop in revenues under the more adverse scenario. However, some BHC officials told us that they would likely cut expenses, including initiating rounds of layoffs, if the economy performed in accordance with the more adverse economic scenario, especially if they were not generating any new business. Federal Reserve officials noted that BHCs were given credit in the stress test for cost cuts made in the first quarter of 2009.

Third, some BHCs were required to assume an increase in their ALLL as of the end of 2010, if necessary, to ensure adequate reserves relative to their year end 2010 portfolio. Some BHC officials believed that this requirement resulted in the BHCs having to raise additional capital because the required ALLL increases were subtracted from the revenue estimates in calculating the resources available to absorb losses. This meant that some BHCs judged to have insufficient year end 2010 reserve adequacy had to account for this shortcoming in the calculation of capital needed to meet the SCAP targeted capital requirements as of the end of 2010 while maintaining a sufficient ALLL for 2011 losses under the more adverse economic scenario. According to some BHCs, the size of the 2010 ALLL was severe given the extent of losses are already included in the 2009 and 2010 loss estimates and effectively stressed BHCs for a third year.

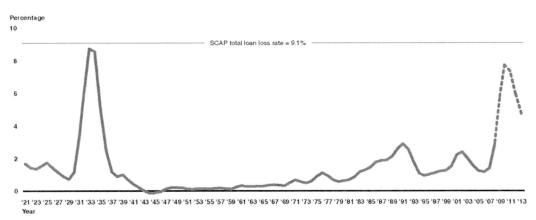

Source: International Monetary F und.

Note: The solid line represents actual loss rates (1921-2008) and the dotted line represents estimated loss rates (2009-2013).

Figure 2. Commercial Bank 2-Year Loan Loss Rates from 1921 through 2013 Compared to SCAP Loan Loss Rate

Finally, according to many BHC officials and others, the calculations used to derive the loan loss rates and other assumptions to stress the BHCs were conservative (i.e., more severe). For example, the total loan loss rate estimated by the SCAP regulators was 9.1 percent, which was greater than the historical 2-year loan loss rates at all commercial banks from 1921 until 2008, including the worst levels seen during the Great Depression (see figure 2). However, the macroeconomic assumptions of the more adverse scenario, which we will discuss later in the report, did not meet the definition of a depression. Specifically, a 25 percent unemployment rate coupled with economic contraction is indicative of a depression. In contrast, the more adverse scenario estimated approximately a 10 percent unemployment rate with some economic growth in late 2010.

SCAP regulators also estimated ranges for loan loss rates within specific loan categories using the baseline and more adverse scenarios as guides. They used a variety of methods to tailor loan losses to each BHC, including an analysis of past BHC losses and quantitative models, and sought empirical support from BHCs regarding the risk level of their portfolios. However, some BHCs told us that the Federal Reserve made substantial efforts to help ensure conformity with the indicative loan loss rates while incorporating BHC-specific information where possible and reliable. Table 1 compares the different indicative loan loss rate ranges under the more adverse scenario for each asset category with actual losses in 2009 for SCAP BHCs and the banking industry.[29] Some BHCs stated that the resulting loan loss rates were indicative of an economy worse off than that represented by the more adverse macroeconomic assumptions, although they recognized the need for the more conservative approach. However, nearly all agreed that the loan loss rates were a more important indication of the stringency of SCAP than the assumptions.

After the public release of the SCAP methodology in April 2009, many observers commented that the macroeconomic assumptions for a more adverse economic downturn were not severe enough given the economic conditions at that time. In defining a more adverse economic scenario, the SCAP regulators made assumptions about the path of the economy using three broad macroeconomic indicators—changes in real GDP, the unemployment rate, and home prices—during the 2-year SCAP period ending December 2010. The actual performances of GDP and home prices have performed better than assumed under the more adverse scenario. However, the actual unemployment rate has more closely tracked the more adverse scenario (see figure 3). Further, as noted earlier, some regulatory and BHC officials have indicated that the loan loss rates that the regulators subsequently developed were more severe than one would have expected under the macroeconomic assumptions. While our analysis of actual and SCAP estimated indicative loan losses (see table 1) is generally consistent with this view, these estimates were developed at a time of significant uncertainty about the direction of the economy and the financial markets, as well as an unprecedented deterioration in the U.S. housing markets.

Table 1. Indicative Loss Rates Estimates and Actual SCAP BHCs and Banking Industry Average Loss Rates, December 31, 2009

Percentage				
	SCAP indicative loss rate estimates		2009 actual loss rates	
Loan category	Federal Reserve's more adverse 2-year loss rate[a]	GAO's more adverse 1-year pro rata loss rate[b]	SCAP BHCs average loss rate	Banking industry average loss rate[c]
First-lien mortgage	7-8.5%	3.5-4.25%	1.9%	1.7%
• Prime	3-4	1.5-2	n/a	0.5
• Alt-A	9.5-13	4.75-6.5	n/a	3.6
• Subprime	21-28	10.5-14	n/a	6.2
Second/junior lien mortgages	12-16	6-8	4.4	3.9
• Closed-end junior liens	22-25	11-12.5	7.5	6.6
• Home lines of credit	8-11	4-5.5	3.6	3.1
Commercial and industrial	5-8	2.5-4	2.5	2.3
Commercial real estate	9-12	4.5-6	2.3	2.4
• Construction	15-18	7.5-9	5.8	6.1
• Multifamily	10-11	5-5.5	1.1	1.1
• Nonfarm, nonresidential	7-9	3.5-4.5	0.9	0.8
Credit cards	18-20	9-10	10.1	10.2
Other consumer	8-12	4-6	4.1	4.4
Other loans	4-10	2-5	1.4	1.1

Sources: Federal Reserve SCAP results report, GAO analysis of SNL Financial Y-9C regulatory data, and Moody's Investors Service for prime, Alt-A, and subprime mortgage loss rates data.

Note: N/a means not available.

[a] Data as of December 31, 2010.

[b] GAO calculated the more adverse 1-year pro rata loss rate by dividing the SCAP more adverse 2-year loss rates by 2 (i.e., the straight-line method). A key limitation of this approach is that it assumes equal distribution of losses, revenues, expenses, and changes to reserves over time, although these items were unlikely to be distributed evenly over the 2-year period. Another important consideration is that actual results were not intended and should not be expected to align with the SCAP projections.

[c] Data are for BHCs with greater than $1 billion in total assets.

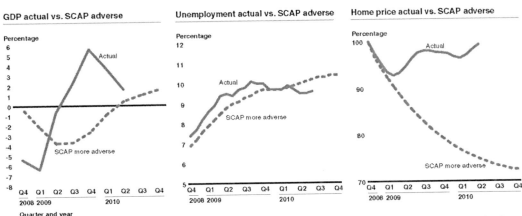

Source: GAO analysis of Bureau of Economic Analysis, Bureau of Labor Statistics, and Standard and
Poor's 10-City Case-Shiller data.

Figure 3. Actual Economic Performance to Date Versus SCAP More Adverse Assumptions

WHILE SCAP INCREASED CAPITAL LEVELS AND IMPROVED CONFIDENCE IN THE BANKING SYSTEM, BHCs COULD FACE ONGOING CHALLENGES

SCAP largely met its goals of increasing the level and quality of capital held by the 19
largest BHCs and, more broadly, of strengthening market confidence in the banking system.
The stress test identified 10 of the 19 BHCs as needing to raise a total of about $75 billion in
additional capital. The Federal Reserve encouraged the BHCs to raise common equity via
private sources—for example, through new common equity issuances, conversion of existing
preferred equity to common equity, and sales of businesses or portfolios of assets. Nine of the
10 BHCs were able to raise the required SCAP amount of new common equity in the private
markets by the November 9, 2009, deadline (see table 2). Some of these BHCs also raised
capital internally from other sources.[30] GMAC LLC (GMAC) was the only BHC that was not
able to raise sufficient private capital by the November 9, 2009, deadline.[31] On December 30,
2009, Treasury provided GMAC with a capital investment of $3.8 billion to help fulfill its
SCAP capital buffer requirement, drawing funds from TARP's Automotive Industry
Financing Program.[32] A unique and additional element of the estimated losses for GMAC
included the unknown impact of possible bankruptcy filings by General Motors Corporation
(GM) and Chrysler LLC (Chrysler). Thus, a conservative estimate of GMAC's capital buffer
was developed in response to this possibility. The Federal Reserve, in consultation with
Treasury, subsequently reduced GMAC's SCAP required capital buffer by $1.8 billion—$5.6
billion to $3.8 billion—primarily to reflect the lower-than-estimated actual losses from the
bankruptcy proceedings of GM and Chrysler. GMAC was the only company to have its
original capital buffer requirement reduced.

Capital adequacy generally improved across all 19 SCAP BHCs during 2009. As shown
in table 3, the largest gains were in tier 1 common capital, which increased by about 51
percent in the aggregate across the 19 BHCs, rising from $412.5 billion on December 31,

2008, to $621.9 billion by December 31, 2009. On an aggregate basis, the tier 1 common capital ratio at BHCs increased from 5.3 percent to 8.3 percent of risk-weighted assets (compared with the SCAP threshold of 4 percent at the end of 2010).[33] The tier 1 risk-based capital ratio also grew from 10.7 percent to 11.3 percent of risk-weighted assets (compared with the SCAP threshold of 6 percent at the end of 2010).[34] While these ratios were helped to some extent by reductions in risk-weighted assets, which fell 4.3 percent from $7.815 trillion on December 31, 2008, to $7.481 trillion on December 31, 2009, the primary driver of the increases was the increase in total tier 1 common capital.

Table 2. Summary of Capital Raised by 10 BHCs to Meet Their SCAP Capital Buffer Amount, as of November 9, 2009

Dollars in billions			
BHC	Sources of capital raised	Required capital buffer amount	Capital raised
Bank of America Corporation	New shares, asset sales, and conversion[a]	$33.9	$35.9
Citigroup Inc.	Conversion	5.5	5.6
Fifth Third Bancorp	New shares, asset sales, and conversion	1.1	1.7
GMAC LLC	New shares	11.5	4.6
KeyCorp	New shares, asset sales, and conversion	1.8	2.3
Morgan Stanley	New shares, asset sales, and conversion	1.8	7.0
PNC Financial Services Group, Inc.	New shares and asset sales	0.6	1.1
Regions Financial Corporation	New shares, asset sales, conversion, and other actions[b]	2.5	2.5
SunTrust Banks, Inc.	New shares, asset sales, conversion, and other actions	2.2	2.2
Wells Fargo & Company	New shares and other actions	13.7	13.7
Total		**$74.6**	**$76.6**

Source: Federal Reserve documentation.

Notes: The following nine BHCs were not required to raise SCAP capital because they had sufficient capital to withstand a worse-than-expected economic downturn through the end of 2010 and continue to meet the SCAP capital buffer targets: American Express Company; BB&T Corporation; The Bank of New York Mellon Corporation; Capital One Financial Corporation; The Goldman Sachs Group, Inc.; JPMorgan Chase & Co.; MetLife, Inc.; State Street Corporation; and U.S. Bancorp. Data in the "capital raised" column is as of November 9, 2009, according to the Federal Reserve.

[a] "New shares" indicates that BHC issued new common equity, "assets sales" represent business lines or products sold to raise cash, and "conversion" shows BHC preferred equity that was converted to common equity.

[b] "Other action" indicates equity raised internally (e.g., sale of equity to employee stock options plans).

Table 3. Capital Measures for SCAP BHCs, December 31, 2008 and December 31, 2009

Dollars in billions			
Capital measures	**2009**	**2008**	**Percent difference**
Capital levels			
• Tier 1 capital	$846.2	$836.7	1.1%
• Tier 1 common capital	$621.9	$412.5	50.8
• Risk-weighted assets	$7,480.8	$7,814.8	-4.3
Capital ratios			
• Tier 1 risk-based capital ratio	11.3%	10.7%	5.6
• Tier 1 common capital ratio	8.3%	5.3%	57.5

Sources: GAO analysis of Federal Reserve SCAP, SNL Financial, and company data.

Table 4. Percentage Change in Tier I Capital Ratios, December 31, 2008, and December 31, 2009

Bank holding company	Tier 1 common capital ratio		Tier 1 risk-based capital ratio	
	2009 (percentage)	Change from 2008 (basis points)	2009 (percentage)	Change from 2008 (basis points)
American Express Company	9.83%	13	9.84%	14
Bank of America Corporation	7.82	322	10.41	-19
BB&T Corporation	8.50	140	11.48	8 - 2
The Bank of New York Mellon Corporation	10.53	103	12.12	-118
Capital One Financial Corporation	10.62	152	13.75	105
Citigroup Inc.	9.77	747	11.67	-23
Fifth Third Bancorp	7.00	260	13.31	271
GMAC LLC	4.85	-155	14.15	405
The Goldman Sachs Group, Inc.	12.20	450	14.97	237
JPMorgan Chase & Co.	8.79	229	11.10	90
KeyCorp	7.50	190	12.75	185
MetLife, Inc.	8.17	-33	8.91	-29
Morgan Stanley	6.71	101	15.30	10
PNC Financial Services Group, Inc.	6.00	130	11.42	182
Regions Financial Corporation	7.15	55	11.54	114
State Street Corporation	15.59	9	17.74	-246
SunTrust Banks, Inc.	7.67	187	12.96	206
U.S. Bancorp	6.76	166	9.61	-99
Wells Fargo & Company	6.46	336	9.25	125
Average (weighted)	8.31%	303	11.31%	60

Sources: GAO analysis of Federal Reserve SCAP, SNL Financial, and company data.

The quality of capital—measured as that portion of capital made up of tier 1 common equity—also increased across most of the BHCs in 2009. The tier 1 common capital ratio increased at 17 of the 19 BHCs between the end of 2008 and the end of 2009 (see table 4). Citigroup Inc. (Citigroup) and The Goldman Sachs Group, Inc. (Goldman Sachs) had the largest increases in tier 1 common capital ratios—747 and 450 basis points, respectively.[35] However, GMAC's tier 1 common capital ratio declined by 155 basis points in this period to 4.85 percent. MetLife, Inc. was the only other BHC to see a drop in its tier 1 common capital ratio, which fell by 33 basis points to 8.17 percent and still more than double the 4 percent target. Based on the SCAP results document, the 2008 balances in the table include the impact of certain mergers and acquisitions, such as Bank of America Corporation's (Bank of America) purchase of Merrill Lynch & Co. Inc. Further, the increase in capital levels reflects the capital that was raised as a result of SCAP

As previously stated by interviewees, the unprecedented public release of the stress test results helped to restore investors' confidence in the financial markets. Some officials from participating BHCs and credit rating agencies also viewed the BHCs' ability to raise the capital required by the stress test as further evidence of SCAP's success in increasing market confidence and reducing uncertainty. But some expressed concerns that the timing of the announcement of SCAP on February 10, 2009—nearly 3 months before the results were released on May 7, 2009—may have intensified market uncertainty about the financial health of the BHCs.

A broad set of market indicators also suggest that the public release of SCAP results may have helped reduce uncertainty in the financial markets and increased market confidence. For example, banks' renewed ability to raise private capital reflects improvements in perceptions of the financial condition of banks. Specifically, banks and thrifts raised significant amounts of common equity in 2008, totaling $56 billion. Banks and thrifts raised $63 billion in common equity in the second quarter of 2009 (see figure 4). The substantial increase in second quarter issuance of common equity occurred after the stress test results were released on May 7, 2009, and was dominated by several SCAP institutions.

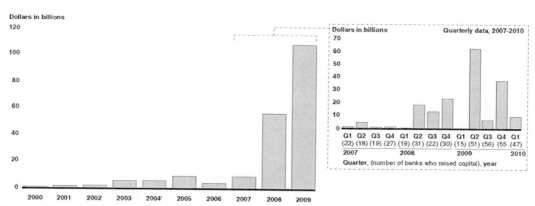

Source: GAO analysis of data from SNLFinancial.

Note: The spike in common equity issuance in the fourth quarter of 2009 primarily relates to Citigroup, Wells Fargo & Company, and other banks raising capital to buy back their TARP capital investment from Treasury. However, the quarterly data do not reflect $19.29 billion of common equivalent securities issued in December 2009 by Bank of America that converted to common stock in February 2010.

Figure 4. Gross Common Equity Issuance by Banks and Thrifts, 2000 to First Quarter 2010

Similarly, stock market prices since the release of the stress test results in May 2009 through October 2009 improved substantially in the overall banking sector and among the 18 public BHCs that participated in SCAP (see figure 5).[36] The initial increase since May 2009 also suggests that SCAP may have helped bolster investor and public confidence. However, equity markets are generally volatile and react to a multitude of events.

Credit default swap spreads, another measure of confidence in the banking sector, also improved. A credit default swap is an agreement in which a buyer pays a periodic fee to a seller in exchange for protection from certain credit events such as bankruptcy, failure to pay debt obligations, or a restructuring related to a specific debt issuer or issues known as the reference entity. Therefore, the credit default swap spread, or market price, is a measure of the credit risk of the reference entity, with a higher spread indicating a greater amount of credit risk. When the markets' perception of the reference entity's credit risk deteriorates or improves, the spread generally will widen or tighten, respectively. Following the SCAP results release in May 2009, the credit default swap spreads continued to see improvements (see figure 6). While many forces interact to influence investors' actions, these declining spreads suggest that the market's perception of the risk of banking sector defaults was falling. Further, the redemption of TARP investments by some banking institutions demonstrated that regulators believed these firms could continue to serve as a source of financial and managerial strength, as well as fulfill their roles as intermediaries that facilitate lending, while both reducing reliance on government funding and maintaining adequate capital levels. This positive view of the regulators may also have helped increase market confidence in the banking system (see appendix II for details on the status of TARP investments in the institutions participating in SCAP).

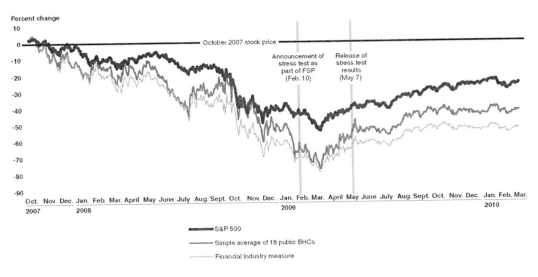

Figure 5. Stock Market Prices, October 2007 through March 2010

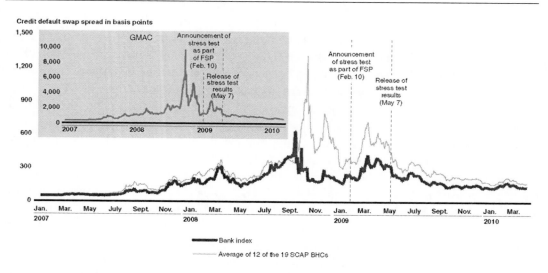

Figure 6. Bank Credit Default Swap Spreads, January 2007 through March 2010

The 19 Tested BHCs Experienced Better Performance Than a Pro Rata Estimate under the More Adverse Scenario

As of the end of 2009, while the SCAP BHCs generally had not experienced the level of losses that were estimated on a pro rata basis under the stress test's more adverse economic scenario, concerns remain that some banks could absorb potentially significant losses in certain asset categories that would erode capital levels. Collectively, the BHCs' total loan losses of $141.2 billion were approximately 38 percent less than the GAO-calculated $229.4 billion in pro rata losses under the more adverse scenario for 2009 (see table 5).[37] The BHCs also experienced significant gains in securities and trading and counterparty credit risk portfolios compared with estimated pro rata losses under SCAP. Total resources other than capital to absorb losses (resources) were relatively close to the pro rata amount, exceeding it by 4 percent.

In tracking BHCs' losses and resources against the SCAP estimates, we compared the actual results with those estimated under the more adverse scenario. We used the 2-year estimates of the more adverse scenario from the SCAP results and annualized those amounts by dividing them in half (the "straight line" method) to get pro rata loss estimates for 2009 because the SCAP regulators did not develop estimates on a quarterly or annual basis. A key limitation of this approach is that it assumes equal distribution of losses, revenues, expenses, and changes to reserves over time, although these items were unlikely to be distributed evenly over the 2-year period. Another important consideration is that actual results were not intended and should not be expected to align with the SCAP projections. Actual economic performance in 2009 differed from the SCAP macroeconomic variable inputs, which were based on a scenario that was more adverse than was anticipated or than occurred, and other forces in the business and regulatory environment could have influenced the timing and level of losses. Appendix I contains additional details on our methodology, including our data sources and calculations, for tracking BHCs' financial performance data.

Table 5. Actual and GAO Pro Rata Estimates of Aggregate Losses and Changes in Resources Other than Capital to Absorb Losses across the 19 SCAP BHCs, December 31, 2009

Dollars in billions Asset category	Actual	GAO pro rata estimate[a]	Percent difference
Consumer and commercial loan losses			
• First-lien mortgages	$19.2	$51.2	-62%
• Second/junior lien mortgages	26.1	41.6	-37
• Commercial and industrial loans	21.2	30.1	-29
• Commercial real estate loans	13.5	26.5	-49
• Credit card loans	31.6	41.2	-23
• Other[b]	29.5	38.9	-24
Total consumer and commercial loans losses	**$141.2**	**$229.4**	**-38%**
Securities—available for sale and held to maturity—losses (gains)	(3.5)	17.6	-120
Trading and counterparty losses (gains)	(56.9)	49.7	-215
Total asset losses	**$80.8**	**$296.7**	**-73%**
Resources other than capital to absorb losses	**$188.4**	**$181.5**	**4%**

Sources: GAO analysis of Federal Reserve SCAP and SNL Financial data.

Notes: A parenthetical number indicates a gain.

The trading and counterparty data in the Y-9C includes both customer derived revenue from transactions for BHCs that operate as broker-dealers, as well as gains and losses from proprietary trading and associated expenses. These items are presented on a net basis in the Y-9C. For the five BHCs that had their trading portfolios stressed (Goldman Sachs, Morgan Stanley, Citigroup, JPMorgan Chase & Co., and Bank of America), the trading and counterparty line item is based on projections of gains or losses from proprietary trading, but preprovision net revenue (specifically noninterest revenue) included projections of gains or losses from customer derived revenue from transactions due to operations as a broker-dealer. These items cannot be segregated based on the Y-9C data and therefore are included in the net amount in both the trading and counterparty and noninterest income line items above. As a result of this limitation, the net amount of the trading gains or losses and preprovision net revenue in the table may be overstated or understated.

[a] GAO calculated 1-year pro rata loss estimates by dividing the SCAP more adverse 2-year loss estimates by 2 (e., the straight-line method). A key limitation of this approach is that it assumes equal distribution of losses, revenues, expenses, and changes to reserves over time, although these items were unlikely to be distributed evenly over the 2-year period. Another important consideration is that actual results were not intended and should not be expected to align with the SCAP projections.

[b] For "Other" we excluded about $6 billion in losses for State Street Corporation realized in 2009. Since this was a one-time charge that was realized in 2009, this effect was segregated from more typical loss amounts for our tracking purposes.

Losses Varied by Individual BHCs

Although the 19 BHCs' actual combined losses were less than the 2009 pro rata loss estimates for the more adverse scenario, the loss rates varied significantly by individual BHCs. For example, most of the BHCs had consumer and commercial loan losses that were below the pro rata loss estimates, but three BHCs—GMAC, Citigroup, and SunTrust Banks Inc. (SunTrust)—exceeded these estimates in at least one portfolio (see figure 7). GMAC was the only one with 2009 loan losses on certain portfolios that exceeded SCAP's full 2-year estimate. Specifically, GMAC exceeded the SCAP 2-year estimated losses in the first-lien, second/junior lien, and commercial real estate portfolios and the 1-year pro rata losses in the "Other" portfolio; Citigroup exceeded the 1-year pro rata estimated losses in the commercial and industrial loan portfolio; and SunTrust exceeded the 1-year estimated losses in the first-lien and credit card portfolios. Appendix III provides detailed data on the individual performance of each of the BHCs.

GMAC faced particular challenges in the first year of the assessment period and posed some risk to the federal government, a majority equity stakeholder.[38] GMAC's loan losses in its first-lien portfolio were $2.4 billion, compared with the $2 billion projected for the full 2-year period. In the second/junior lien portfolio, GMAC saw losses of $1.6 billion, compared with the $1.1 billion estimated losses for the 2 years. GMAC experienced losses of $710 million in its commercial real estate portfolio, compared with $600 million projected for the full 2-year period. Further, in its "Other" portfolio (which is comprised of auto leases and consumer auto loans), GMAC's losses were $2.1 billion, exceeding the 1-year pro rata $2 billion loss estimate. With a tier 1 common capital ratio of 4.85 percent—just more than the SCAP threshold of 4 percent—at the end of 2009, GMAC has a relatively small buffer in the face of potential losses.

GMAC's position should be placed in context, however, because it is relatively unique among the SCAP participants. It was the only nonpublicly traded participant, and the federal government owns a majority equity stake in the company as a result of capital investments made through the Automotive Industry Financing Program under TARP. Further, GMAC's core business line—financing for automobiles—is dependent on the success of efforts to restructure, stabilize, and grow General Motors Company and Chrysler Group LLC.[39] Finally, the Federal Reserve told us that because GMAC only recently became a BHC and had not previously been subject to banking regulations, it would take some time before GMAC was fully assimilated into a regulated banking environment.[40] To improve its future operating performance and better position itself to become a public company in the future, GMAC officials stated that the company posted large losses in the fourth quarter of 2009 as result of accelerating its recognition of lifetime losses on loans.[41] In addition, the company has been restructuring its operations and recently sold off some nonperforming assets.[42] However, the credit rating agencies we met with generally believed that there could still be further losses at GMAC, although the agencies were less certain about the pace and level of those losses. Two of the agencies identified GMAC's Residential Capital, LLC mortgage operation as the key source of potential continued losses.

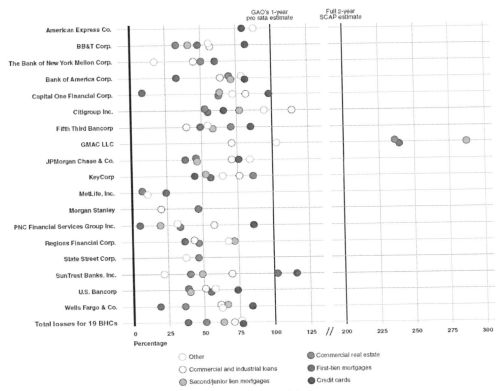

Source: GAO analysis of Federal Reserve and SNLFinancial data.

Notes: Figure shows only those loan loss categories that were applicable under SCAP and that showed losses in 2009. In addition, Goldman Sachs was not included in the figure because it had no losses or recoveries for these loan categories in 2009. The "Other" category for State Street Corporation does not include one-time items in the actual or estimated amounts. See table 27 in appendix III for additional details.

GAO calculated 1-year pro rata loss estimates by dividing the SCAP more adverse 2-year loss estimates by 2 (i.e., the straight-line method). A key limitation of this approach is that it assumes equal distribution of losses, revenues, expenses, and changes to reserves over time, although these items were unlikely to be distributed evenly over the 2-year period. Another important consideration is that actual results were not intended and should not be expected to align with the SCAP projections.

Figure 7. Comparison of Actual and GAO Pro Rata Estimated Losses for Consumer and Commercial Loans, December 31, 2009

BHCs Are Generally Not Experiencing the Level of Securities and Trading Losses That Were Estimated under the Pro Rata More Adverse Scenario, and Some Have Recorded Gains

Given that market conditions have generally improved, the BHCs' investments in securities and trading account assets performed considerably better in 2009 than had been estimated under the pro rata more adverse scenario.[43] The SCAP assessment of the securities portfolio consisted of an evaluation for possible impairment of the portfolio's assets, including Treasury securities, government agency securities, sovereign debt, and private sector securities. In the aggregate, the securities portfolio has experienced a gain of $3.5 billion in 2009, compared with a pro rata estimated loss of $17.6 billion under the stress test's more adverse scenario. As figure 8 shows, 5 of the 19 BHCs recorded securities losses in 2009,[44] 13 recorded gains, and 1 (Morgan Stanley) recorded no gain or loss. Losses were projected at 17 of the BHCs under the pro rata more adverse scenario, and SCAP regulators did not consider the remaining 2 BHCs (American Express Company and Morgan Stanley) to be applicable for this category. In the securities portfolio, The Bank of New York Mellon Corporation had losses greater than estimated under SCAP for the full 2-year period.[45] The variances could be due to a number of factors, including the extent to which a BHC decides to deleverage, how their positions react to changing market values, and other factors.

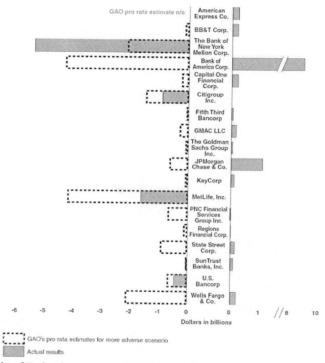

Source: GAO analysis of Federal Reserve and SNLFinancial data.

Notes: Morgan Stanley was not included in the figure because it has not had any available for sale or held to maturity securities gains (losses) in 2009 and was deemed to be not applicable for this category in SCAP. American Express Company was also deemed not applicable for this category in SCAP, but was included in the figure because it had securities gains in 2009.

GAO calculated 1-year pro rata loss estimates by dividing the SCAP more adverse 2-year loss estimates by 2 (i.e., the straight-line method). A key limitation of this approach is that it assumes equal distribution of losses, revenues, expenses, and changes to reserves over time, although these items were unlikely to be distributed evenly over the 2-year period. Another important consideration is that actual results were not intended and should not be expected to align with the SCAP projections.

Figure 8. Comparison of Actual and GAO Pro Rata Estimated Gains and Losses for Securities Available for Sale and Held to Maturity, December 31, 2009

To estimate trading and counterparty losses, SCAP regulators assumed that these investments would be subject to the change in value of a proportional level as experienced in the last half of 2008.[46] The trading portfolio shows an even greater difference between the 1-year pro rata estimates and the actual performance—a gain of $56.9 billion in 2009 rather than the pro rata $49.7 billion estimated loss under the more adverse scenario (see table 5). The stress test only calculated trading and counterparty credit loss estimates for the five BHCs with trading assets that exceeded $100 billion.[47] All five had trading gains as opposed to losses, based on the publicly available data from the Y-9C.[48] These gains were the result of a number of particular circumstances. First, the extreme spreads and risk premium resulting from the lack of liquidity during the financial crisis—especially in the second half of 2008—reversed in 2009, improving the pricing of many risky trading assets that remained on BHCs' balance sheets. Because the trading portfolio is valued at fair value, it had been written down for the declines in value that occurred throughout 2008 and the first quarter of 2009 and saw significant gains when the market rebounded through the remainder of 2009. Second, the crisis led to the failure or absorption of several large investment banks, reducing the number of competitors and, according to our analysis of Thomson Reuters Datastream, increased market share and pricing power for the remaining firms.[49] Finally, the Federal Reserve's low overnight bank lending rates (near 0 percent) have prevailed for a long period and have facilitated a favorable trading environment for BHCs. This enabled BHCs to fund longer-term, higher yielding assets in their trading portfolios with discounted wholesale funding (see figure 9).[50]

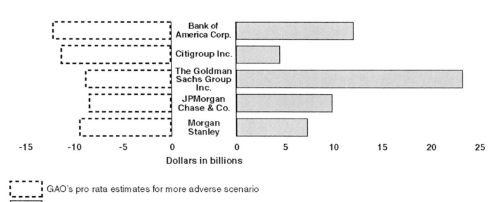

Source: GAO analysis of Federal Reserve and SNLFinancial data.

Notes: SCAP regulators only generated trading and counterparty estimates for the 5 BHCs with a trading book (assets) greater than $100 billion, therefore this comparison is not applicable to the other 14 BHCs.

GAO calculated 1-year pro rata loss estimates by dividing the SCAP more adverse 2-year loss estimates by 2 (i.e., the straight-line method). A key limitation of this approach is that it assumes equal distribution of losses, revenues, expenses, and changes to reserves over time, although these items were unlikely to be distributed evenly over the 2-year period. Another important consideration is that actual results were not intended and should not be expected to align with the SCAP projections.

Figure 9. Comparison of Actual and GAO Pro Rata Estimated Gains and Losses for Trading and Counterparty, December 31, 2009

Potential Losses in Consumer and Commercial Credit Continue to Pose a Challenge

Potentially large losses in consumer and commercial loans continue to challenge SCAP BHCs, and addressing these challenges depends on a variety of factors, including, among other things, the effectiveness of federal efforts to reduce foreclosures in the residential mortgage market. The BHCs absorbed nearly $400 billion in losses in the 18 months ending December 31, 2008. As they continue to experience the effects of the recent financial crisis, estimating precisely how much more they could lose is difficult. In March 2010, officials from two credit rating agencies indicated that 50 percent or more of the losses the banking industry was expected to incur during the current financial crisis could still be realized if the economy were to suffer further stresses.

Data for the 19 BHCs show a rapid rise in the percentage of nonperforming loans over the course of 2009 (see figure 10).[51] Specifically, total nonperforming loans grew from 1 percent in the first quarter of 2007 to 6.6 percent in the fourth quarter of 2009 for SCAP BHCs. In particular, increases in total nonperforming loans were driven by significant growth in nonperforming first-lien mortgages and commercial real estate loans. Standard & Poor's Corporation noted that many nonperforming loans may ultimately have to be charged-off, exposing the BHCs to further potential losses. According to the credit rating agencies that we interviewed, federal housing policy to aid homeowners who are facing foreclosures, as well as time lags in the commercial real estate markets, will likely continue to affect the number of nonperforming loans for the remainder of the SCAP time frame (December 2010).

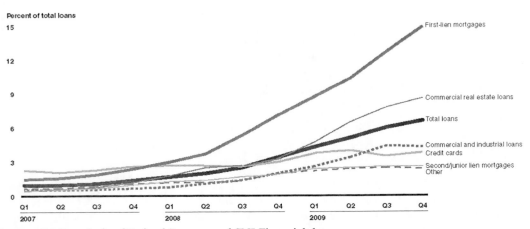

Source: GAO analysis of Federal Reserve and SNLFinancial data.

Note: Because they converted to BHCs in late 2008, American Express Company, Goldman Sachs, and Morgan Stanley did not submit Y-9Cs to the Federal Reserve until the first quarter of 2009, and GMAC did not submit its Y-9C until the second quarter of 2009. As a result, the data do not include information on these holding companies before those dates.

Figure 10. Change in the Percentage of Nonperforming Loans for Applicable SCAP BHCs, by Loan Type, First Quarter 2007 through Fourth Quarter 2009

The Economic and Regulatory Environment Could Impact BHCs' Net Revenues and Loss Reserves

The total amount of resources other than capital to absorb losses (resources) has tracked the amount GAO prorated under the stress test's more adverse scenario. Resources measure how much cushion the BHCs have to cover loans losses. As shown previously in table 5, the aggregate actual results through the end of 2009 for resources showed a total of $188.4 billion, or 4 percent more than GAO's pro rata estimated $181.5 billion in the stress test's more adverse scenario. Eleven of the 19 BHCs tracked greater than the pro rata estimated amount in 2009, while the remaining 8 tracked less than the estimate (see figure 11). GMAC and MetLife, Inc. had negative resources in 2009, although only GMAC was projected to have negative resources over the full 2-year period.

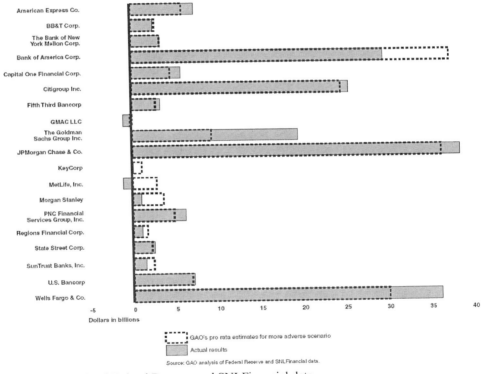

Source: GAO analysis of Federal Reserve and SNLFinancial data.
Notes: Resources other than capital to absorb losses are calculated as preprovision net revenue less the change in allowance for loan and lease losses.
GAO calculated 1-year pro rata loss estimates by dividing the SCAP more adverse 2-year loss estimates by 2 (i.e., the straight-line method). A key limitation of this approach is that it assumes equal distribution of losses, revenues, expenses, and changes to reserves over time, although these items were unlikely to be distributed evenly over the 2-year period. Another important consideration is that actual results were not intended and should not be expected to align with the SCAP projections.

Figure 11. Comparison of Actual and GAO Pro Rata Estimated Resources Other Than Capital to Absorb Losses, December 31, 2009

Our calculation considers increases in ALLL during 2009 to be a drain on resources in order to mirror the regulators' calculation for the full 2-year projection. However, the ALLL may ultimately be used as a resource in 2010, causing available resources to be higher than they currently appear in our tracking. PPNR is based on numerous factors, including interest income, trading revenues, and expenses. The future course of this resource will be affected by factors such as the performance of the general economy, the BHCs' business strategies, and regulatory changes, including the Dodd-Frank Wall Street Reform and Consumer Protection Act of 2010 (Dodd-Frank Act) and the Credit Card Accountability, Responsibility, and Disclosure Act of 2009.[52] Such regulatory changes could impose additional costs or reduce future profitability, either of which would impact future PPNR.

SCAP PROVIDED LESSONS THAT COULD HELP REGULATORS STRENGTHEN SUPERVISORY OVERSIGHT AND BHCS IMPROVE RISK MANAGEMENT PRACTICES

The SCAP stress test provided lessons in a number of areas that can be incorporated in the bank supervision process and used to improve BHCs' risk management practices. First, the transparency that was part of SCAP helped bolster market confidence, but the Federal Reserve has not yet developed a plan that incorporates transparency into the supervisory process. Second, the SCAP experience highlighted that BHCs' stress tests in the past were not sufficiently comprehensive and we found that regulators' oversight of these tests has been generally weak. Third, we identified opportunities to enhance both the process and data inputs for conducting stress testing in the future. Finally, SCAP demonstrated the importance of robust coordination and communication among the different regulators as an integral part of any effective supervisory process. By incorporating these lessons going forward, regulators will be able to enhance their ability to efficiently and effectively oversee the risk-taking in the banking industry.

SCAP's Transparency Helped Bolster Market Confidence, but the Federal Reserve Has yet to Implement a Plan to Incorporate Greater Transparency into the Supervisory Process

As stated earlier and as agreed generally by market participants, the public release of the SCAP design and results helped restore confidence in the financial system during a period of severe turmoil. Some agency officials stated that their experience in implementing SCAP suggested that greater transparency would also be beneficial in the supervisory process. In recent statements, the chairman and a governor of the Federal Reserve have both stated that, while protecting the confidentiality of firm-specific proprietary information is imperative, greater transparency about the methods and conclusions of future stress tests could benefit from greater scrutiny by the public.[53] The Federal Reserve governor also noted that feedback from the public could help to improve the methodologies and assumptions used in the supervisory process. In addition, they noted that more transparency about the central bank's activities overall would ultimately enhance market discipline and that the Federal Reserve is looking at ways to enhance its disclosure policies.[54]

Consistent with the goal of greater transparency, we previously recommended that the Federal Reserve consider periodically disclosing to the public the aggregate performance of the 19 BHCs against the SCAP estimates for the 2-year forecast period.[55] Subsequently, the chairman and a governor of the Federal Reserve have publicly disclosed 2009 aggregate information about the performance of the 19 BHCs based on the Federal Reserve's internal tracking. As the 2-year SCAP period comes to a close at the end of 2010, completing a final analysis that compares the performance of BHCs with the estimated performance under the more adverse economic scenario would be useful; however, at the time of the review, Federal Reserve officials told us that they have not decided whether to conduct and publicly release any type of analysis. Given that the chairman and a governor of the Federal Reserve have already publicly disclosed some aggregate BHC performance against the more adverse scenario for 2009, providing the 2-year results would provide the public with consistent and reliable information from the chief architect of the stress test that could be used to further establish the importance of understanding such tests and consider lessons learned about the rigor of the stress test estimates.

Increasing transparency in the bank supervisory process is a more controversial issue to address. Supervisory officials from OCC (including the then Comptroller) and the Federal Reserve question the extent to which greater transparency would improve day-to-day bank supervision. And, some BHCs we interviewed also were against public disclosure of future stress tests results. They noted that SCAP was a one-time stress test conducted under unique circumstances. Specifically, during the financial crisis, Treasury had provided a capital backstop for BHCs that were unable to raise funds privately. They expressed concern that public disclosure of certain unfavorable information about individual banks in a normal market environment could cause depositors to withdraw funds en masse creating a "run" on the bank. In addition, banks that appear weaker than their peers could be placed at a competitive disadvantage and may encourage them to offer more aggressive rates and terms for new depositors, thereby increasing their riskiness and further affecting their financial stability. While these concerns are valid and deserve further consideration, they have to be weighed against the potential benefits of greater transparency about the financial health of financial institutions and the banking system in general to investors, creditors, and counterparties.

The Dodd-Frank Act takes significant steps toward greater transparency. For example, the act requires the Federal Reserve to perform annual stress tests on systematically significant institutions and publicly release a summary of results. Also, the act requires each of the systematically significant institutions to publicly report the summary of internal stress tests semiannually.[56] Given comments by its senior leadership, the Federal Reserve is willing to engage in a constructive dialogue about creating a plan for greater transparency that could benefit the entire financial sector. The other federal bank regulators—FDIC, OCC, and the Office of the Thrift Supervision—are also critical stakeholders in developing such a plan. While Federal Reserve officials have discussed possible options for increasing transparency, the regulators have yet to engage in a formal dialogue about these issues and have not formalized a plan for the public disclosure of regulatory banking information or developed a plan for integrating public disclosures into the ongoing supervisory process. Without a plan for reconciling these divergent views and for incorporating steps to enhance transparency into the supervisory process and practices, including the public disclosure of certain information, bank regulators may miss a significant opportunity to enhance market discipline by providing investors, creditors, and counterparties with information such as bank asset valuations.

Limited Use and Weak Oversight of BHCs' Stress Tests Prior to SCAP Highlights the Need for More Rigorous Testing and Better Monitoring of Tests

SCAP highlighted that the development and utilization of BHCs' stress tests were limited. Further, BHC officials noted that they failed to adequately stress test for the effects of a severe economic downturn scenario and did not test on a firmwide basis or test frequently enough. We also found that the regulator's oversight of these tests were weak, reinforcing the need for more rigorous and firmwide stress testing, better risk governance processes by BHCs, and more vigorous oversight of BHCs' stress tests by regulators. Going forward, as stress tests become a fundamental part of oversights of individual banks and the financial system, more specific guidance needs to be developed for examiners. BHCs and regulators stated that they are taking steps to address these shortcomings.

BHCs Generally Did Not Perform Firmwide Stress Tests Prior to SCAP

Prior to SCAP, many BHCs generally performed stress tests on individual portfolios, such as commercial real estate or proprietary trading, rather than on a firmwide basis. SCAP led some institutions to look at their businesses in the aggregate to determine how losses would affect the holding company's capital base rather than individual portfolios' capital levels. As a result, some BHC officials indicated that they had begun making detailed assessments of their capital adequacy and risk management processes and are making improvements. Officials from one BHC noted that before SCAP their financial and risk control teams had run separate stress tests, but had not communicate or coordinate with each other about their stress testing activities. Officials from another BHC noted that their senior management and board of directors were not actively involved in the oversight of the stress testing process. These officials said that since participating in SCAP, they have improved in these areas by institutionalizing the internal communication and coordination procedures between the financial risk and control teams, and by increasing communication with senior management and board of directors about the need for active involvement in risk management oversight, respectively. These improvements can enhance the quality of the stress testing process. Moreover, officials of BHCs that were involved in ongoing bank mergers during the SCAP process credited SCAP with speeding up of the conversion process of the two institutions' financial systems since the BHCs' staff had to work together to be able to quickly provide, among other things, the aggregate asset valuations and losses of the combined firm's balance sheets to the regulators.

BHC officials also stated that their stress tests would take a firmwide view, that is, taking into account all business units and risks within the holding company structure and would include updates of the economic inputs used to determine potential losses and capital needs in adverse scenarios. One BHC noted that it had developed several severe stress scenarios for liquidity because the recent financial crisis had shown that liquidity could deteriorate more quickly than capital, endangering a company's prospects for survival. This danger became evident in the failures of major financial institutions during the recent financial crisis—for example, IndyMac Bank, Lehman Brothers, and Bear Stearns.

BHCs Did Not Sufficiently Stress Their Portfolios for Unexpected Losses Prior to SCAP

Officials from many SCAP BHCs and the Federal Reserve noted that internal bank stress test models generally did not use macroeconomic assumptions and loss rates inputs as conservative as those used in the SCAP stress test. According to Federal Reserve officials, using the SCAP macroeconomic assumptions, most of the 19 BHCs that took part in SCAP initially determined that they would not need additional capital to weather the more adverse scenario. However, the SCAP test results subsequently showed that more than half of them (10 of 19) did need to raise capital to meet the SCAP capital buffer requirements. Some BHCs indicated that future stress tests would be more comprehensive than SCAP. BHCs can tailor their stress test assumptions to match their specific business models, while SCAP generally used a one-size-fits-all assumptions approach. For example, some BHCs noted that they use macroeconomic inputs (such as disability claims, prolonged stagflation, or consumer confidence) that were not found in the SCAP stress test.

Although the Federal Reserve has required BHCs to conduct stress tests since 1998, officials from several BHCs noted that their institutions had not conducted rigorous stress tests in the years prior to SCAP, a statement that is consistent with regulatory findings during the same period. To some degree, this lack of rigorous testing reflected the relatively good economic times that preceded the financial crisis. According to one credit rating agency and a BHC, stress test assumptions generally tend to be more optimistic in good economic times and more pessimistic in bad economic times. In addition, one BHC noted that it had conducted stress tests on and off for about 20 years, but usually only as the economy deteriorated. To address this issue, many BHC officials said that they have incorporated or are planning to incorporate more conservative inputs into their stress test models and are conducting more rigorous, firmwide stress testing more frequently.

Regulators Required Stress Tests Prior to SCAP, but Oversight Was Limited

Although regulators' guidelines have required for over 10 years that financial institutions use stress tests to assess their capacity to withstand losses, we found that regulators' oversight of these tests had been limited. Horizontal examinations by the regulators from 2006 through 2008 identified multiple weaknesses in institutions' risk management systems, including deficiencies in stress testing. Areas of weaknesses found during examination included that the BHCs' stress testing of their balance sheets lacked severity, were not performed frequently enough, and were not done on a firmwide basis. Also, it was found that BHCs' risk governance process lacked the active and effective involvement of BHC senior management and board of directors. The SCAP stress test and the financial crisis revealed the same shortcomings in BHCs' risk management and stress testing practices.

However, we previously found that regulators did not always effectively address these weaknesses or in some cases fully appreciate their magnitude.[57] Specifically, regulators did not take measures to push forcefully for institutions to better understand and manage risks in a timely and effective manner. In addition, according to our discussions with some SCAP participants, oversight of these tests through routine examinations was limited in scope and tended to be discretionary. For example, regulators would review firms' internal bank stress tests of counterparty risk and would make some suggestions, but reviews of these tests were done at the discretion of the individual supervisory team and were not consistently performed across teams. Even though BHCs have for many years performed stress tests to one degree or another, they have not been required to report the results of their testing to the Federal Reserve unless it specifically requested the information.

The Federal Reserve recently issued a letter to the largest banking organizations outlining its view on good practices with respect to the use of stress testing in the context of internal capital adequacy assessment practices (ICAAP). For example, some areas highlighted in the letter include how frequent a stress test should be performed, the minimum time frame that the test should cover, documentation of the process, involvement of senior management and board of directors, and types of scenarios and risks to include in such tests. Some BHC officials believed that stress testing would become an integral part of future risk management practices and noted that SCAP helped them see how bank examiners would want them to stress their portfolios in the future. In anticipation of future action by regulators, many BHCs were designing at least part of their stress tests along the lines of SCAP. However, a few BHC officials hoped that future stress tests would not be performed in the same manner as SCAP, with the largest institutions tested simultaneously in a largely public setting, but rather as part of the confidential supervisory review process.

Regulatory Oversight Is to Focus on More Rigorous Stress Testing, but Examiners Need More Specific Guidance

Federal Reserve officials stated that going forward, stress tests will become a fundamental part of the agency's oversight of individual banks and the financial system. As a result of SCAP, Federal Reserve officials stated that they are placing greater emphasis on the BHCs' internal capital adequacy planning through their ICAAP. This initiative is intended to improve the measurement of firmwide risk and the incorporation of all risks into firms' capital planning assessment and planning processes. In addition to enhanced supervisory focus on these practices across BHCs, stress testing is also a key component of the Basel II capital framework (Pillar 2).[58] Under Pillar 2, supervisory review is intended to help ensure that banks have adequate capital to support all risks and to encourage that banks develop and use better risk management practices. All BHCs, including those adopting Basel II, must have a rigorous process of assessing capital adequacy that includes strong board and senior management oversight, comprehensive assessment of risks, rigorous stress testing and scenario analyses, validation programs, and independent review and oversight. In addition, Pillar 2 requires supervisors to review and evaluate banks' internal capital adequacy assessments and monitor compliance with regulatory capital requirements. The Federal Reserve wants the large banks to conduct this work for themselves and report their findings to their senior management and boards of directors. According to Federal Reserve officials, for BHCs to satisfy the totality of expectations for ICAAP it may take 18 to 24 months, partly because the BHCs are taking actions to enhance practices where needed—including with respect to the use of stress testing and scenario analyses in internal capital assessments—and the Federal Reserve then needs to evaluate these actions across a relatively large number of BHCs.

In addition, the Federal Reserve is finalizing guidance for examiners to assess the capital adequacy process, including stress testing, for BHCs. Examiners are expected to evaluate how BHCs' stress tests inform the process for identifying and measuring risk and decisions about capital adequacy. Federal Reserve officials stated that examiners are expected to look closely at BHCs' internal stress test methodologies and results. In a letter to BHCs, the Federal Reserve also emphasized that institutions should look at time frames of 2 or more years and considers losses firmwide. It also suggested that BHCs develop their own stress test scenarios and then review these scenarios and the results for appropriate rigor and quantification of risk.

While these are positive steps, examiners do not have specific criteria for assessing the quality of these tests. For example, the Federal Reserve has not established criteria for assessing the severity of the assumptions used to stress BHCs' balance sheets. The Federal Reserve officials stated that they intend to have technical teams determine the type of criteria that will be needed to evaluate these assumptions, but they are in the early planning stages. Development of such criteria will be particularly helpful in ensuring the effective implementation of the stress test requirements under the Dodd-Frank Act. Without specific criteria, Federal Reserve examiners will not be able to ensure the rigor of BHCs' stress tests—an important part of the capital adequacy planning. Furthermore, the absence of such guidance could lead to variations in the intensity of these assessments by individual examiners and across regional districts.

Risk Identification and Assessment Infrastructure Needs to be Upgraded to Improve Oversight

Following SCAP, regulatory and BHC officials we met with identified opportunities to enhance both the process and data inputs for conducting stress testing in the future. This would include processes for obtaining, analyzing, and sharing data and capabilities for data modeling and forecasting, which potentially could increase the Federal Reserve's abilities to assess risks in the banking system. According to the Federal Reserve, an essential component of this new system will be a quantitative surveillance mechanism for large, complex financial institutions that will combine a more firmwide and multidisciplinary approach for bank supervision. This quantitative surveillance mechanism will use supervisory information, firm-specific data analysis, and market-based indicators to identify developing strains and imbalances that may affect multiple institutions, as well as emerging risks within specific institutions. This effort by the Federal Reserve may also improve other areas of supervision which rely on data and quantitative analysis, such as assessing the process used by BHC's to determine their capital adequacy, forecasting revenue, and assessing and measuring risk, which is critical to supervising large, complex banks. Officials at the Federal Reserve told us that examiners should be analyzing BHC performances versus their stress test projections to provide insight into the agency's loss forecasting approach. Moreover, Federal Reserve officials stated that they are always looking to increase their analytical capabilities, and they have recently implemented a new governance structure to address some of their management information infrastructure challenges. However, not enough time has passed to determine the extent to which such measures will improve banking supervision.

In addition, some other deficiencies were found in the data reported to the Federal Reserve by BHCs using the Y-9C, as well as the Federal Reserve's ability to analyze the risk of losses pertaining to certain portfolios that were identified during the SCAP stress test. This led the Federal Reserve to develop a more robust risk identification and assessment infrastructure including internally developed models or purchased analytical software and tools from data vendors. Going forward, such models and analytics would facilitate improved risk identification and assessment capabilities and oversight, including the oversight of systemic risk. Moreover, a risk identification and assessment system that can gauge risk in the banking sector by collecting data on a timelier basis is necessary to better ensure the safety and soundness of the banking industry. Specific areas in which data collection and risk identification and assessment could be enhanced include mortgage default modeling to include more analysis of nontraditional mortgage products, counterparty level exposures, country and currency exposures, and commodity exposures. An example of where the Federal Reserve used SCAP to significantly upgrade its ability to assess risks across large BHCs is the development of a system that allowed BHCs to submit their securities positions and market values at a fixed date and apply price shocks. This process was enhanced during SCAP to facilitate the stress analysis of securities portfolios held by SCAP BHCs.[59] This system allowed the Federal Reserve to analyze approximately 100,000 securities in a relatively short time period. The Federal Reserve intends to continue using this database to receive and analyze updated positions from BHCs.

With other portfolios, the Federal Reserve contracted with outside data and analytical systems providers. For multifamily loan portfolios, nonfarm loans, and nonresidential loans with a maturity beyond 2 years, all of which are subsets of commercial and industrial loans or commercial real estate portfolios, the Federal Reserve used internal models and purchased an outside vendor service that allowed it to estimate losses for these portfolios. For the remaining commercial portfolios, the Federal Reserve used different existing models found at both the Federal Reserve and Federal Reserve district banks and new models developed to meet the needs of SCAP. When analyzing BHCs' mortgage portfolios, the consumer loans Supervisory Analytical and Advisory Team provided templates to the BHCs to collect granular data for such analysis, allowing the system to separate BHCs' mortgage portfolios into much more granular tranches than would be possible using data from regulatory filings. The Federal Reserve further used data from various sources, including a large comprehensive loan-level database of most mortgages that have been securitized in the United States to assist in developing its own loss estimates to benchmark against the BHCs' proprietary estimates.

These examples point to enhancements in the ability to assess risks to individual firms and across the banking sector that resulted from the SCAP stress test. The Federal Reserve has made clear that it views many of these innovations in its ability to assess and model risks and potential losses as permanent additions to its toolkit, and has also recognized the need for more timely and granular information to improve its supervision of BHCs and other institutions. However, the extent to which these models and tools will be distributed across the Federal Reserve district banks and other federal banking regulators is unclear. In addition, as the stress test applied to trading positions was limited to those BHCs that held trading positions of at least $100 billion as of February 20, 2009, the Federal Reserve has not indicated that it will roll out its new system to BHCs with smaller trading positions. The Federal Reserve has taken steps to maintain and enhance the tools and data used during SCAP. Further, improving the Federal Reserve's financial data collection and supervisory tools will require additional resources, training for bank examiners, coordination in the dissemination of new infrastructure across all U.S. financial regulators, and, according to a Federal Reserve governor, would benefit from relief from the Paperwork Reduction Act of 1980 as well.

The Federal Reserve lacks a complete plan on how it will achieve permanent improvements in its risk identification and assessment infrastructure, but according to officials, such a plan is in development. The Federal Reserve has finalized a plan that describes a governance structure for overseeing large, complex financial organizations. The plan defines the roles and responsibilities of various committees and teams within the Federal Reserve that will carry out its supervisory responsibilities over these organizations. However, further planning is needed to incorporate lessons learned from SCAP for addressing data and modeling gaps that existed prior to the crisis and a structure for disseminating improvements to risk identification and assessment. Specifically, this plan will also be critical to addressing improvements to data and modeling infrastructure in supervising not only large financial holding companies but also smaller institutions. A fully developed plan would also consider how to disseminate data, models, and other infrastructure to the entire Federal Reserve System and bank regulatory agencies, as well as the newly established Financial Stability Oversight Council and Treasury's Office of Financial Research. Without such a plan, the agency runs the risk of not optimizing its oversight responsibilities, especially in light of its new duties as the systemic risk regulator under the Dodd-Frank Act.

More Coordination and Communication across Regulators Is Critical for Understanding Risks to Individual Institutions and Financial Markets

Another critical lesson from SCAP was the need for robust coordination and communication among the regulators in examining large, complex financial institutions. Officials from the regulatory agencies and BHCs stated that the degree of cooperation among the SCAP regulators was unprecedented and improved the understanding of the risks facing the individual BHCs and the financial market. Such coordination and communication will become increasingly important as banking regulators increase their oversight role. Even with recent major reform to the financial regulatory structure, multiple regulatory agencies continue to oversee the banking industry, and regulators will need to prioritize efforts to promote coordination and communication among staff from these agencies so that emerging problematic issues affecting the financial industry are identified in a timely manner and effectively addressed.

Going forward, based on our discussions with various SCAP participants and statements by Federal Reserve officials, including the chairman, the regulators' experience with SCAP is anticipated to lead to the expanded use of horizontal examinations and multidisciplinary staff that will require extensive interagency coordination. Horizontal examinations may involve multiple regulators and underscore the importance of effective coordination and communication.

Currently, regulators are conducting horizontal examinations of internal processes that evaluate the capital adequacy at the 28 largest U.S. BHCs. Their focus is on the use of stress testing and scenario analyses in ICAAP, as well as how shortcomings in fundamental risk management practices and governance and oversight by the board of directors for these processes could impair firms' abilities to estimate their capital needs. Regulators recently completed the initial phase of horizontal examinations of incentive compensation practices at 25 large U.S. BHCs. As part of this review, each organization was required to submit an analysis of shortcomings or "gaps" in its existing practices relative to the principles contained in the proposed supervisory guidance issued by the Federal Reserve in the fall of 2009 as well as plans—including timetables—for addressing any weaknesses in the firm's incentive compensation arrangements and related risk-management and corporate governance practices. In May 2010, regulators provided the banking organizations feedback on the firms' analyses and plans. These organizations recently submitted revised plans to the Federal Reserve for addressing areas of deficiencies in their incentive compensation programs. In a June 2010 press release, the Federal Reserve noted that to monitor and encourage improvements in compensation practices by banking organizations, its staff will prepare a report after 2010 on trends and developments in such practices at banking organizations.

Our prior work has found that coordination and communication among regulatory agencies is an ongoing challenge.[60] For example, in 2007, OCC onsite examiners, as well as officials in headquarters, told us that coordination issues hampered the Federal Reserve's horizontal examinations. Also, in 2007, a bank told us that it had initially received conflicting information from the Federal Reserve, its consolidated supervisor, and the OCC, its primary bank supervisor, regarding a key policy interpretation. Officials from the bank also noted that when the Federal Reserve collected information, it did not coordinate with OCC, the primary bank examiner of the lead bank, resulting in unnecessary duplication. We noted that to improve oversight in the future, regulators will need to work closely together to expedite examinations and avoid such duplications.

Since the SCAP stress test was concluded, the following examples highlight ongoing challenges in coordination and communication:

- Officials from OCC and FDIC indicated that they were not always involved in important discussions and decisions. For example, they were not involved in the decision to reduce GMAC's SCAP capital requirement, even though they were significantly involved in establishing the original capital requirement. Also, FDIC noted that it was excluded from such decision even though it is the primary federal bank regulator for GMAC's retail bank (Ally Bank).

- The Federal Reserve held an internal meeting to discuss lessons learned from SCAP, but has yet to reach out to the other SCAP regulators. The OCC and FDIC told us that they had not met with the Federal Reserve as a group to evaluate the SCAP process and document lessons learned. As a result, the FDIC and OCC did not have an opportunity to share their views on what aspects of SCAP worked and did not work, as well as any potential improvements that can be incorporated into future horizontal reviews or other coordinated efforts.

- In the recent horizontal examinations, both FDIC and OCC noted that the interagency process for collaboration—especially in the initial design stages—was not as effective as it was for SCAP. OCC commented that more collaboration up front would have been preferable. Also, FDIC stated that the Federal Reserve did not include it in meetings to formulate aggregate findings for the horizontal examination of incentive compensation programs, and it experienced difficulties in obtaining aggregate findings from the Federal Reserve. The Federal Reserve commented that the FDIC was involved in the development of findings for those organizations that control an FDIC-supervised subsidiary bank and that FDIC has since been provided information on the findings across the full range of organizations included in the horizontal review, the majority of which do not control an FDIC-supervised subsidiary bank.

These continued challenges in ensuring effective coordination and communication underscore the need for sustained commitment and effort by the regulators to ensure the inclusion of all relevant agencies in key discussions and decisions regarding the design, implementation, and results of multiagency horizontal examinations. As the SCAP process has shown, active participation by all relevant regulators can strengthen approaches used by examiners in performing their supervisory activities. Without continuous coordination and communication, the regulators will miss opportunities to leverage perspectives and experiences that could further strengthen the supervision of financial institutions, especially during horizontal examinations of financial institutions.

CONCLUSIONS

Publicly reporting a comparison of the actual performance of the SCAP BHCs and the estimated performance under a more adverse scenario provides insights into the financial strength of the nation's largest BHCs. Senior Federal Reserve officials have publicly disclosed select aggregate information about the performance of the 19 BHCs consistent with the recommendation in our June 2009 report. Specifically, we recommended that the Federal Reserve consider periodically disclosing to the public the performance of the 19 BHCs against the SCAP estimates during the 2-year period. However, the Federal Reserve has yet to commit to completing a final analysis that compares the BHCs' actual performance with the estimated performance under SCAP's more adverse economic scenario for the entire 2-year period and making this analysis public. Such an analysis is important for the market and BHCs to assess the rigor of the stress test methodology. Publicly releasing the results also would allow the public to gauge the health of the BHCs that participated in SCAP, which is a strong proxy for the entire U.S. banking industry. And public disclosure of this analysis could act as a catalyst for a public discussion of the value of effective bank risk management and enhance confidence in the regulatory supervision of financial institutions.

The public release of the stress test methodology and results helped improve market confidence in the largest BHCs during the recent financial crisis and provided an unprecedented window into bank supervision process. Subsequently, the Chairman of the Federal Reserve and a Federal Reserve governor have publicly stated that greater transparency should be built into the supervisory process and that feedback from the public could help increase the integrity of the supervisory process. Increased transparency can also augment the information that is available to investors and counterparties of the institutions tested and enhance market discipline. Despite these statements, the Federal Reserve and other bank regulators have yet to start a formal dialogue about this issue, nor have they developed a plan for integrating public disclosures into the ongoing supervisory process. Such a plan could detail the types of information that would benefit the markets if it were publicly released; the planned methodology for the stress tests, including assumptions; the frequency with which information would be made public; and the various means of disseminating the information. Taking into account the need to protect proprietary information and other market-sensitive information would be an important part of such a plan. While regulators will undoubtedly face challenges in determining how best to overcome skepticism about the potential effects on the financial markets of disclosing sensitive information on the financial health of banks, the Dodd-Frank Act requires that the Federal Reserve and certain banks publicly release a summary of results from periodic stress tests. Without a plan for enhancing the transparency of supervisory processes and practices, bank regulators may miss a significant opportunity to further strengthen market discipline and confidence in the banking industry by providing investors, creditors, and counterparties with useful information.

The SCAP stress test shed light on areas for further improvement in the regulators' bank supervision processes, including oversight of risk management practices at BHCs. Prior to SCAP, regulatory oversight of stress tests performed by the BHCs themselves was ineffective. Specifically, although regulators required stress tests, the guidelines for conducting them were more than a decade old, and the individual banks were responsible for designing and executing them. The Federal Reserve's reviews of the internal stress tests were done at the discretion of the BHCs' individual supervisory teams and were not consistently performed. Further, even though BHCs performed stress tests, they were not required to report the results of their stress testing to the Federal Reserve without a specific request from regulators. Post-SCAP, however, the Federal Reserve has stated that stress testing will now be a fundamental part of their oversight of individual banks. The Federal Reserve expects to play a more prominent role in reviewing assumptions, results, and providing input into the BHCs' risk management practices. While the Federal Reserve has begun to take steps to augment its oversight, currently Federal Reserve examiners lack specific criteria for assessing the severity of BHCs' stress tests. Without specific criteria, Federal Reserve examiners will not be able to ensure the rigor of BHCs' stress tests. Furthermore, the absence of such criteria could lead to variations in the intensity of these assessments by individual examiners and across regional districts.

The experience with SCAP also showed that regulators needed relevant and detailed data to improve oversight of individual banks and to identify and assess risks. As the Federal Reserve and the other regulators conduct more horizontal reviews, they will need a robust plan for quantitatively assessing the risk in the banking sector. Collecting timely data for the annual stress testing and other supervisory actions will be critical in order to better ensure the safety and soundness of the banking industry. The Federal Reserve has finalized a plan that describes a governance structure for overseeing large, complex financial organizations. However, further planning is needed to incorporate lessons learned from SCAP for addressing data and modeling gaps and a structure for disseminating improvements to risk identification and assessment. Further, efforts to improve the risk identification and assessment infrastructure will need to be effectively coordinated with other regulators and the newly established Financial Stability Oversight Council and Treasury's Office of Financial Research in order to ensure an effective systemwide risk assessment. Without fully developing a plan that can identify BHCs' risks in time to take appropriate supervisory action, the Federal Reserve may not be well-positioned to anticipate and minimize future banking problems and ensure the soundness of the banking system.

Despite the positive coordination and communication experience of the SCAP stress test, developments since the completion of SCAP have renewed questions about the effectiveness of regulators' efforts to strengthen their coordination and communication. For example, on important issues, such as finalizing GMAC's SCAP capital amount, the Federal Reserve chose not to seek the views of other knowledgeable bank regulators. While the Dodd-Frank Act creates formal mechanisms that require coordination and communication among regulators, the experiences from SCAP point to the need for a sustained commitment by each of the banking regulators to enhance coordination and communication. In particular, ensuring inclusion of relevant agencies in key discussions and decisions regarding the design, implementation, and results of multiagency horizontal examinations will be critical. If regulators do not consistently coordinate and communicate effectively during horizontal examinations, they run the risk of missing opportunities to leverage perspectives and experiences that could further strengthen bank supervision.

RECOMMENDATIONS

To gain a better understanding of SCAP and inform the use of similar stress tests in the future, we recommend that the Chairman of the Federal Reserve direct the Division of Banking Supervision and Regulation to:

- Compare the performance of the 19 largest BHCs against the more adverse scenario projections following the completion of the 2-year period covered in the SCAP stress test ending December 31, 2010, and disclose the results of the analysis to the public. To leverage the lessons learned from SCAP to the benefit of other regulated bank and thrift institutions, we recommend that the Chairman of the Federal Reserve in consultation with the heads of the FDIC and OCC take the following actions:
- Follow through on the Federal Reserve's commitment to improve the transparency of bank supervision by developing a plan that reconciles the divergent views on transparency and allows for increased transparency in the regular supervisory process. Such a plan should, at a minimum, outline steps for releasing supervisory methodologies and analytical results for stress testing.
- Develop more specific criteria to include in its guidance to examiners for assessing the quality of stress tests and how these tests inform BHCs' capital adequacy planning. These guidelines should clarify the stress testing procedures already incorporated into banking regulations and incorporate lessons learned from SCAP.
- Fully develop its plan for maintaining and improving the use of data, risk identification and assessment infrastructure, and requisite systems in implementing its supervisory functions and new responsibilities under the Dodd-Frank Act. This plan should also ensure the dissemination of these enhancements throughout the Federal Reserve System and other financial regulators, as well as new organizations established in the Dodd-Frank Act.
- Take further steps to more effectively coordinate and communicate among themselves. For example, ensuring that all applicable regulatory agencies are included in discussions and decisions regarding the development, implementation,

and results of multiagency activities, such as horizontal examinations of financial institutions.

List of Committees
The Honorable Daniel K. Inouye
Chairman The Honorable Thad Cochran
Vice Chairman Committee on Appropriations United
States Senate

The Honorable Christopher J. Dodd
Chairman
The Honorable Richard C. Shelby
Ranking Member
Committee on Banking, Housing, and Urban Affairs
United States Senate

The Honorable Kent Conrad
Chairman
The Honorable Judd Gregg
Ranking Member
Committee on the Budget
United States Senate

The Honorable Max Baucus
Chairman
The Honorable Charles E. Grassley
Ranking Member
Committee on Finance
United States Senate

The Honorable David R. Obey
Chairman
The Honorable Jerry Lewis
Ranking Member
Committee on Appropriations
House of Representatives

The Honorable John M. Spratt Jr.
Chairman
The Honorable Paul Ryan
Ranking Member
Committee on the Budget
House of Representatives

The Honorable Barney Frank
Chairman

The Honorable Spencer Bachus
Ranking Member
Committee on Financial Services
House of Representatives

The Honorable Sander M. Levin
Chairman
The Honorable Dave Camp
Ranking Member
Committee on Ways and Means
House of Representatives

APPENDIX I. OBJECTIVES, SCOPE, AND METHODOLOGY

The objectives of this chapter were to (1) describe the process used to design and conduct the stress test and participants views' of the process, (2) describe the extent to which the stress test achieved its goals and compare its estimates with the bank holding companies' (BHC) actual results, and (3) identify the lessons regulators and BHCs learned from the Supervisory Capital Assessment Program (SCAP) and examine how each are using those lessons to enhance their risk identification and assessment practices.

To meet the report's objectives, we reviewed the Board of Governors of the Federal Reserve System's (Federal Reserve) *The Supervisory Capital Assessment Program: Design and Implementation* (SCAP design and implementation document) dated April 24, 2009, and *The Supervisory Capital Assessment Program: Overview of Results* (SCAP results document) dated May 7, 2009. We analyzed the initial stress test data that the Federal Reserve provided to each BHC, the subsequent adjustments the Federal Reserve made to these estimates, and the reasons for these adjustments. We reviewed BHC regulatory filings such as the Federal Reserve's 2009 Consolidated Financial Statements for Bank Holding Companies—FR Y-9C (Y-9C);[61] company quarterly 10-Qs and annual 10-Ks; speeches and testimonies regarding SCAP and stress testing; BHCs' presentations to shareholders and earnings reports; bank supervision guidance issued by the Federal Reserve, Office of the Comptroller of the Currency (OCC), and the Federal Deposit Insurance Corporation (FDIC); and documents regarding the impact of SCAP and the financial crisis and proposed revisions to bank regulation and supervisory oversight.[62] To further understand these documents and obtain different perspectives on the SCAP stress test, we interviewed officials from the Federal Reserve, OCC, FDIC, and the Office of the Thrift Supervision, as well as members of the multidisciplinary teams created to execute SCAP.[63]

We also collected data from SNL Financial—a private financial database that contains publicly filed regulatory and financial reports, including those of the BHCs involved in SCAP—in order to compare the BHCs' actual performance in 2009 against the regulators' 2-year SCAP loss estimates and GAO's 1-year pro rata loss estimates. To obtain additional background information regarding the tracking of the BHCs, perspectives on their performance, anticipated loan losses, and the success of SCAP in achieving its goals, we interviewed relevant officials (e.g., chief risk officers and chief financial officers) from 11 of the 19 BHCs that participated in the SCAP stress test. The BHCs we interviewed were the American Express Company; Bank of America Corporation; The Bank of New York Mellon Corporation; BB&T Corporation; Citigroup Inc.; GMAC LLC;[64] The Goldman Sachs Group, Inc.; JPMorgan Chase & Co.; MetLife, Inc.; Regions Financial Corporation; and Wells Fargo & Company. We selected these BHCs to reflect differences in size, types of financial services provided, geographic location, primary bank regulator, and participation in the Troubled Asset Relief Program (TARP). In addition, we met with credit rating agency officials from the Standard and Poor's Corporation, Moody's Corporation, and Fitch Ratings Inc. for their perspective on SCAP and their own stress test practices. To more completely understand the execution of SCAP, we completed a literature search of stress tests conducted by others—for example, the Committee on European Banking Supervisors and the International Monetary Fund. We also reviewed relevant credit rating agency reports and the reports of other oversight bodies such as the Congressional Oversight Panel and the Special Inspector General for the Troubled Asset Relief Program on topics related to stress testing and TARP. We also reviewed our past work on the bank supervisory process and SCAP.[65]

In addition, to track the actual performance of the 19 BHCs, we collected data from several sources. We then compared the BHCs' actual performance to the December 31, 2008, capital levels presented in SCAP and the projections made under the more adverse scenario for estimated losses for loans, securities (available for sale and held to maturity), trading and counterparty, and resources other than capital to absorb losses.[66] Our primary source for SCAP estimates was the May 7, 2009, SCAP results document, which contained the estimates for each of the 19 BHCs and aggregate data for all BHCs. We also reviewed the confidential April 24, 2009, and May 5, 2009, presentations that the SCAP regulators made to each of the 19 BHCs to identify estimates of preprovision net revenue (PPNR) and changes in allowance for loan and lease losses (ALLL) for the 2 years ended 2010. Our primary source for the actual results at the BHCs was the Federal Reserve's Y-9C. In doing so, we used the SNL Financial database to extract data on the Y-9C and the Securities and Exchange Commission forms 10-K and 10-Q. These data were collected following the close of the fourth quarter of 2009, the halfway point of the SCAP's 2-year time frame.

Since losses were not estimated on a quarter-by-quarter or yearly basis but projected for the full 2-year period, we assumed that losses and revenue estimates under the more adverse scenario were distributed at a constant rate across the projection period. Thus, we compared the actual 2009 year end values with half of the Federal Reserve's 2-year SCAP projections. This methodology has some limitations because losses, expenses, revenues, and changes to reserves are historically unevenly distributed and loss rates over a 2-year period in an uncertain economic environment can follow an inconsistent path. However, the Federal Reserve, OCC, credit rating agencies, an SNL Financial analyst, and most of the BHCs we interviewed who are tracking performance relative to SCAP estimates are also using the same methodology. We assessed the reliability of the SNL Financial database by following GAO's best practices for data reliability and found that the data was sufficiently reliable for our purposes.[67] To confirm the accuracy of our BHC tracking data, we shared our data with the Federal Reserve and the 19 SCAP BHCs. We received comments and incorporated them as appropriate.

Some of the data that we collected were not in a form that was immediately comparable to the categories used in the SCAP results, and we had to make adjustments in order to make the comparison. For tier 1 common capital, most asset categories, and resources other than capital to absorb losses, we had to find a methodology suited to aggregating these data so that we could compare it to the corresponding SCAP data. For example, net-charge offs for the various loan categories are broken out into more subcategories in the Y-9C than those listed in the SCAP results. In addition, we calculated "Resources Other than Capital to Absorb Losses" to correspond to the SCAP definition of PPNR minus the change in ALLL, which required obtaining data from multiple entries within the Y-9C. When calculating noninterest expense we removed the line item for goodwill impairment losses because this item was not included in the SCAP regulators' projections. We also used the calculation of a change in ALLL until December 31, 2009. But the SCAP regulators considered an increase in ALLL over the full 2-year period to be a drain on resources, because the provisions made to increase the ALLL balance would not be available to absorb losses during the 2-year SCAP time frame. This notion creates a problem in using the formula for 1-year tracking purposes because an increase in ALLL during 2009 would require provisions for that increase, but those added reserves could ultimately be used to absorb losses during 2010. To maintain consistency, our calculation considers ALLL increases during 2009 to be a drain on resources, but we recognize that this money could act as a resource to absorb losses rather than a drain on those resources.

We faced an additional limitation pertaining to the ALLL calculation and a challenge with regard to the treatment of trading and counterparty revenues. In our review of SCAP documentation, we found that SCAP regulators used two different ALLL calculations—1 calculation for 4 of the BHCs that included a reserve for off-balance sheet items and another for the remaining 15 BHCs that did not include off-balance sheet reserves. The Federal Reserve confirmed that there were two different calculations that were not adjusted for consistency. In order to be consistent across the BHCs, we applied the same methodology that the regulators used for 15 of the BHCs to the 4 that remained. The treatment of trading and counterparty revenue created a challenge because the data in the Y-9C includes both customer derived revenue from transactions for BHCs that operate as broker-dealers and gains (or losses) from proprietary trading and certain associated expenses. These items are presented only in net form in the Y-9C. However, for the five BHCs (Bank of America Corporation; Citigroup, Inc.; Goldman Sachs Group, Inc.; JPMorgan Chase & Co.; and Morgan Stanley) that had their trading portfolios stressed, the trading and counterparty line is based on projections of gains (losses) from proprietary trading, but PPNR (specifically noninterest revenue) is based on gains from customer derived revenue from transactions for BHCs that operate as broker-dealers. Because we could not segregate these items based on the Y-9C, we have included the net amount in both the trading and counterparty and noninterest income line items. This means that the net amount of the trading gains or losses as reported in the Y-9C are included in two places in our tracking table for those five BHCs. For the remaining 14 BHCs, we included the entire line item in noninterest income, as that is where it was located in the SCAP projections.

Table 6 shows the items we used to calculate tier 1 capital, asset losses, PPNR, and ALLL as of December 31, 2009 and the specific sources we used. We also included specific references to the sources we used. Some elements within the table required a more detailed aggregation or calculation and are therefore explained further in tables 7 and 8 below. For reporting these capital measures and asset balances for the year ending December 31, 2008, we generally relied on the figures published in various SCAP documents.

Table 6. Items Used to Calculate Tier 1 Capital, Asset Losses, PPNR, and ALLL

Actual at 12/31/09 and source	
Capital measures	
Tier 1 capital	From line 11 ("tier 1 capital") of Schedule HC-R (page 40) of the FR Y-9C
Tier 1 common capital	See table 7
Risk-weighted assets	From line 62 ("total risk-weighted assets") of Schedule HC-R (page 43) of the FR Y-9C
Tier 1 risk-based ratio	Calculated as tier 1 capital divided by risk-weighted assets
Tier 1 common capital ratio	Calculated as tier 1 common capital divided by risk-weighted assets
Asset category[a]	
First-lien mortgages	See table 8
Second/junior lien mortgages	See table 8
Commercial and industrial loans	See table 8
Commercial real estate loans	See table 8
Credit card loans	See table 8
Securities (available for sale and held to maturity)	Calculated as: total of line 6a ("realized gains (losses) on held-to-maturity securities") and line 6b ("realized gains (losses) on available-for-sale securities") of Schedule HI (page 2) of the FR Y-9C
Trading and counterparty	For the 5 BHCs that had their trading and counterparty portfolio stressed: line 5c ("trading revenue") of Schedule HI (page 1) of the FR Y-9C. For all other BHCs, this line item was left blank.
Other	See table 8
One-time items (included in "Other" in SCAP results)	If one-time losses (gains) could be identified, they were located here and removed from the respective category above. This only applies to State Street Corporation.
Resources other than capital to absorb losses (Total PPNR less change in ALLL)[b]	
Preprovision net revenue (PPNR)[c]	
Net interest income (expense)	Line 3 ("net interest income") of Schedule HI (page 1) of the FR Y-9C.
Noninterest income	Line 5m ("total noninterest income") of Schedule HI (page 2) of the FR Y-9C.
Less noninterest expense	Calculated as: line 7e ("total noninterest expense") less Line 7c (1) ("goodwill impairment losses") of Schedule HI (page 2) of the FR Y-9C.
Change in allowance for loan and lease losses (ALLL)[d]	
ALLL at 12/31/08	Line 1 ("balance most recently reported at the end of previous year") of Part II of the Schedule HI-B (page 7) of the 12/31/09 FR Y-9C.
ALLL at 12/31/09	Line 7 ("balance at end of current period") of Part II of the Schedule HI-B (page 7) of the 12/31/09 FRY-9C.

Source: GAO analysis of Federal Reserve 2009 Y-9C information.

[a] Calculated as the total of the losses (gains) below. Categories that were n/a in the SCAP were included in this total.

[b] Calculated as Total PPNR less the change in ALLL.

[c] Calculated as net interest income (expense) plus noninterest income less noninterest expense.

[d] Calculated as ALLL at 12/31/09 less ALLL at 12/31/08.

Table 7 shows our methodology for calculating tier 1 common capital, including the part of the Y-9C in which the data can be found. Currently, there is no defined regulatory method for calculating tier 1 common capital, and it is not a required data field for BHCs to file in their Y-9C submissions. As a result, we developed a formula consistent with the Federal Reserve's by reviewing the guidance available in the SCAP design and implementation and SCAP results documents and consulting with SNL Financial regarding its methodology.

Table 7. Tier 1 Common Capital Calculation

Location within the FR Y 9-C	Tier 1 common capital calculation
Line 11 of Schedule HC-R (page 40)	Tier 1 capital
Line 23 of Schedule HC (page 12)	Less: perpetual preferred stock and related surplus
Line 6a of Schedule HC-R (page 40)	Less: qualifying Class A noncontrolling (minority) interests in consolidated subsidiaries
Line 6b of Schedule HC-R (page 40)	Less: qualifying restricted core capital elements (other than cumulative perpetual preferred stock)
Line 6c of Schedule HC-R (page 40)	Less: qualifying mandatory convertible preferred securities of internationally active bank holding companies
Line 1 of the "notes to the balance sheet-other" (page 49)	Less: amount of excess restricted core capital elements included in Schedule HC- R, item 10
Line 5 of Schedule HC-R (page 40)	Add: nonqualifying perpetual preferred stock
	Total = Tier 1 common capital

Source: Federal Reserve 2009 Y-9C documentation.

Table 8 provides a crosswalk for the asset classification we used to group the various charge-off categories listed in the Y-9C.

To ensure additional comparability with SCAP, we attempted to identify any unique circumstances that could skew the results. For example, after we shared our initial tracking estimates with the 19 BHCs, one BHC had identified an issue with our calculation of tier 1 common capital that resulted from the way information is reported on the Y-9C. After discussing the issue with the BHC and verifying their explanation, we adjusted our calculation to more accurately reflect their position. Another BHC also had a one-time charge that had been included in the "Other" loss category, and we decided to segregate this item as a separate line item. We have also submitted our tracking spreadsheet to the Federal Reserve and to each BHC to give them an opportunity to provide input and ensure the accuracy and comparability of our numbers. Appropriate adjustments to 2009 numbers based on information received from the Federal Reserve and individual BHCs are noted, where applicable, in the tables in appendix III.

Some items that impact precise comparisons between actual results and the pro rata estimates are disclosed in our footnotes, rather than as adjustments to our calculations. For example, the stress test was applied to loan and other asset portfolios as of December 31, 2008, without including a calculation for ongoing banking activities. Because the Y-9C data includes ongoing activity as of the date of the report, the actual results are slightly different than the performance of the stressed assets as the BHCs were treated as liquidating concerns rather than going concerns in the SCAP stress test. Distinguishing between the gains (losses) from legacy assets and those that resulted from new assets is not possible using public data. Other examples are that SCAP did not include the impact of the owned debt value adjustment or one-time items (occurring subsequent to SCAP) in their projections of PPNR.[68] As credit default swap spreads narrowed in 2009,[69] liability values increased at most banks, causing a negative impact on revenue at those banks that chose to account for their debt at fair value; but these losses were not included in the SCAP estimates. One-time items, such as sales of business lines, were also not included in the SCAP estimates of PPNR, as these events occurred subsequent to the stress test and, in part, could not be fully predicted as a part of SCAP. Rather than remove the losses from the owned debt value adjustments and the gains (or losses) due to one-time items from the BHCs' 2009 PPNR results, we disclosed the amounts in footnotes for the applicable BHCs. We chose this treatment so that PPNR would reflect actual results at the BHCs, while still disclosing the adjustments needed for more precise comparability to SCAP.

Table 8. Crosswalk of Y-9C Net Charge-Offs and Asset Classifications to Classifications Used by SCAP

Y-9C classification	Classification used in GAO analysis		
	Overall category	Primary category	Sub-category
1. Loans secured by real estate			
a. Construction, land development, and other land loans in domestic offices:			
(1) One to four family residential construction loans	Commercial real estate	Commercial real estate	Construction
(2) Other construction loans and all land development and other land loans	Commercial real estate	Commercial real estate	Construction
b. Secured by farmland in domestic offices	Other	Other loans	n/a
c. Secured by one to four family residential properties in domestic offices:			
(1) Revolving, open-end loans secured by one to four family residential properties under lines of credit	Second/junior lien	Second/junior lien	Home equity line of credit
(2) Closed-end loans secured by one to four family residential properties in domestic offices:			
(a) Secured by first liens	First lien	First lien	n/a
(b) Secured by junior liens	Second/ junior lien	Second/ junior lien	Closed-end junior liens
d. Secured by mutlifamily (five or more) residential properties in domestic offices	Commercial real estate	Commercial real estate	Multifamily
e. Secured by nonfarm nonresidential properties in domestic offices:			
(1) Loans secured by owner-occupied nonfarm nonresidential properties	Commercial real estate	Commercial real estate	Nonfarm, nonresidential
(2) Loans secured by other nonfarm nonresidential properties	Commercial real estate	Commercial real estate	Nonfarm, nonresidential
f. In foreign offices	Other	Other loans	n/a
2. Loans to depository institutions and acceptances of other banks:			
a. To U.S. banks and other U.S. depository institutions	Other	Other loans	n/a
b. To foreign banks	Other	Other loans	n/a
3. Loans to finance agricultural production and other loans to farmers	Other	Other loans	n/a
4. Commercial and industrial loans:			
a. To U.S. addresses (domicile)	Commercial and industrial	Commercial and industrial	n/a
b. To non-U.S. addresses (domicile)	Commercial and industrial	Commercial and industrial	n/a
5. Loans to individuals for household, family, and other personal expenditures			
a. Credit cards	Credit cards	Credit cards	n/a
b. Other (includes single payment, installment, all student loans, and revolving credit plans other than credit cards)	Other	Other consumer	n/a
6. Loans to foreign governments and official institutions	Other	Other loans	n/a
7. All other loans	Other	Other loans	n/a
8. Lease financing receivables:			
a. Leases to individuals for household, family, and other personal expenditures	Other	Other consumer	n/a
b. All other leases	Other	Other loans	n/a

Source: Federal Reserve 2009 Schedule HI-B of the Y-9C.

Note: N/a means not applicable.

We identified the TARP status of each of the 19 BHCs that participated in SCAP by reviewing data from the Treasury's Office of Financial Stability's *TARP Transactions Report for the Period Ending September 22, 2010* (TARP Transactions Report) and the SCAP results document. We used the SCAP results document to identify BHCs that were required to raise capital. The TARP Transactions Report, was then used to identify the program under which TARP funds were received (if any), the amount of funds received, capital repayment date, amount repaid, and warrant disposition date and to determine whether the warrants were repurchased or sold by Treasury in a public offering.

To gain a better understanding of future potential losses, we determined the percentage of BHCs' total loans that are either nonaccrual or more than 90 days past due using Y-9C data from the SNL Financial database.[70] We used quarterly data for the period 2007 through 2009 on nonaccrual loans and past due balances of more than 90 days, for each of the BHCs. We aggregated the data into the same six loan categories used in SCAP: first-lien mortgages, second/junior-lien mortgages, commercial and industrial loans, commercial real estate loans, credit card balances, and "Other." (See tables 8 and 9 for details.) Once the data were aggregated, we divided that data by the applicable total loan balance for each category at each point in time (i.e., quarterly basis). One limitation is that Y-9C data were not available for all periods for four of the BHCs (American Express Company; GMAC LLC; The Goldman Sachs Group, Inc.; and Morgan Stanley) because they had recently became BHCs.[71] As a result, we did not include these BHCs in the calculation during those periods where their Y-9Cs were not available (fourth quarter of 2008 and earlier for all except GMAC LLC, which also did not have a Y-9C in the first quarter of 2009).

Table 9. Crosswalk of Y-9C Loans and Lease Financing Receivables to and Classifications used by SCAP

Y-9C classification	Classification used in GAO analysis		
	Overall category	Primary category	Sub-category
1. Loans secured by real estate			
a. Construction, land development, and other land loans in domestic offices:			
(1) One to four family residential construction loans	Commercial real estate	Commercial real estate	Construction
(2) Other construction loans and all land development and other land loans	Commercial real estate	Commercial real estate	Construction
b. Secured by farmland	Other	Other loans	n/a
c. Secured by one to four family residential properties:			
(1) Revolving, open-end loans secured by one to four family residential properties and extended under lines of credit	Second/ junior lien	Second/ junior lien	Home equity lines of credit
(2) Closed-end loans secured by one to four family residential properties:			
(a) Secured by first liens	First lien	First lien	n/a
(b) Secured by junior liens	Second/ junior lien	Second/ junior lien	Closed-end junior liens
d. Secured by mutlifamily (five or more) residential properties	Commercial real estate	Commercial real state	Multifamily
e. Secured by nonfarm nonresidential properties:			
(1) Loans secured by owner-occupied nonfarm nonresidential properties	Commercial real estate	Commercial real estate	Nonfarm, nonresidential

Table 9. (Continued)

(2) Loans secured by other nonfarm nonresidential properties	Commercial real estate	Commercial real estate	Nonfarm, nonresidential
2. Loans to depository institutions and acceptances of other banks:			
a. To U.S. banks and other U.S. depository institutions	Other	Other loans	n/a
b. To foreign banks	Other	Other loans	n/a
3. Loans to finance agricultural production and other loans to farmers	Other	Other loans	n/a
4. Commercial and industrial loans:			
a. To U.S. addresses (domicile)	Commercial and industrial	Commercial and industrial	n/a
b. To non-U.S. addresses (domicile)	Commercial and industrial	Commercial and industrial	n/a
6. Loans to individuals for household, family, and other personal expenditures			
a. Credit cards	Credit cards	Credit cards	n/a
b. Other revolving credit plans	Other	Other consumer	n/a
b. Other consumer (includes single payment, installment, and all student loans)	Other	Other consumer	n/a
7. Loans to foreign governments and official institutions (including foreign central banks)	Other	Other loans	n/a
9. a. Loans for purchasing and carrying securities (secured and unsecured)	Other	Other loans	n/a
b. All other loans	Other	Other loans	n/a
10. Lease financing receivables (net of unearned income):			
a. Leases to individuals for household, family, and other personal expenditures	Other	Other consumer	n/a
b. All other leases	Other	Other loans	n/a
11. Less: Any unearned income on loans reflected in items 1-9 above.	-[a]	-[a]	-[a]

Source: Federal Reserve 2009 Schedule HC-C of the Y-9C.

Notes: Foreign office real estate was also included in our calculation of the total loans, but is not distinguishable in the table above. We pulled it directly from the SNL Financial database. This amount equates to the difference, in Schedule HC-C, between line item 1 for the "Consolidated" and "In Domestic Offices" columns (these columns are not depicted above). The classification of these loans in our calculations was as "Other" and the primary category was "Other loans."

N/a means not applicable.

[a] For calculations for the 19 SCAP BHCs, unearned income was distributed to all loan balances based on the percent that each line item represented of total loans for that BHC (excludes lease financing receivables). For calculations for all BHCs with total assets greater than $1 billion, unearned income was distributed to the aggregate balances for each line item based on the respective percentage that each balance represented of the total.

We collected Y-9C data from the SNL Financial database to calculate the loan loss rates across BHCs with more than $1 billion of assets and compare the 19 BHCs with the indicative loss rates provided by the SCAP regulators. We used annual data for the year ended December 31, 2009, on loan charge-offs. We also used average total loan balances. In the Y-9C total loan balances were categorized somewhat differently from charge-offs. Table 9 provides a crosswalk for the asset classification. We aggregated loan balance data into the same categories that were used in the indicative loss rate table in SCAP: first-lien mortgages, prime mortgages, Alt-A mortgages, subprime mortgages, second/junior lien mortgages, closed-end junior liens, home equity lines of credit, commercial and industrial loans, commercial real estate loans, construction loans, multifamily loans, nonfarm nonresidential loans, credit card balances, other consumer, and other loans. Once the data were aggregated into these categories, we divided the net charge-offs by the applicable average loan balance. This calculation showed the loss rate for each category (e.g., first-lien mortgages and commercial real estate) for the year ended December 31, 2009. This methodology was applied to calculate the loss rates for the 19 SCAP BHCs and all BHCs with more than $1 billion of assets, respectively. Because those institutions had recently converted to being BHCs, Y-9C data on loan balances was not available for the fourth quarter of 2008 for American Express Company; The Goldman Sachs Group, Inc.; and Morgan Stanley, and was not available for GMAC LLC for both the first quarter of 2009 and the fourth quarter of 2008. Therefore, we approximated the loan balances in these periods for GMAC LLC and American Express Company based on their Form 10-Q for these time periods. Because The Goldman Sachs Group, Inc. and Morgan Stanley have considerably smaller loan balances, in general, than the other BHCs; the fourth quarter of 2008 balance was not approximated for these BHCs. Instead, the average loan balance was simply based on the available data (e.g., first quarter of 2009 through fourth quarter of 2009).

We conducted this performance audit from August 2009 to September 2010 in accordance with generally accepted government auditing standards. Those standards require that we plan and perform the audit to obtain sufficient, appropriate evidence to provide a reasonable basis for our findings and conclusions based on our audit objectives. We believe that the evidence obtained provides a reasonable basis for our findings and conclusions based on our audit objectives.

APPENDIX II. STATUS OF BANK HOLDING COMPANIES' TARP INVESTMENTS AS SEPTEMBER 22, 2010

Twelve of the 19 bank holding companies (BHC) that participated in the Supervisory Capital Assessment Program (SCAP) had redeemed their Troubled Asset Relief Program (TARP) investments and had their warrants disposed of as of September 22, 2010, and most of them were not required to raise capital under SCAP (table 10). Six of the 19 BHCs tested under SCAP have not repaid TARP investments or disposed of warrants, and one, MetLife, Inc., did not receive any TARP investments. BHCs participating in SCAP must follow specific criteria to repay TARP funds. In approving applications from participating banks that want to repay TARP funds, the Federal Reserve considers various factors. Some of these factors[72] include whether the banks can demonstrate an ability to access the long-term debt market without relying on the Federal Deposit Insurance Corporation's (FDIC) Temporary Liquidity Guarantee Program and whether they can successfully access the public equity markets, remain in a position to facilitate lending, and maintain capital levels in accord with supervisory expectations.[73] BHCs intending to repay TARP investments must have post repayment capital ratios that meet or exceed SCAP requirements.

Table 10. Status of TARP Investments for the 19 BHCs Participating in SCAP, as of September 22, 2010

Dollars in billions							
Bank holding company	Required to raise capital under SCAP?	Type of TARP received	Capital amount received	Capital repayment date	Capital amount repaid	Warrant disposition date	Warrants repurchased (R) or sold via auction (A)[a]
BHC that was not a recipient of TARP funding							
MetLife, Inc.	No	n/a	n/a	n/a	n/a	n/a	n/a
BHCs that were recipients of TARP funding and have exited TARP							
American Express Company	No	CPP[b]	$3.4	06/17/09	$3.4	07/29/09	R
Bank of America Corporation	Yes	CPP	25.0	12/09/09	25.0	03/03/10	A
		TIP[c]	20.0	12/09/09	20.0	03/03/10	A
BB&T Corporation	No	CPP	3.1	06/17/09	3.1	07/22/09	R
The Bank of New York Mellon Corporation	No	CPP	3.0	06/17/09	3.0	08/05/09	R
Capital One Financial Corporation	No	CPP	3.6	06/17/09	3.6	12/03/09	A
The Goldman Sachs Group, Inc.	No	CPP	10.0	06/17/09	10.0	07/22/09	R
JPMorgan Chase & Co.	No	CPP	25.0	06/17/09	25.0	12/10/09	A
Morgan Stanley	Yes	CPP	10.0	06/17/09	10.0	08/12/09	R
PNC Financial Services Group, Inc	Yes	CPP	7.6	02/02/10	7.6	04/29/10	A
State Street Corporation	No	CPP	2.0	06/17/09	2.0	07/08/09	R
U.S. Bancorp	No	CPP	6.6	06/17/09	6.6	07/15/09	R
Wells Fargo & Company	Yes	CPP	25.0	12/23/09	25.0	05/21/10	A
BHCs that have not fully repaid TARP funding or disposed of warrants							
Citigroup Inc.[d]	Yes	CPP	25.0	-	-	-	-
		TIP	20.0	12/23/09	20.0	-	-
Fifth Third Bancorp	Yes	CPP	3.4	-	-	-	-
GMAC LLC[e]	Yes	AIFP	16.3	-	-	-	-
KeyCorp	Yes	CPP	2.5	-	-	-	-
Regions Financial Corporation	Yes	CPP	3.5	-	-	-	-
SunTrust Banks, Inc.	Yes	CPP	4.9	-	-	-	-

Sources: Federal Reserve's SCAP results document and Treasury's TARP Transactions Report for the Period Ending September XX, 2010.

Note: N/a means not applicable since MetLife, Inc. did not receive any TARP funding.

[a] "R" indicates that the warrants were repurchased by the financial institution via negotiations with Treasury. "A" indicates that Treasury sold the warrants in a registered public auction.

[b] The Capital Purchase Program (CPP) is a program in which Treasury invests in preferred securities issued by qualified financial institutions.

[c] Treasury created the Targeted Investment Program (TIP) to stabilize the financial system by making investments in institutions that are determined to be critical to the functioning of the financial system.

[d] As part of an exchange offer designed to strengthen Citigroup Inc.'s capital, in June 2009, Treasury agreed to exchange its $25 billion of CPP preferred stock in Citigroup for 7.7 billion shares of Citigroup Inc. common stock at a price of $3.25 per common share. In May 2010, Treasury sold 1.5 billion of its 7.7 billion common shares. In June 2010, Treasury sold 1.1 billion shares and has a remaining ownership of 5.1 billion common shares.

[e] On June 30, 2009, GMAC LLC changed its corporate structure and became GMAC Inc., and on May 10, 2010, GMAC Inc. changed its name to Ally Financial Inc.

APPENDIX III. ONE-YEAR ACTUAL PERFORMANCE COMPARED TO GAO'S PRO RATA STRESS TEST LOSS PROJECTIONS FOR EACH OF THE 19 SCAP BHCs

Table 11 shows the names, location, and total assets as of December 31, 2008, of the 19 bank holding companies (BHC) subject to the Supervisory Capital Assessment Program (SCAP) stress test that was conducted by the federal bank regulators in the spring of 2009. The stress test was a forward-looking exercise intended to help federal banking regulators gauge the extent of the additional capital buffer necessary to keep the BHCs strongly capitalized and lending even if economic conditions are worse than had been expected between December 2008 and December 2010.

The following tables (12 through 30) compare the 2009 performance of the 19 BHCs involved in SCAP to the 2-year SCAP estimates and the GAO 1-year pro rata estimates for the more adverse economic scenario. Specifically, these tables include comparison of actual and estimates of losses and gains associated with loans, securities, trading and counterparty, resources, preprovision net revenue (PPNR), and allowance for loan and lease losses (ALLL). These tables also include a comparison of actual capital levels at December 31, 2009, and December 31, 2008. Totals may not add due to rounding. For a more detailed explanation of the calculations made in constructing this analysis, see appendix I.

Table 11. Identification of 19 BHCs Subject to the Stress Test

Dollars in thousands			
Table number	Name of bank holding company	Location of headquarters	Total assets as of December 31, 2008
12	American Express Company	New York, NY	$126,074,000
13	Bank of America Corporation	Charlotte, NC	1,817,943,000
14	BB&T Corporation	Winston-Salem, NC	152,015,000
15	The Bank of New York Mellon Corporation	New York, NY	237,512,000
16	Capital One Financial Corporation	McLean, VA	165,913,452
17	Citigroup Inc.	New York, NY	1,938,470,000
18	Fifth Third Bancorp	Cincinnati, OH	119,764,000
19	GMAC LLC	Detroit, MI	189,476,000
20	The Goldman Sachs Group, Inc.	New York, NY	884,547,000
21	JPMorgan Chase & Co.	New York, NY	2,175,052,000
22	KeyCorp	Cleveland, OH	104,531,000
23	MetLife, Inc.	New York, NY	501,678,000
24	Morgan Stanley	New York, NY	676,764,000
25	PNC Financial Services Group, Inc.	Pittsburgh, PA	291,081,000
26	Regions Financial Corporation	Birmingham, AL	146,247,810
27	State Street Corporation	Boston, MA	173,631,000
28	SunTrust Banks, Inc.	Atlanta, GA	189,137,961
29	U.S. Bancorp	Minneapolis, MN	265,912,000
30	Wells Fargo & Company	San Francisco, CA	1,309,639,000

Source: GAO.

Table 12. American Express Company

Dollars in billions	Actual at 12/31/09	12/31/08 balance per SCAP	Difference	12/31/09 as a percent of the 12/31/08 balance
Tier 1 capital	$11.5	$10.1	$1.4	113.5%
Tier 1 common capital	$11.5	$10.1	$1.4	113.5%
Risk-weighted assets	$116.6	$104.4	$12.2	111.6%
Tier 1 risk-based ratio	9.8%	9.7%	0.1%	101.4%
Tier 1 common capital ratio	9.8%	9.7%	0.1%	101.4%

	Actual for year ended 12/31/09	2-year SCAP estimate	GAO 1-year pro rata estimate	Difference	Actual as a percent of the pro rata estimate
Total asset losses	**$4.4**	**$11.2**	**$5.6**	**$(1.2)**	**78.0%**
• First-lien mortgages	0.0	n/a	n/a	n/a	n/a
Second/junior lien mortgages	0.0	n/a	n/a	n/a	n/a
• Commercial and industrial Loans	0.0	n/a	n/a	n/a	n/a
• Commercial real estate loans	0.0	n/a	n/a	n/a	n/a
• Credit card loans	3.4	8.5	4.3	(0.9)	79.9
• Securities (available for sale and held to maturity)	(0.2)	n/a	n/a	n/a	n/a
• Trading and counterparty	-[a]	n/a	n/a	n/a	n/a
• Other	1.2	2.7	1.4	(0.2)	88.0
Resources other than capital To absorb losses (Total PPNR less change in ALLL)	**$7.4**	**$11.9**	**$6.0**	**$1.4**	**123.8%**
PPNR	**$7.8**	-	-	-	-
• Net interest income (expense)	5.3	-	-	-	-
• Noninterest income	19.0[a]	-	-	-	-
• Less: noninterest expense	16.5	-	-	-	-
Change in allowance for loan and lease losses (ALLL)	**$0.4**	-	-	-	-
• ALLL at 12/31/08	3.4	-	-	-	-
• ALLL at 12/31/09	3.8	-	-	-	-

Source: GAO analysis of Federal Reserve and SNL Financial data.

Note: N/a means not applicable.

[a] Trading and counterparty positions were not stressed because the total portfolio is less than the $100 billion required for stress testing in SCAP, but trading (gain) loss information for this BHC was included in the "trading revenue" line of Schedule HI of the Y-9C in 2009. In SCAP, the projections of trading gains or losses for this BHC were included in the estimate of PPNR rather than the trading and counterparty line. Therefore, we have included the actual trading results in PPNR (specifically noninterest income).

Table 13. Bank of America Corporation

Dollars in billions	Actual at 12/31/09	12/31/08 balance per SCAP	Difference	12/31/09 as a percent of the 12/31/08 balance
Tier 1 capital	$160.6	$173.2	$(12.6)	92.7%
Tier 1 common capital	$120.6[a]	$74.5	$46.1	161.9%
Risk-weighted assets	$1,541.6	$1,633.8	$(92.2)	94.4%
Tier 1 risk-based ratio	10.4%	10.6%	(0.2)%	98.3%
Tier 1 common capital ratio	7.8%	4.6%	3.2%	170.1%

	Actual for year ended 12/31/09	2-year SCAP estimate	GAO 1-year pro rata estimate	Difference	Actual as a percent of the pro rata estimate
Total asset losses	**$12.3**	**$136.6**	**$68.4**	**$(56.0)**	**18.1%**
• First-lien mortgages	3.6	22.1	11.1	(7.5)	32.5
• Second/junior lien Mortgages	7.6	21.4	10.7	(3.1)	70.9
• Commercial and industrial loans	5.0	15.7	7.9	(2.8)	63.8
• Commercial real estate loans	3.3	9.4	4.7	(1.4)	69.4
• Credit card loans	7.8	19.1	9.6	(1.8)	81.5
• Securities (available for sale and held to maturity)	(9.3)	8.5	4.3	(13.5)	(218.4)
• Trading and counterparty	(12.1)[b]	24.1	12.1	(24.1)	(100.1)
• Other	6.4	16.4	8.2	(1.8)	78.7
Resources other than capital to absorb losses (total PPNR less change in ALLL)	**$29.5**	**$74.5**	**$37.3**	**$(7.7)**	**79.3%**
PPNR	**$43.7[c,d]**	-	-	-	-
• Net interest income (expense)	47.8	-	-	-	-
• Noninterest income	62.6[b]	-	-	-	-
• Less: noninterest expense	66.7	-	-	-	-
Change in allowance for loan and lease losses (ALLL)	**$14.1**	-	-	-	-
• ALLL at 12/31/08	23.1	-	-	-	-
• ALLL at 12/31/09	37.2	-	-	-	-

Source: GAO analysis of Federal Reserve and SNL Financial data.

Note: N/a means not applicable.

[a] Tier 1 common capital includes $19.29 billion of common equivalent securities (CES) issued in December 2009. As described in Bank of America Corporation's (Bank of America) Form 10-K for the year ended December 31, 2009, CES are included in tier 1 common capital based upon applicable regulatory guidance and the expectation that the underlying securities would convert to common stock following shareholder approval of additional authorized shares. Shareholders approved the increase in the number of authorized shares of common stock at the special meeting of shareholders held on February 23, 2010, and the CES converted to common stock on February 24, 2010.

[b] The trading and counterparty data in the Y-9C includes both customer derived revenue from transactions for BHCs that operate as broker-dealers as well as gains and losses from proprietary trading and associated expenses. These items are presented in net form only in the Y-9C. For the five BHCs that had their trading portfolios stressed (including Bank of America), the trading and counterparty line is based on projections of (gains) losses from proprietary trading, but PPNR (specifically noninterest revenue) included projections of gains (losses) from customer derived revenue from transactions due to operations as a broker-dealer. Because we could not segregate these items based on the Y-9C, we have included the net amount in the trading and counterparty and noninterest income line items above. As a

result of this limitation, the net amount of the trading gains or losses and PNNR in the table may be overstated or understated.

[c] PPNR includes an owned debt value adjustment of ($4.80) billion, which was not stressed in SCAP. As Bank of America's credit spreads narrowed during 2009, this caused the liability values to increase. This offsets the gains Bank of America experienced in 2008 when its credit spreads widened.

[d] PPNR includes one-time items totaling $4.90 billion, which were not included in SCAP.

Table 14. BB&T Corporation

Dollars in billions	Actual at 12/31/09	12/31/08 balance per SCAP	Difference	12/31/09 as a percent of the 12/31/08 balance
Tier 1 capital	$13.5	$13.4	$0.1	100.4%
Tier 1 common capital	$10.0	$7.8	$2.2	127.7%
Risk-weighted assets	$117.2	$109.8	$7.4	106.7%
Tier 1 risk-based ratio	11.5%	12.3%	(0.8)%	93.4%
Tier 1 common capital ratio	8.5%	7.1%	1.4%	119.7%

	Actual for year ended 12/31/09	2-year SCAP estimate	GAO 1-year pro rata estimate	Difference	Actual as a percent of the pro rata estimate
Total asset losses	**$1.6**	**$8.7**	**$4.4**	**$(2.8)**	**36.2%**
• First-lien mortgages	0.3	1.1	0.6	(0.3)	47.8
• Second/junior lien mortgages	0.1	0.7	0.4	(0.2)	40.9
• Commercial and industrial loans	0.2	0.7	0.4	(0.2)	56.5
• Commercial real estate Loans	0.7	4.5	2.3	(1.5)	32.3
• Credit card loans	0.1	0.2	0.1	(0.0)	81.6
• Securities (available for sale and held to maturity)	(0.2)	0.2	0.1	(0.3)	-199.3
• Trading and counterparty	-[a]	n/a	n/a	-	-
• Other	0.4	1.3	0.7	(0.3)	55.6
Resources other than capital to absorb losses (total PPNR less change in ALLL)	**$2.6**	**$5.5**	**$2.8**	**$(0.1)**	**94.9%**
PPNR	**$3.6**	-	-	-	-
• Net interest income (expense)	4.8	-	-	-	-
• Noninterest income	3.5[a]	-	-	-	-
• Less: noninterest expense	4.7	-	-	-	-
Change in allowance for loan and lease losses (ALLL)	**$1.0**	-	-	-	-
• ALLL at 12/31/08	1.6	-	-	-	-
• ALLL at 12/31/09	2.6	-	-	-	-

Source: GAO analysis of Federal Reserve and SNL Financial data.

Note: N/a means not applicable.

On August 14, 2009, BB&T Corporation (BB&T) entered into a purchase and assumption agreement with the Federal Deposit Insurance Corporation (FDIC) to acquire certain assets and assume substantially all of the deposits and certain liabilities of Colonial Bank, an Alabama state-chartered bank headquartered in Montgomery, Alabama. As further discussed in BB&T's Form 10-K for the year ended December 31, 2009, BB&T entered into loss sharing agreements with the FDIC related to certain loans, securities, and other assets. The actual results include BB&T's performance including the Colonial Bank acquisition.

[a] Trading and counterparty positions were not stressed because the total portfolio is less than the $100 billion required for stress testing in SCAP, but trading (gain) loss information for this BHC was included in the

"trading revenue" line of Schedule HI of the Y-9C in 2009. In SCAP, the projections of trading gains or losses for this BHC were included in the estimate of PPNR rather than the trading and counterparty line. Therefore, we have included the actual trading results in PPNR (specifically noninterest income).

Table 15. The Bank of New York Mellon Corporation

Dollars in billions					
	Actual at 12/31/09	12/31/08 balance per SCAP	Difference		12/31/09 as a percent of the 12/31/08 balance
Tier 1 capital	$12.9	$15.4	$(2.5)		83.7%
Tier 1 common capital	$11.2	$11.0	$0.2		101.8%
Risk-weighted assets	$106.3	$115.8	$(9.5)		91.8%
Tier 1 risk-based ratio	12.1%	13.3%	(1.2)%		91.1%
Tier 1 common capital ratio	10.5%	9.5%	1.0%		110.8%
	Actual for year ended 12/31/09	2-year SCAP estimate	GAO 1-year pro rata estimate	Difference	Actual as a percent of the pro rata estimate
Total asset losses	**$5.6**	**$5.4**	**$2.7**	**$2.9**	**207.6%**
• First-lien mortgages	0.1	0.2	0.1	(0.0)	60.0
• Second/junior lien mortgages	0.0	n/a	n/a		
• Commercial and industrial loans	0.1	0.4	0.2	(0.1)	45.0
• Commercial real estate loans	0.1	0.2	0.1	(0.1)	50.0
• Credit card loans	0.0	n/a	n/a		
• Securities (available for sale and held to maturity)	5.4[a]	4.2	2.1	3.3	255.7
• Trading and counterparty	-[b]	n/a	n/a		
• Commercial and industrial loans	0.1	0.4	0.2	(0.1)	45.0
• Commercial real estate loans	0.1	0.2	0.1	(0.1)	50.0
• Credit card loans	0.0	n/a	n/a		
• Other	0.0	0.4	0.2	(0.2)	17.0
Resources other than capital to absorb losses (total PPNR less change in ALLL):	**$3.4**	**$6.7**	**$3.4**	**$(0.0)**	**100.2%**
• PPNR	$3.5	-	-	-	-
• Net interest income (expense)	2.9	-	-	-	-
• Noninterest income	10.1[b]	-	-	-	-
• Less: noninterest expense	9.6	-	-	-	-
Change in allowance for loan and lease losses (ALLL)	$0.1	-	-	-	-
• ALLL at 12/31/08	.4	-	-	-	-
• ALLL at 12/31/09	.5	-	-	-	-

Source: GAO analysis of Federal Reserve and SNL Financial data.

Note: N/a means not applicable.

[a] Based on discussions with Bank of New York Mellon Corporation (Bank of New York Mellon) officials, the company's securities portfolio underwent a significant restructuring in the third quarter of 2009 in order to de-risk this portfolio, causing the recognition of significant losses in that period. However, The Bank of New York Mellon sold off many of its riskiest holdings in that period, including many Alt-A residential mortgage-backed securities, so that it expects to see gains in this portfolio in the future, causing the final 2-year loss amount to be less than the amount projected under SCAP in the securities (available for sale and held to maturity) portfolio. See the Bank of New York Mellon's Form 10-K for the year ended December 31, 2009, and other public disclosures for additional information. As a result of the write downs taken due to the restructuring of the securities portfolio, Bank of New York Mellon

expects an increase in net interest revenue of $200 million in 2010. As of the second quarter of 2010 year to date, the BHC experienced a gain of $20 million in this portfolio.

[b] Trading and counterparty positions were not stressed because the total portfolio is less than the $100 billion required for stress testing in SCAP, but trading (gain) loss information for this BHC was included in the "trading revenue" line of Schedule HI of the Y-9C in 2009. In SCAP, the projections of trading gains or losses for this BHC were included in the estimate of PPNR rather than the trading and counterparty line. Therefore, we have included the actual trading results in PPNR (specifically noninterest income).

Table 16. Capital One Financial Corporation

Dollars in billions				
	Actual at 12/31/09	12/31/08 balance per SCAP	Difference	12/31/09 as a percent of the 12/31/08 balance
Tier 1 capital	$16.0	$16.8	$(0.8)	95.2%
Tier 1 common capital	$12.4	$12.0	$0.4	103.0%
Risk-weighted assets	$116.3	$131.8	$(15.5)	88.2%
Tier 1 risk-based ratio	13.7%	12.7%	1.0%	108.2%
Tier 1 common capital ratio	10.6%	9.1%	1.5%	116.7%
	Actual for year ended 12/31/09	2-year SCAP estimate	GAO 1-year pro rata estimate	Difference	Actual as a percent of the pro rata estimate
Total asset losses	**$4.4**	**$13.4**	**$6.7**	**$(2.3)**	**65.1%**
• First-lien mortgages	0.1	1.8	0.9	(0.8)	7.8%
• Second/junior lien mortgages	0.2	0.7	0.4	(0.1)	63.0
• Commercial and industrial loans	0.6	1.5	0.8	(0.1)	81.5
• Commercial real estate loans	0.3	1.1	0.6	(0.2)	62.4
• Credit card loans	1.8	3.6	1.8	(0.0)	98.0
• Securities (available for sale and held to maturity)	(0.2)	0.4	0.2	(0.4)	(103.1)
• Trading and counterparty	-[a]	n/a	n/a	-	-
• Other	1.6	4.3	2.2	(0.6)	72.5
Resources other than capital to absorb losses (total PPNR less change in ALLL):	**$5.8**	**$9.0**	**$4.5**	**$1.3**	**128.0%**
PPNR	**$5.4**	-	-	-	-
• Net interest income (expense)	7.7	-	-	-	-
• Noninterest income	5.0[a]	-	-	-	-
• Less: noninterest expense	7.3	-	-	-	-
Change in allowance for loan and lease losses (ALLL)	**$(0.4)**	-	-	-	-
• ALLL at 12/31/08	4.5	-	-	-	-
• ALLL at 12/31/09	4.1	-	-	-	-

Source: GAO analysis of Federal Reserve and SNL Financial data.

Note: N/a means not applicable.

[a] Trading and counterparty positions were not stressed because the total portfolio is less than the $100 billion required for stress testing in SCAP, but trading (gain) loss information for this BHC was included in the "trading revenue" line of Schedule HI of the Y-9C in 2009. In SCAP, the projections of trading gains or

losses for this BHC were included in the estimate of PPNR rather than the trading and counterparty line. Therefore, we have included the actual trading results in PPNR (specifically noninterest income).

Table 17. Citigroup Inc.

Dollars in billions	Actual at 12/31/09	12/31/08 balance per SCAP	Difference	12/31/09 as a percent of the 12/31/08 balance
Tier 1 capital	$127.0	$118.8	$8.2	106.9%
Tier 1 common capital	$106.4	$22.9	$83.5	464.5%
Risk-weighted assets	$1088.5	$996.2	$92.3	109.3%
Tier 1 risk-based ratio	11.7%	11.9%	(0.2)%	98.1%
Tier 1 common capital ratio	9.8%	2.3%	7.5%	424.9%

	Actual for year ended 12/31/09	2-year SCAP estimate	GAO 1-year pro rata estimate	Difference	Actual as a percent of the pro rata estimate
Total asset losses	**$27.2**	**$104.7**	**$52.4**	**$(25.1)**	**52.0%**
• First-lien mortgages	4.2	15.3	7.7	(3.5)	54.5
• Second/junior lien mortgages	4.7	12.2	6.1	(1.4)	76.8
• Commercial and industrial loans	5.1	8.9	4.5	0.6	113.6
• Commercial real estate loans	0.7	2.7	1.4	(0.6)	52.2
• Credit card loans	6.5	19.9	10.0	(3.4)	65.4
• Securities (available for sale and held to maturity)	0.9	2.9	1.5	(0.5)	62.8
• Trading and counterparty	(4.4)[a]	22.4	11.2	(15.6)	(39.7)
• Other	9.6	20.4	10.2	(0.6)	94.3
Resources other than capital to absorb losses (total PPNR less change in ALLL):	**$25.5**	**$49.0**	**$24.5**	**$1.0**	**103.9%**
PPNR	$31.9[b,c]	-	-	-	-
• Net interest income (expense)	50.4	-	-	-	-
• Noninterest income	32.1[a]	-	-	-	-
• Less: noninterest expense	50.6	-	-	-	-
Change in allowance for loan and lease losses (ALLL)	**$6.4**	-	-	-	-
• ALLL at 12/31/08	29.6	-	-	-	-
• ALLL at 12/31/09	36.0	-	-	-	-

Source: GAO analysis of Federal Reserve and SNL Financial data.

Note: N/a means not applicable.

[a]The trading and counterparty data in the Y-9C includes both customer derived revenue from transactions for BHCs that operate as broker-dealers as well as gains and losses from proprietary trading and associated expenses. These items are presented in net form only in the Y-9C. For the five BHCs that had their trading portfolios stressed (including Citigroup Inc.), the trading and counterparty line is based on projections of (gains) losses from proprietary trading, but PPNR (specifically noninterest revenue) included projections of gains (losses) from customer derived revenue from transactions due to operations as a broker-dealer. Because we could not segregate these items based on the Y-9C, we have

included the net amount in both the trading and counterparty and noninterest income line items above. As a result of this limitation, the net amount of the trading gains or losses and PPNR in the table may be overstated or understated.

[b] PPNR includes an owned debt value adjustment of ($4.23) billion, which was not included stressed in SCAP. As Citigroup's credit spreads narrowed during 2009, this caused the liability values to increase. This offsets the gains Citigroup Inc. experienced in 2008 when its credit spreads widened.

[c] PPNR includes one-time items totaling $2.73 billion, which were not included in SCAP.

Table 18. Fifth Third Bancorp

Dollars in billions	Actual at 12/31/09	12/31/08 balance per SCAP	Difference	12/31/09 as a percent of the 12/31/08 balance
Tier 1 capital	$13.4	$11.9	$1.5	112.8%
Tier 1 common capital	$7.1	$4.9	$2.2	144.0%
Risk-weighted assets	$100.9	$112.6	$(11.7)	89.6%
Tier 1 risk-based ratio	13.3%	10.6%	2.7%	125.6%
Tier 1 common capital ratio	7.0%	4.4%	2.6%	159.0%

	Actual for year ended 12/31/09	2-year SCAP estimate	GAO 1-year pro rata estimate	Difference	Actual as a percent of the pro rata estimate
Total asset losses	**$2.5**	**$9.1**	**$4.6**	**$(2.1)**	**54.6%**
• First-lien mortgages	0.3	1.1	0.6	(0.3)	49.1
• Second/junior lien Mortgages	0.3	1.1	0.6	(0.2)	57.8
• Commercial and industrial loans	0.6	2.8	1.4	(0.8)	39.4
• Commercial real estate loans	1.0	2.9	1.5	(0.4)	70.8
• Credit card loans	0.2	0.4	0.2	(0.0)	84.6
• Securities (available for sale and held to maturity)	(0.1)	0.1	0.0	(0.1)	-227.5
• Trading and counterparty	-[a]	n/a	n/a		-
• Other	0.2	0.9	0.5	(0.2)	54.6
Resources other than capital to absorb losses (total PPNR less change in ALLL):	**$3.3**	**$5.5**	**$2.8**	**$0.5**	**119.7%**
PPNR	$4.3[b]	-	-	-	-
• Net interest income (expense)	3.5	-	-	-	-
• Noninterest income	4.6[a]	-	-	-	-
• Less: noninterest expense	3.8	-	-	-	-
Change in allowance for loan and lease losses (ALLL)	**$1.0**	**-**	**-**	**-**	**-**
• ALLL at 12/31/08	2.8	-	-	-	-
• ALLL at 12/31/09	3.7	-	-	-	-

Source: GAO analysis of Federal Reserve and SNL Financial data.

Note: N/a means not applicable.

[a]Trading and counterparty positions were not stressed because the total portfolio is less than the $100 billion required for stress testing in SCAP, but trading (gain) loss information for this BHC was included in the "trading revenue" line of Schedule HI of the Y-9C in 2009. In SCAP, the projections of trading gains or losses for this BHC were included in the estimate of PPNR rather than the trading and counterparty line. Therefore, we have included the actual trading results in PPNR (specifically noninterest income).

[b]Fifth Third Bancorp's PPNR includes one-time items totaling $2.05 billion, which were not included in SCAP.

Table 19. GMAC LLC

Dollars in billions	Actual at 12/31/09	12/31/08 balance per SCAP	Difference		12/31/09 as a percent of the 12/31/08 balance
Tier 1 capital	$22.4	$17.4	$5.0		128.7%
Tier 1 common capital	$7.7	$11.1	$(3.4)		69.2%
Risk-weighted assets	$158.3	$172.7	$(14.4)		91.7%
Tier 1 risk-based ratio	14.1%	10.1%	4.0%		140.1%
Tier 1 common capital ratio	4.8%	6.4%	(1.6)%		75.8%
	Actual for year ended 12/31/09	2-year SCAP estimate	GAO 1-year pro rata estimate	Difference	Actual as a percent of the pro rata estimate
Total asset losses[a]	$6.9	$9.2	$4.6	$2.3	150.7%
• First-lien mortgages	2.4	2.0	1.0	1.4	239.9
• Second/junior lien mortgages	1.6	1.1	0.6	1.0	287.3
• Commercial and industrial loans	0.4	1.0	0.5	(0.1)	71.2
• Commercial real estate loans	0.7	0.6	0.3	0.4	236.7
• Credit card loans	0.0	n/a	n/a		
• Securities (available for sale and held to maturity)	(0.2)	0.5	0.3	(0.4)	(66.4)
• Trading and counterparty	-[b]	n/a	n/a	-	-
• Other[c]	2.1	4.0	2.0	0.1	102.7
Resources other than capital to absorb losses (total PPNR less change in ALLL):	$(1.1)	$(0.5)	$(0.3)	$(0.8)	(429.6)%
PPNR	$(2.1)	-	-	-	-
• Net interest income (expense)	0.1	-	-	-	-
• Noninterest income	10.1	-	-	-	-
• Less: noninterest expense	12.3	-	-	-	-
Change in allowance for loan and lease losses (ALLL)	$(1.0)	-	-	-	-
• ALLL at 12/31/08	3.4	-	-	-	-
• ALLL at 12/31/09	2.4	-	-	-	-

Source: GAO analysis of Federal Reserve and SNL Financial data.

Notes: N/a means not applicable.

GMAC LLC (GMAC) experienced a loss from discontinued operations totaling $2.4 billion in 2009. The item was not included in our calculation of PPNR.

GMAC changed its corporate name to GMAC Inc. on June 30, 2009. On May 10, 2010, GMAC Inc. changed its name to Ally Financial Inc.

[a] According to GMAC officials, in order to be positioned for better future performance the company pulled losses forward into the fourth quarter of 2009 by recognizing the lifetime losses on assets in that period;

and as a result of the accelerated loss recognition less losses would be expected in 2010. GMAC had a profit in the first and second quarters of 2010, its first profits since the fourth quarter of 2008. GMAC's tier 1 common capital ratio also improved to 5 percent and 5.2 percent, respectively.

[b] Trading and counterparty positions were not stressed because the total portfolio is less than the $100 billion required for stress testing in SCAP, but trading (gain) loss information for this BHC was included in the "trading revenue" line of Schedule HI of the Y-9C in 2009. In SCAP, the projections of trading gains or losses for this BHC were included in the estimate of PPNR rather than the trading and counterparty line. Therefore, we have included the actual trading results in PPNR (specifically noninterest income).

[c] GMAC's "Other" loans category per SCAP included only automobile-related loans. However, our classification of "Other" using Y-9C data includes automobile loans and other loans such as European home mortgages, which had substantial losses in 2009. Automobile loan losses totaled about $600 million in 2009 compared to the $2.0 billion prorated SCAP estimate, according to GMAC officials. On April 12, 2010, GMAC's mortgage subsidiary, Residential Capital, LLC agreed to sell its European mortgage assets and business. The assets in the transactions are valued at approximately the levels established in the fourth quarter of 2009, and there is no material gain or loss expected.

Table 20. The Goldman Sachs Group, Inc.

Dollars in billions	Actual at 12/31/09	12/31/08 balance per SCAP	Difference	12/31/09 as a percent of the 12/31/08 balance
Tier 1 capital	$64.6	$55.9	$8.7	115.6%
Tier 1 common capital	$52.7	$34.4	$18.3	153.2%
Risk-weighted assets	$431.9	$444.8	$(12.9)	97.1%
Tier 1 risk-based ratio	15.0%	12.6%	2.4%	118.8%
Tier 1 common capital ratio	12.2%	7.7%	4.5%	158.4%

	Actual for year ended 12/31/09	2-year SCAP estimate	GAO 1-year pro rata estimate	Difference	Actual as a percent of the pro rata estimate
Total asset losses	**$(23.3)**	**$17.8**	**$8.9**	**$(32.2)**	**(261.3)%**
• First-lien mortgages	0.0	n/a	n/a	n/a	-
• Second/junior lien Mortgages	0.0	n/a	n/a	n/a	-
• Commercial and industrial Loans	0.0	0.0	0.0	(0.0)	0.0%
• Commercial real estate loans	0.0	n/a	n/a	n/a	-
• Credit card loans	0.0	n/a	n/a	n/a	-
• Securities (available for sale and held to maturity)	(0.0)	0.1	0.1	(0.1)	(72.0)
• Trading and counterparty	(23.2)[a]	17.4	8.7	(31.9)	(267.10)
• Other	0.0	0.3	0.2	(0.2)	0.0
Resources other than capital to absorb losses (total PPNR less change in ALLL):	**$19.4**	**$18.5**	**$9.3**	**$10.2**	**209.9%**
PPNR	**$19.4[b]**	-	-	-	-
• Net interest income (expense)	7.4	-	-	-	-
• Noninterest income	37.3[a]	-	-	-	-
• Less: noninterest expense	25.3	-	-	-	-
Change in allowance for loan and lease losses (ALLL)	**$0.0**	-	-	-	-
• ALLL at 12/31/08	0.0	-	-	-	-
• ALLL at 12/31/09	0.0	-	-	-	-

Source: GAO analysis of Federal Reserve and SNL Financial data.

Note: N/a means not applicable.

[a]The trading and counterparty data in the Y-9C includes both customer derived revenue from transactions for BHCs that operate as broker-dealers as well as gains and losses from proprietary trading and associated expenses. These items are presented in net form only in the Y-9C. For the five BHCs that had their trading portfolios stressed (including Goldman Sachs Group, Inc.), the trading and counterparty line is based on projections of (gains) losses from proprietary trading, but PPNR (specifically noninterest revenue) included projections of gains (losses) from customer derived revenue from transactions due to operations as a broker-dealer. Because we could not segregate these items based on the Y-9C, we have included the net amount in both the trading and counterparty and noninterest income line items above. As a result of this limitation, the net amount of the trading gains or losses and PPNR in the table may be overstated or understated.

[b]PPNR includes an owned debt value adjustment of ($770) million, which was not stressed in SCAP. As Goldman Sachs Group, Inc.'s credit spreads narrowed during 2009, this caused the liability values to increase. This offsets the gains Goldman Sachs Group, Inc. experienced in 2008 when its credit spreads widened.

Table 21.JPMorgan Chase & Co.

Dollars in billions	Actual at 12/31/09	12/31/08 balance per SCAP	Difference	12/31/09 as a percent of the 12/31/08 balance
Tier 1 capital	$133.0	$136.2	$(3.2)	97.6%
Tier 1 common capital	$105.3	$87.0	$18.3	121.0%
Risk-weighted assets	$1,198.0	$1,337.5	$(139.5)	89.6%
Tier 1 risk-based ratio	11.1%	10.2%	0.9%	108.8%
Tier 1 common capital ratio	8.8%	6.5%	2.3%	135.2%

	Actual for year ended 12/31/09	2-year SCAP estimate	GAO 1-year pro rata estimate	Difference	Actual as a percent of the pro rata estimate
Total asset losses	**$12.0**	**$97.4**	**$48.7**	**$(36.7)**	**24.6%**
• First-lien mortgages	3.5	18.8	9.4	(5.9)	37.7
• Second/junior lien mortgages	4.7	20.1	10.1	(5.4)	46.3
• Commercial and industrial loans	3.6	10.3	5.2	(1.5)	70.8
• Commercial real estate loans	0.8	3.7	1.9	(1.0)	45.4
• Credit card loans	8.1	21.2	10.6	(2.5)	76.1
• Securities (available for sale and held to maturity)	(1.1)	1.2	0.6	(1.7)	(185.0)
• Trading and counterparty	(9.9)[a]	16.7	8.4	(18.2)	(118.2)
• Other	2.2	5.3	2.7	(0.4)	83.7
Resources other than capital to absorb losses (total PPNR less change in ALLL):	**$38.3**	**$72.4**	**$36.2**	**$2.1**	**105.9%**
PPNR	**$46.8[b]**	-	-	-	-
• Net interest income (expense)	51.3	-	-	-	-
• Noninterest income	48.5[a]	-	-	-	-
• Less: noninterest expense	53.0	-	-	-	-
Change in allowance for loan and lease losses (ALLL)	**$8.4**	-	-	-	-
• ALLL at 12/31/08	23.2	-	-	-	-
• ALLL at 12/31/09	31.6	-	-	-	-

Source: GAO analysis of Federal Reserve and SNL Financial data.

[a] The trading and counterparty data in the Y-9C includes both customer derived revenue from transactions for BHCs that operate as broker-dealers as well as gains and losses from proprietary trading and associated expenses. These items are presented in net form only in the Y-9C. For the five BHCs that had their trading portfolios stressed (including JPMorgan Chase & Co.), the trading and counterparty line is based on projections of (gains) losses from proprietary trading, but PPNR (specifically noninterest revenue) included projections of gains (losses) from customer derived revenue from transactions due to operations as a broker-dealer. Because we could not segregate these items based on the Y-9C, we have included the net amount in both the trading and counterparty and noninterest income line items above. As a result of this limitation, the net amount of the trading gains or losses and PPNR in the table may be overstated or understated.

[b] PPNR includes an owned debt value adjustment of ($1.57) billion, which was not stressed in SCAP. As JPMorgan Chase & Co.'s credit spreads narrowed during 2009, this caused the liability values to increase. This offsets the gains JPMorgan Chase & Co. experienced in 2008 when its credit spreads widened.

Table 22. KeyCorp

Dollars in billions	Actual at 12/31/09	12/31/08 balance per SCAP	Difference	12/31/09 as a percent of the 12/31/08 balance
Tier 1 capital	$11.0	$11.6	$(0.6)	94.4%
Tier 1 common capital	$6.4	$6.0	$0.4	107.4%
Risk-weighted assets	$85.9	$106.7	$(20.8)	80.5%
Tier 1 risk-based ratio	12.8%	10.9%	1.9%	117.0%
Tier 1 common capital ratio	7.5%	5.6%	1.9%	133.9%

	Actual for year ended 12/31/09	2-year SCAP estimate	GAO 1-year pro rata estimate	Difference	Actual as a percent of the pro rata estimate
Total asset losses	**$2.3**	**$6.7**	**$3.3**	**$(1.0)**	**69.3%**
• First-lien mortgages	0.0	0.1	0.1	(0.0)	55.7
• Second/junior lien mortgages	0.2	0.6	0.3	(0.1)	52.3
• Commercial and industrial loans	0.6	1.7	0.9	(0.2)	76.0
• Commercial real estate loans	1.0	2.3	1.2	(0.2)	85.8
• Credit card loans	0.0	0.0	0.0	(0.0)	44.4
• Securities (available for sale and held to maturity)	(0.1)	0.1	0.1	(0.2)	-225.7
• Trading and counterparty	-[a]	n/a	n/a	n/a	n/a
• Other	0.6	1.8	0.9	(0.3)	64.6
Resources other than capital to absorb losses (total PPNR less change in ALLL):	**$0.1**	**$2.1**	**$1.1**	**$(1.0)**	**5.3%**
PPNR	**$0.9**	-	-	-	-
• Net interest income (expense)	2.4	-	-	-	-
• Noninterest income	1.8[a]	-	-	-	-
• Less: noninterest expense	3.3	-	-	-	-
Change in allowance for loan and lease losses(ALLL)	**$0.9**	-	-	-	-
• ALLL at 12/31/08	1.8	-	-	-	-
• ALLL at 12/31/09	2.7	-	-	-	-

Source: GAO analysis of Federal Reserve and SNL Financial data.

Note: N/a means not applicable.

[a]Trading and counterparty positions were not stressed because the total portfolio is less than the $100 billion required for stress testing in SCAP, but trading (gain) loss information for this BHC was included in the "trading revenue" line of Schedule HI of the Y-9C in 2009. In SCAP, the projections of trading gains or losses for this BHC were included in the estimate of PPNR rather than the trading and counterparty line. Therefore, we have included the actual trading results in PPNR (specifically noninterest income).

Table 23. MetLife, Inc.

Dollars in billions	Actual at 12/31/09	12/31/08 balance per SCAP	Difference	12/31/09 as a percent of the 12/31/08 balance
Tier 1 capital	$28.8	$30.1	$(1.3)	95.6%
Tier 1 common capital	$26.4	$27.8	$(1.4)	94.8%
Risk-weighted assets	$322.8	$326.4	$(3.6)	98.9%
Tier 1 risk-based ratio	8.9%	9.2%	-0.3%	96.9%
Tier 1 common capital ratio	8.2%	8.5%	-0.3%	96.1%

	Actual for year ended 12/31/09	2-year SCAP estimate	GAO 1-year pro rata estimate	Difference	Actual as a percent of the pro rata estimate
Total asset losses	**$1.7**	**$9.6**	**$4.8**	**$(3.1)**	**35.1%**
• First-lien mortgages	0.0	0.0	0.0	(0.0)	24.0
• Second/junior lien mortgages	0.0	0.0	0.0	(0.0)	0.0
• Commercial and industrial loans	0.0	0.0	0.0	0.0	0.0
• Commercial real estate loans	0.0	0.8	0.4	(0.4)	6.9
• Credit card loans	0.0	n/a	n/a	n/a	n/a
• Securities (available for sale and held to maturity)	1.6	8.3	4.2	(2.5)	39.3
• Trading and counterparty	-[a]	n/a	n/a	n/a	n/a
• Other	0.0	0.5	0.3	(0.2)	10.7
Resources other than capital to absorb losses (total PPNR less change in ALLL):	**$(1.1)**	**$5.6**	**$2.8**	**$(3.9)**	**(38.9)%**
PPNR	$(0.7)	-	-	-	-
• Net interest income (expense)	14.1	-	-	-	-
• Noninterest income	29.4[a]	-	-	-	-
• Less: noninterest expense	44.1[b]	-	-	-	-
Change in allowance for loan and lease losses (ALLL)	**$0.4**	-	-	-	-
• ALLL at 12/31/08	0.3	-	-	-	-
• ALLL at 12/31/09	0.7	-	-	-	-

Source: GAO analysis of Federal Reserve and SNL Financial data.

Note: N/a means not applicable.

[a] Trading and counterparty positions were not stressed because the total portfolio is less than the $100 billion required for stress testing in SCAP, but trading (gain) loss information for this BHC was included in the "trading revenue" line of Schedule HI of the Y-9C in 2009. In SCAP, the projections of trading gains or losses for this BHC were included in the estimate of PPNR rather

than the trading and counterparty line. Therefore, we have included the actual trading results in PPNR (specifically noninterest income).

[b] MetLife, Inc. (MetLife) experienced high noninterest expense in 2009 largely due to derivative losses from interest rate hedging, which protects MetLife against lower interest rates among other things. Similar to the owned debt value adjustment, as MetLife's credit spreads narrowed during 2009, this caused the liability values to increase. This offsets the gains MetLife experienced in 2008 when its credit spreads widened.

Table 24. Morgan Stanley

Dollars in billions	Actual at 12/31/09	12/31/08 balance per SCAP	Difference	12/31/09 as a percent of the 12/31/08 balance
Tier 1 capital	$46.7	$47.2	$(0.5)	98.9%
Tier 1 common capital	$20.5	$17.8	$2.7	115.0%
Risk-weighted assets	$305.0	$310.6	$(5.6)	98.2%
Tier 1 risk-based ratio	15.3%	15.2%	0.1%	100.7%
Tier 1 common capital ratio	6.7%	5.7%	1.0%	117.8%

	Actual for year ended 12/31/09	2-year SCAP estimate	GAO 1-year pro rata estimate	Difference	Actual as a percent of the pro rata estimate
Total asset losses	**$(7.1)**	**$19.7**	**$9.8**	**$(16.9)**	**-72.7%**
• First-lien mortgages	0.0	n/a	n/a	n/a	n/a
• Second/junior lien mortgages	0.0	n/a	n/a	n/a	n/a
• Commercial and industrial loans	0.0	0.1	0.1	(0.0)	20.0
• Commercial real estate loans	0.1	0.6	0.3	(0.2)	46.7
• Credit card loans	0.0	n/a	n/a	n/a	n/a
• Securities (available for sale and held to maturity)	0.0	n/a	n/a	n/a	n/a
• Trading and counterparty	(7.3)[a]	18.7	9.4	(16.6)	-77.9
• Other	0.0	0.2	0.1	(0.1)	0.0
Resources other than capital to absorb losses (total PPNR less change in ALLL):	**$1.0**	**$7.1**	**$3.6**	**$(2.5)**	**28.4%**
PPNR	$1.1[b,c]	-	-	-	-
• Net interest income (expense)	0.9	-	-	-	-
• Noninterest income	22.7[a]	-	-	-	-
• Less: noninterest expense	22.5	-	-	-	-
Change in allowance for loan and lease losses (ALLL)	**$0.1**	**-**	**-**	**-**	**-**
• ALLL at 12/31/08	0.0	-	-	-	-
• ALLL at 12/31/09	0.2	-	-	-	-

Source: GAO analysis of Federal Reserve and SNL Financial data.

Note: N/a means not applicable.

[a] The trading and counterparty data in the Y-9C includes both customer derived revenue from transactions for BHCs that operate as broker-dealers as well as gains and losses from proprietary trading and associated expenses. These items are presented in net form only in the Y-9C. For the five BHCs that had their trading portfolios stressed (including Morgan Stanley), the trading and counterparty line is based on

projections of (gains) losses from proprietary trading, but PPNR (specifically noninterest revenue) included projections of gains (losses) from customer derived revenue from transactions due to operations as a broker-dealer. Because we could not segregate these items based on the Y-9C, we have included the net amount in both the trading and counterparty and noninterest income line items above. As a result of this limitation, the net amount of the trading gains or losses and preprovision net revenue in the table may be overstated or understated.

[b] PPNR includes an owned debt value adjustment of ($5.30) billion, which was not included as a stress in SCAP. As Morgan Stanley's credit spreads narrowed during 2009, this caused the liability values to increase. This offsets the gains Morgan Stanley experienced in 2008 when its credit spreads widened.

[c] PPNR includes one-time items totaling $710 million, which were not included in SCAP.

Table 25. PNC Financial Services Group, Inc.

Dollars in billions	Actual at 12/31/09	12/31/08 balance per SCAP	Difference	12/31/09 as a percent of the 12/31/08 balance
Tier 1 capital	$26.5	$24.1	$2.4	110.1%
Tier 1 common capital	$13.9	$11.7	$2.2	119.2%
Risk-weighted assets	$232.3	$250.9	$(18.6)	92.6%
Tier 1 risk based ratio	11.4%	9.6%	1.8%	119.0%
Tier 1 common capital ratio	6.0%	4.7%	1.3%	127.7%

	Actual for year ended 12/31/09	2-year SCAP Estimate	GAO 1-year pro rata estimate	Difference	Actual as a percent of the pro rata estimate
Total asset losses	**$2.7**	**$18.8**	**$9.4**	**$(6.6)**	**29.3%**
• First-lien mortgages	0.1	2.4	1.2	(1.1)	4.6
• Second/junior lien mortgages	0.4	4.6	2.3	(1.9)	19.4
• Commercial and industrial loans	0.9	3.2	1.6	(0.7)	57.8
• Commercial real estate loans	0.8	4.5	2.3	(1.5)	33.4
• Credit card loans	0.2	0.4	0.2	(0.0)	85.6
• Securities (available for sale and held to maturity)	0.0	1.3	0.7	(0.6)	4.2
• Trading and counterparty	-[a]	n/a	n/a	n/a	n/a
• Other	0.4	2.3	1.2	(0.8)	31.4
Resources other than capital to absorb losses (Total PPNR less change in ALLL):	**$6.2**	**$9.6**	**$4.8**	**$1.4**	**128.6%**
PPNR	$7.3[b]	-	-	-	-
• Net interest income expense)	9.1	-	-	-	-
• Noninterest income	7.9[a]	-	-	-	-
• Less: noninterest expense	9.6	-	-	-	-
Change in allowance for loan and lease losses (ALLL)	**$1.2**	-	-	-	-
• ALLL at 12/31/08	3.9	-	-	-	-
• ALLL at 12/31/09	5.1	-	-	-	-

Source: GAO analysis of Federal Reserve and SNL Financial data.

Note: N/a means not applicable.

[a] Trading and counterparty positions were not stressed because the total portfolio is less than the $100 billion required for stress testing in SCAP, but trading (gain) loss information for this BHC was included in the "trading revenue" line of Schedule HI of the Y-9C in 2009. In SCAP, the projections of trading gains or

losses for this BHC were included in the estimate of PPNR rather than the trading and counterparty line. Therefore, we have included the actual trading results in PPNR (specifically noninterest income).
[b] PPNR includes one-time items totaling $1.08 billion, which were not included in SCAP.

Table 26. Regions Financial Corporation

Dollars in billions	Actual at 12/31/09	12/31/08 balance per SCAP	Difference	12/31/09 as a percent of the 12/31/08 balance
Tier 1 capital	$11.9	$12.1	$(0.2)	98.5%
Tier 1 common capital	$7.4	$7.6	$(0.2)	97.2%
Risk-weighted assets	$103.3	$116.3	$(13.0)	88.8%
Tier 1 risk-based ratio	11.5%	10.4%	1.1%	111.0%
Tier 1 common capital ratio	7.1%	6.6%	0.5%	108.3%

	Actual for year ended 12/31/09	2-year SCAP estimate	GAO 1-year pro rata estimate	Difference	Actual as a percent of the pro rata estimate
Total asset losses	**$2.2**	**$9.2**	**$4.6**	**$(2.4)**	**48.8%**
• First-lien mortgages	0.2	1.0	0.5	(0.3)	36.7
• Second/junior lien mortgages	0.4	1.1	0.6	(0.2)	72.0
• Commercial and industrial loans	0.3	1.2	0.6	(0.3)	43.2
• Commercial real estate Loans	1.1	4.9	2.5	(1.3)	46.7
• Credit card loans	0.0	n/a	n/a	n/a	n/a
• Securities (available for sale and held to maturity)	(0.0)	0.2	0.1	(0.1)	(6.4)
• Trading and counterparty	-[a]	n/a	n/a	n/a	n/a
• Other	0.3	0.8	0.4	(0.1)	67.9
Resources other than capital to absorb losses (total PPNR less change in ALLL):	**$1.1**	**$3.3**	**$1.7**	**$(0.6)**	**64.9%**
PPNR	$2.4[b]	-	-	-	-
• Net interest income (expense)	3.3	-	-	-	-
• Noninterest income	3.5[a]	-	⌐	-	-
• Less: noninterest expense	4.5	-	-	-	-
Change in allowance for loan and lease losses (ALLL)	**$1.3**	-	-	-	-
• ALLL at 12/31/08	1.8	-	-	-	-
• ALLL at 12/31/09	3.1	-	-	-	-

Source: GAO analysis of Federal Reserve and SNL Financial data.
Note: N/a means not applicable.
[a] Trading and counterparty positions were not stressed because the total portfolio is less than the $100 billion required for stress testing in SCAP, but trading (gain) loss information for this BHC was included in the "trading revenue" line of Schedule HI of the Y-9C in 2009. In SCAP, the projections of trading gains or losses for this BHC were included in the estimate of PPNR rather than the trading and counterparty line. Therefore, we have included the actual trading results in PPNR (specifically noninterest income).
[b] PPNR includes one-time items totaling $140 million, which were not included in SCAP.

Table 27. State Street Corporation

Dollars in billions	Actual at 12/31/09	12/31/08 balance per SCAP	Difference	12/31/09 as a percent of the 12/31/08 balance
Tier 1 capital	$12.0	$14.1	$(2.1)	85.1%
Tier 1 common capital	$10.6	$10.8	$(0.2)	97.7%
Risk-weighted assets	$67.7	$69.6	$(1.9)	97.3%
Tier 1 risk-based ratio	17.7%	20.2%	(2.5)%	87.8%
Tier 1 common capital ratio	15.6%	15.5%	0.1%	100.6%

	Actual for year ended 12/31/09	2-year SCAP estimate	GAO 1-year pro rata estimate	Difference	Actual as a percent of the pro ata estimate
Total asset losses	**$(0.1)**	**$2.2**	**$1.1**	**$(1.2)**	**(4.7)%**
• First-lien mortgages	0.0	n/a	n/a	n/a	n/a
• Second/junior lien mortgages	0.0	n/a	n/a	n/a	n/a
• Commercial and industrial Loans	0.0	0.0	0.0	(0.0)	0.0
• Commercial real estate loans	0.1	0.3	0.2	(0.1)	46.5
• Credit card loans	0.0	n/a	n/a	n/a	n/a
• Securities (available for sale and held to maturity)	(0.1)	1.8	0.9	(1.0)	-15.6
• Trading and counterparty	-[a]	n/a	n/a	n/a	n/a
• Other	0.0	0.1	0.1	(0.0)	37.5
• One-time items in SCAP[b]	$6.1	$5.9	n/a	$0.2	103.4%
Resources other than capital to absorb losses (total PPNR less change in ALLL):	**$2.5**	**$4.3**	**$2.2**	**$0.3**	**115.1%**
PPNR	**$2.5**	-	-	-	-
• Net interest income (expense)	2.6	-	-	-	-
• Noninterest income	5.9[a]	-	-	-	-
• Less: noninterest expense	6.0	-	-	-	-
Change in allowance for loan and lease losses (ALLL)	**$0.1**	-	-	-	-
• ALLL at 12/31/08	0.0	-	-	-	-
• ALLL at 12/31/09	0.1	-	-	-	-

Source: GAO analysis of Federal Reserve and SNL Financial data.

Note: N/a means not applicable.

[a] Trading and counterparty positions were not stressed because the total portfolio is less than the $100 billion required for stress testing in SCAP, but trading (gain) loss information for this BHC was included in the "trading revenue" line of Schedule HI of the Y-9C in 2009. In SCAP, the projections of trading gains or losses for this BHC were included in the estimate of PPNR rather than the trading and counterparty line. Therefore, we have included the actual trading results in PPNR (specifically noninterest income)

[b] We broke out "other" losses into two categories—"Other" and "One-time items." As discussed in State Street Corporation's (State Street) May 7, 2009, press release, $5.9 billion of the amount listed in the "Other" category in the SCAP results was a pretax charge that was expected to occur when certain asset-backed commercial paper conduits administered by State Street were consolidated onto its balance sheet in 2009. Since this was a one-time charge that was realized in 2009, this effect was segregated from more typical loss amounts for tracking purposes. Upon consolidation, the actual amount realized was $6.1 billion, as reported in State Street's Form 10-Q for the second quarter of 2009.

Table 28. SunTrust Banks, Inc.

Dollars in billions	Actual at 12/31/09	12/31/08 balance per SCAP	Difference	12/31/09 as a percent of the 12/31/08 balance
Tier 1 capital	$18.1	$17.6	$0.5	102.7%
Tier 1 common capital	$10.7	$9.4	$1.3	113.7%
Risk-weighted assets	$139.4	$162.0	$(22.6)	86.0%
Tier 1 risk-based ratio	13.0%	10.9%	2.1%	118.9%
Tier 1 common capital ratio	7.7%	5.8%	1.9%	132.3%

	Actual for year ended 12/31/09	2-year SCAP estimate	GAO 1-year pro rata estimate	Difference	Actual as a percent of the pro rata estimate
Total asset losses	**$3.1**	**$11.8**	**$5.9**	**$(2.8)**	**53.1%**
• First-lien mortgages	1.1	2.2	1.1	0.0	101.5
• Second/junior lien mortgages	0.8	3.1	1.6	(0.8)	48.8
• Commercial and industrial loans	0.5	1.5	0.8	(0.2)	69.9
• Commercial real estate loans	0.6	2.8	1.4	(0.8)	39.8
• Credit card loans	0.1	0.1	0.1	0.0	115.3
• Securities (available for sale and held to maturity)	(0.1)	0.0	0.0	(0.1)	(980.2)
• Trading and counterparty	-[a]	n/a	n/a	n/a	n/a
• Other	0.2	2.1	1.1	(0.8)	21.6
Resources other than capital to absorb losses (total PPNR less change in ALLL):	**$1.4**	**$4.7**	**$2.4**	**$(0.9)**	**61.3%**
PPNR	$2.2[b,c]	-	-	-	-
• Net interest income (expense)	4.5	-	-	-	-
• Noninterest income	3.6[a]	-	-	-	-
• Less: noninterest expense	5.9	-	-	-	-
Change in allowance for loan and lease losses (ALLL)	**$0.8**	-	-	-	-
• ALLL at 12/31/08	2.4	-	-	-	-
• ALLL at 12/31/09	3.1	-	-	-	-

Source: GAO analysis of Federal Reserve and SNL Financial data.

Note: N/a means not applicable.

[a] Trading and counterparty positions were not stressed because the total portfolio is less than the $100 billion required for stress testing in SCAP, but trading (gain) loss information for this BHC was included in the "trading revenue" line of Schedule HI of the Y-9C in 2009. In SCAP, the projections of trading gains or losses for this BHC were included in the estimate of PPNR rather than the trading and counterparty line. Therefore, we have included the actual trading results in PPNR (specifically noninterest income).

[b] PPNR includes an owned debt value adjustment of ($150) million, which was not stressed in SCAP. As SunTrust Banks Inc.'s credit spreads narrowed during 2009, this caused the liability values to increase. This offsets the gains SunTrust experienced in 2008 when its credit spreads widened.

[c] PPNR includes one-time items totaling $110 million, which were not included in SCAP.

Table 29. U.S. Bancorp

Dollars in billions	Actual at 12/31/09	12/31/08 balance per SCAP	Difference	as a percent of the 12/31/08
Tier 1 capital	$22.6	$24.4	$(1.8)	92.7%
Tier 1 common capital	$15.9	$11.8	$4.1	134.7%
Risk-weighted assets	$235.2	$230.6	$4.6	102.0%
Tier 1 risk-based ratio	9.6%	10.6%	(1.0)%	90.7%
Tier 1 common capital ratio	6.8%	5.1%	1.7%	132.5%

	Actual for year ended 12/31/09	2-year SCAP estimate	GAO 1-year pro rata estimate	Difference	Actual as a percent of the pro rata estimate
Total asset losses	**$4.3**	**$15.7**	**$8.0**	**$(3.6)**	**54.3%**
• First-lien mortgages	0.5	1.8	0.9	(0.4)	54.3
• Second/junior lien Mortgages	0.3	1.7	0.9	(0.5)	39.8
• Commercial and industrial loans	0.6	2.3	1.2	(0.6)	50.9
• Commercial real estate loans	0.6	3.2	1.6	(1.0)	38.6
• Credit card loans	1.0	2.8	1.4	(0.4)	73.6
• Securities (available for Sale and held to maturity)	0.5	1.3	0.7	(0.2)	69.4
• Trading and counterparty	-[a]	n/a	n/a	n/a	n/a
• Other	0.8	2.8	1.4	(0.6)	57.7
Resources other than capital to absorb losses (total PPNR less change in ALLL):	**$7.1**	**$13.7**	**$6.9**	**$0.2**	**103.3%**
PPNR	**$8.6**	-	-	-	-
• Net interest income (expense)	8.5	-	-	-	-
• Noninterest income	8.4[a]	-	-	-	-
• Less: noninterest expense	8.3	-	-	-	-
Change in allowance for loan and lease losses (ALLL)	**$1.6**	-	-	-	-
• ALLL at 12/31/08	3.5	-	-	-	-
• ALLL at 12/31/09	5.1	-	-	-	-

Source: GAO analysis of Federal Reserve and SNL Financial data.

Note: N/a means not applicable.

[a] Trading and counterparty positions were not stressed because the total portfolio is less than the $100 billion required for stress testing in SCAP, but trading (gain) loss information for this BHC was included in the "trading revenue" line of Schedule HI of the Y-9C in 2009. In SCAP, the projections of trading gains or losses for this BHC were included in the estimate of PPNR rather than the trading and counterparty line. Therefore, we have included the actual trading results in PPNR (specifically noninterest income).

Table 30. Wells Fargo & Company

Dollars in billions	Actual at 12/31/09	12/31/08 balance per SCAP	Difference	12/31/09 as a percent of the 12/31/08 balance
Tier 1 capital	$93.8	$86.4	$7.4	108.6%
Tier 1 common capital	$65.5[a]	$33.9	$31.6	193.2%
Risk-weighted assets	$1,013.6	$1,082.3	$(68.7)	93.7%
Tier 1 risk-based ratio	9.3%	8.0%	1.3%	115.7%
Tier 1 common capital ratio	6.5%	3.1%	3.4%	208.4%

	Actual for year ended 12/31/09	2-year SCAP estimate	GAO 1-year pro rata estimate	Difference	Actual as a percent of the pro rata estimate
Total asset losses	**$18.0**	**$86.1**	**$43.1**	**$(25.1)**	**41.7%**
• First-lien mortgages	3.0	32.4	16.2	(13.2)	18.4
• Second/junior lien mortgages	4.9	14.7	7.4	(2.5)	66.1
• Commercial and industrial loans	2.8	9.0	4.5	(1.7)	61.5
• Commercial real estate loans	1.5	8.4	4.2	(2.7)	35.8
• Credit card loans	2.6	6.1	3.1	(0.5)	83.7
• Securities (available for sale and held to maturity)	(0.2)	4.2	,	(2.3)	(9.8)
• Trading and counterparty	-[b]	n/a	n/a	n/a	n/a
• Other	3.5	11.3	5.7	(2.1)	62.1
Resources other than capital to absorb losses (total PPNR less change in ALLL):	**$36.1**	**$60.0**	**$30.0**	**$6.1**	**120.5%**
PPNR	**$39.6**	-	-	-	-
• Net interest income (expense)	46.9	-	-	-	-
• Noninterest income	41.5[b]	-	-	-	-
• Less: noninterest expense	48.8	-	-	-	-
Change in allowance for loan and lease losses (ALLL)	**$3.5**	-	-	-	-
• ALLL at 12/31/08	21.0	-	-	-	-
• ALLL at 12/31/09	24.5	-	-	-	-

Source: GAO analysis of Federal Reserve and SNL Financial data.

Note: N/a means not applicable.

[a] The tier 1 common calculation has been adjusted to provide for appropriate treatment of preferred shares Wells Fargo & Company (Wells Fargo) issued as a part of its Employee Stock Ownership Plan (ESOP). Each share of ESOP preferred stock released from the unallocated reserve of the 401(k) plan is converted into shares of Wells Fargo's common stock based on the stated value of the ESOP preferred stock and the current market price of Wells Fargo's common stock. Wells Fargo sells ESOP preferred stock to its 401(k) plan and lends the 401(k) plan cash to purchase those shares. The loan is recorded as "Unearned ESOP Preferred Shares." While the ESOP preferred shares are counted as an addition to equity, the loans recorded as Unearned ESOP Preferred Shares are treated as a reduction to equity, and so there is no net impact on the equity accounts (including tier 1 capital). However, the tier 1 common capital calculation removes the ESOP preferred shares without also removing the corresponding loans recorded as Unearned ESOP Preferred Shares. After consulting with Wells Fargo, GAO adjusted the tier 1 common capital calculation by removing the $442 million of Unearned ESOP Preferred Shares outstanding as of December 31, 2009 (the Unearned ESOP Preferred Shares is a negative amount; thus, removing this item leads to the addition of $442 million in tier 1 capital), which is consistent with SCAP's treatment.

[b] Trading and counterparty positions were not stressed because the total portfolio is less than the $100 billion required for stress testing in SCAP, but trading (gain) loss information for this BHC was included in the

"trading revenue" line of Schedule HI of the Y-9C in 2009. In SCAP, the projections of trading gains or losses for this BHC were included in the estimate of PPNR rather than the trading and counterparty line. Therefore, we have included the actual trading results in PPNR (specifically noninterest income).

APPENDIX IV. COMMENTS FROM THE BOARD OF GOVERNORS OF THE FEDERAL RESERVE SYSTEM

BOARD OF GOVERNORS
OF THE
FEDERAL RESERVE SYSTEM
WASHINGTON, D. C. 20551

BEN S. BERNANKE
CHAIRMAN

September 27, 2010

Ms. Orice M. Williams
Director
Financial Markets and Community Investment
Government Accountability Office
441 G Street, NW
Washington, D.C. 20548

Dear Ms. Williams:

The Supervisory Capital Assessment Program (SCAP) was a very successful program that helped to restore confidence in the banking system by assessing the potential capital needs of the largest bank holding companies under a scenario of an economic environment that was more adverse than anticipated at the time. The program resulted in significant additional capital being raised by the banking industry and provided the public with assurance that these very large and complex institutions would remain viable even in the face of more severely negative economic conditions.

The Government Accountability Office's (GAO's) report "Bank Stress Test Offers Lesson as Regulators Take Further Actions to Strengthen Supervisory Oversight," GAO-10-861, recognizes the success of the SCAP and recommends five ways to build on those successes. These recommendations relate to actions the Federal Reserve already is undertaking, either on its own initiative or as part of the implementation of the Dodd-Frank Wall Street Reform and Consumer Protection Act of 2010 (Dodd-Frank Act).

Recommendation One: The Chairman of the Federal Reserve should direct the Division of Banking Supervision and Regulation to compare the performance of the 19 bank holding companies against the more adverse scenario projections following the completion of the two-year period covered in the SCAP exercise ending December 31, 2010, and disclose the results of the analysis to the public.

As we have noted in the past, the size and character of the bank holding companies has, in many cases, changed materially over the interim period, making before-and-after comparisons difficult and potentially misleading. In addition, the SCAP process was not designed as a tool for measuring bank holding company performance over the course of the 2009 to 2010 period, but rather was designed to estimate the potential capital needs of bank holding companies under a more-adverse–than-anticipated

Ms. Orice M. Williams
September 27, 2010
Page 2

economic environment and during a very turbulent time for the economy in early 2009.
Given that the SCAP was designed to estimate potential losses and resulting capital needs
in a worse-than-anticipated scenario, measuring performance against the estimates may
imply an attempt to test the accuracy of these estimates. By design, the SCAP used
estimates of potential losses in a scenario that has not materialized, and thus would not be
expected to accurately reflect the BHC's losses and overall operating performance over
the two-year period ending at year-end 2010. With these important considerations and
limitations in mind, the Federal Reserve intends to provide a public assessment of the
performance of the firms relative to the loss and pre-provision net revenue estimates
under the "more adverse scenario" used in the SCAP. The Federal Reserve will
coordinate with the Federal Deposit Insurance Corporation (FDIC) and the Office of the
Comptroller of the Currency (OCC) on this assessment, as well as on designing the
specifics of what will be publicly reported.

**Recommendation Two: That the Chairman of the Federal Reserve, in consultation
with the heads of the FDIC and OCC, should develop a plan that reconciles
divergent views on transparency and allows for increased transparency in the
regular supervisory process, specifically addressing steps for releasing supervisory
methodologies and analytical results for stress testing.**

The recently passed Dodd-Frank Act requires annual stress tests for certain
financial institutions and further requires the disclosure of certain stress test results. The
Dodd-Frank Act also requires the federal regulatory agencies, including the Federal
Reserve, FDIC, and OCC, to develop consistent and comparable regulations governing
the publications of the results of these required stress tests. The Federal Reserve will
coordinate with the other agencies in the development of these regulations. In addition,
the Federal Reserve will continue to examine options for increasing the information that
supervisors may make valuable.

**Recommendation Three: That the Chairman of the Federal Reserve, in
consultation with the heads of the FDIC and OCC, should develop more specific
criteria to include in its guidance to examiners for assessing the quality of stress
tests that are used in firms' internal capital assessment and capital planning
processes, and for how these tests inform bank holding companies' internal capital
adequacy assessments and capital planning.**

The Federal Reserve is in the process of developing guidance for its examiners
regarding the assessment of stress testing procedures. Once the guidance is completed it
will be supplemented in a manner that is consistent with this recommendation. For
purposes of sharing best practices and carrying out the Dodd-Frank Act, the Federal
Reserve will continue to consult with the FDIC and OCC regarding general principles,
common to all supervisors, to guide regulatory agencies when evaluating stress testing.

Ms. Orice M. Williams
September 27, 2010
Page 3

Recommendation Four: That the Chairman of the Federal Reserve, in consultation with the heads of the FDIC and OCC, should fully develop the Federal Reserve's plan for maintaining and improving the use of data, risk identification and assessment infrastructure, and requisite systems consistent with new responsibilities under the Dodd-Frank Act, and should disseminate these enhancements among the Federal Reserve System and other regulators and new organizations established under the Dodd-Frank Act.

As the recommendation suggests, the Federal Reserve has taken a number of steps to enhance risk identification, including data collection and dissemination.

The Federal Reserve will continue to consult with the FDIC and OCC on best practices in the areas of risk assessment and data collection and sharing, and will ensure the continued dissemination of these improvements throughout the Federal Reserve System. The Federal Reserve will also continue to provide information about these enhancements to other regulators and, as appropriate, to new organizations established by the Dodd-Frank Act.

Recommendation Five: That the Chairman of the Federal Reserve, in consultation with the heads of the FDIC and OCC, should take further steps to more effectively coordinate and communicate multiagency activities.

As noted in the GAO report, the SCAP process is considered by many to be an example of effective inter-agency coordination and communication in relation to a multiagency activity, but it should be noted that it is simply the most public example. The agencies coordinate on supervisory issues on a daily basis and have done so for many years. The Federal Reserve believes these consultations result in more effective and uniform supervisory practices and will continue its practice of consulting with the FDIC and OCC, especially in the context of implementation of the Dodd-Frank Act.

Sincerely,

APPENDIX V. COMMENTS FROM THE DEPARTMENT OF THE TREASURY'S OFFICE OF FINANCIAL STABILITY

DEPARTMENT OF THE TREASURY
WASHINGTON, D.C. 20220

ASSISTANT SECRETARY

September 14, 2010

Thomas J. McCool
Director, Center for Economics
Applied Research and Methods
U.S. Government Accountability Office
441 G Street, N.W.
Washington, D.C. 20548

Dear Mr. McCool:

Thank you for providing the Department of the Treasury ("Treasury") an opportunity to review and comment on your recent report on the Troubled Asset Relief Program ("TARP") titled, *Bank Stress Test Offers Lessons as Regulators Take Further Actions to Strengthen Supervisory Oversight* ("Draft Report").

Treasury appreciates the GAO's comprehensive review of the Supervisory Capital Assessment Program ("SCAP") and its acknowledgement that SCAP met its goals of providing a comprehensive, forward-looking assessment of risk on the balance sheets of our largest banks. By doing so with unprecedented transparency, the SCAP strengthened market confidence in the banking system and led to significant increase in the level and quality of capital held by the largest banks. The GAO issued no recommendations to Treasury in the Draft Report.

Treasury looks forward to reviewing the final audit report when issued. We thank you again for your diligence and continuing work in reviewing Treasury's efforts to stabilize the financial system.

Sincerely,

Herbert M. Allison, Jr.
Assistant Secretary for Financial Stability

End Notes

[1] Treasury, *Financial Stability Plan* (Feb. 10, 2009). SCAP was a key component of the Capital Assistance Program.

[2] The other federal banking regulators involved in SCAP were the Federal Deposit Insurance Corporation and the Office of the Comptroller of the Currency. The Office of Thrift Supervision did not participate. The Federal Reserve led the SCAP stress test since it is the primary federal bank regulator for bank holding companies.

[3] The 19 BHCs each had at least $100 billion in risk-weighted assets as of December 31, 2008, meeting the established threshold for required participation in the SCAP stress test. Risk-weighted assets are the total assets and off-balance sheet items, adjusted for risks that institutions hold. A BHC is a company that owns or controls one or more banks or one that owns or controls one or more BHCs. See 12 U.S.C. § 1841(a). Since a BHC may also own another BHC, which in turn owns or controls a bank, the company at the top of the ownership chain is commonly called the top holder. The Federal Reserve is responsible for regulating and supervising BHCs, even if the bank owned by the holding company is under the primary supervision of a different federal banking agency. For example, the Federal Reserve is responsible for regulating and supervising Citigroup Inc. (the BHC) and the Office of the Comptroller of the Currency is responsible for regulating and supervising Citibank N.A. (the main bank in the holding company structure).

[4] Capital is a source of long-term funding, contributed largely by a bank's equity stockholders and its own returns in the form of retained earnings that provides banks with a cushion to absorb unexpected losses. A stress test is a "what-if" scenario that is not a prediction or expected outcome of the economy.

[5] GAO is required to report at least every 60 days on TARP activities and performance. TARP was authorized under the Emergency Economic Stabilization Act of 2008 (EESA), Pub. L. No. 110-343, 122 Stat. 3765 (2008), codified at 12 U.S.C. §§ 5201 et seq. EESA originally authorized Treasury to purchase or guarantee up to $700 billion in troubled assets. The Helping Families Save Their Homes Act of 2009, Pub. L. No. 111-22, Div. A, 123 Stat. 1632 (2009), codified at 12 U.S.C. § 5225(a)(3), amended ESSA to reduce the maximum allowable amount of outstanding troubled assets under ESSA by almost $1.3 billion, from $700 billion to $698.741 billion.

[6] 12 U.S.C. § 5226.

[7] GAO, *Troubled Asset Relief Program: June 2009 Status of Efforts to Address Transparency and Accountability Issues*, GAO-09-658 (Washington, D.C.: June 2009).

[8] Percent change in the annual average of real GDP. GDP is defined as the total market value of goods and services produced domestically during a given period (i.e., one year).

[9] Financial institutions that were not subject to the stress test could, after supervisory review, also apply for capital from CAP if they were in need of additional capital.

[10] Common stock is a security that represents ownership in a company and gives the stockholder the right to vote for the company's board of directors and benefit from its financial success. Noncumulative perpetual preferred stock is a security that has no fixed maturity date and pays its stated dividend forever or "in perpetuity," but any unpaid dividends do not accumulate or accrue to stockholders.

[11] In general, tier 1 common capital is voting common equity subject to certain deductions from capital.

[12] For example, to be well-capitalized under Federal Reserve definitions, on a consolidated basis, a BHC must have a tier 1 risk-based capital ratio of at least 6 percent of total risk-weighted assets, among other things, 12 C.F.R. § 225.2(r)(1)(ii).

[13] PPNR is defined as net interest income plus noninterest income minus noninterest expense.

[14] Trading book positions and counterparty exposures were stress tested as of February 20, 2009.

[15] These statements became effective on January 1, 2010, and require banking organizations to bring onto their balance sheets off-balance sheet positions. However, for regulatory purposes, the BHCs and other institutions may defer bringing such positions onto their balance sheets until the end of 2010.

[16] Subprime mortgages are mortgages granted to borrowers whose credit history includes significant impairments resulting in lower credit scores.

[17] For a more detailed discussion about risk management practices in place during the market turmoil, see the following reports: Senior Supervisors Group, *Observations on Risk Management Practices during the Recent Market Turbulence* (New York, Mar. 6, 2008); The President's Working Group on Financial Markets, *Policy Statement on Financial Market Developments* (March 2008); International Monetary Fund, *Global Financial Stability Report: Containing Systemic Risk and Restoring Financial Soundness* (Washington, D.C., April 2008); Financial Stability Forum, *Report of the Financial Stability Forum on Enhancing Market and Institutional Resilience* (April 2008); Institute of International Finance, *Final Report of the IIF Committee on Market Best Practices: Principles of Conduct and Best Practice Recommendations* (July 2008); Credit Risk Management Policy Group III, *Containing Systemic Risk: The Road to Reform* (August 2008); and Senior Supervisors Group, *Risk Management Lessons from the Global Banking Crisis of 2008* (Oct. 21, 2009).

[18] The Basel Committee seeks to improve the quality of banking supervision worldwide, in part by developing broad supervisory standards. The Basel Committee consists of central bank and regulatory officials from 27 member

countries. The Basel Committee's supervisory standards are also often adopted by nonmember countries. See Basel Committee on Banking Supervision, *Principles for Sound Stress Testing Practices and Supervision.* (Basel, Switzerland, May 2009).

[19] Regulators used the Case-Shiller 10-City Composite index to forecast changes in housing prices.

[20] The unemployment rate is the number of jobless people who are available for work but not currently employed and are actively seeking jobs, expressed as a percentage of the labor force.

[21] According to the Federal Reserve's SCAP design and implementation document, the professionals are the Consensus Forecasts, Blue Chip survey, and Survey of Professional Forecasters.

[22] ALLL is the capital reserve set aside to cover anticipated losses.

[23] Resources available to absorb losses is defined as PPNR less the change in ALLL from December 31, 2008, to December 31, 2010.

[24] Financial Accounting Standards Board position numbers 115-2 and 124-2 focus on whether firms with debt securities held in the available for sale and held to maturity accounts intended or would be required to sell securities at a lower price than its cost basis. Generally accepted accounting principles are a widely accepted set of rules, conventions, standards, and procedures for reporting financial information established by the Financial Accounting Standards Board.

[25] Other than temporarily impaired write down is measured as the difference between a security's book value and market value.

[26] See Financial Accounting Statements No. 166 and 167.

[27] In its June 2009 SCAP analysis report, the Congressional Oversight Panel also noted that there was a lack of transparency about the linkage between the loan losses and the three macroeconomic assumptions.

[28] According to the Federal Reserve, legacy loans refer to those bank loans made during the 2005 to 2007 period. Underwriting standards refer to guidelines used by lenders to ensure that loans meet credit standards and that the terms and conditions of a loan are appropriate to its risk and maturity.

[29] Loss rate ranges under the more adverse scenario were later tailored to each BHC.

[30] Other forms of raising capital included the use of deferred tax assets (DTA), employee stock option awards, and restriction on dividend payments. A DTA represents the amount by which taxes can be reduced in future years as a result of temporary tax differences for financial reporting and tax reporting purposes. DTAs are includable as tier 1 capital up to no more than 10 percent of a BHC's tier 1 capital.

[31] The SCAP results required GMAC to raise a total of $11.5 billion in capital, of which $9.1 billion had to be in new equity capital. On May 21, 2009, Treasury made a capital investment of $3.5 billion in GMAC via the TARP Automotive Industry Financing Program to be applied as a down payment towards GMAC's SCAP capital buffer of $9.1 billion in new equity capital. GMAC had to raise the remaining amount of $5.6 billion by the November 9, 2009, deadline from either the private markets or through further Treasury assistance. In December 2009, Treasury converted its existing $5.25 billion of preferred stock into mandatorily convertible preferred stock and converted $3 billion of existing GMAC mandatorily convertible preferred securities into common equity that allowed GMAC to meet its total SCAP capital requirement of $11.5 billion.

[32] The Automotive Industry Financing Program was created in December 2008 by Treasury under TARP to prevent a significant disruption of the American automotive industry. Treasury determined that such a disruption would pose a systemic risk to financial market stability and have a negative effect on the U.S. economy.

[33] Tier 1 common capital ratio equals tier 1 common capital divided by total risk-weighted assets.

[34] Tier 1 risk-based capital ratio equals tier 1 capital divided by total risk-weighted assets.

[35] A basis point is a common measure used in quoting yields on bills, notes, and bonds and represents 1/100 of a percent of yield. For example, an increase from 4.35 percent to 4.45 percent would be an increase of 10 basis points.

[36] GMAC is the only nonpublic BHC that was included in SCAP.

[37] The asset categories are first-lien mortgages consisting of prime, Alt-A, and subprime residential mortgages; second/junior lien mortgages consisting of closed-end junior liens and home equity line of credit residential mortgages; commercial and industrial loans consisting of large corporate and middle market, small business, and asset-based lending loans; commercial real estate loans consisting of construction and land development, multifamily, and nonfarm nonresidential loans; credit card loans, consisting of credit cards; other loans consisting of auto, personal, and student loans, and farmland lending, loans to depository institutions, loans to governments, and other categories; securities (available for sale and held to maturity) consisting of a majority of Treasury securities, government agency securities, sovereign debt, and high-grade municipal securities and corporate bonds, equities, asset-backed securities, commercial mortgage-backed securities, and nonagency residential mortgage-backed securities; and trading and counterparty, or trading book positions (e.g., securities such as common stock and derivatives).

[38] As of September 22, 2010, Treasury has a 56.3 percent ownership stake in GMAC.

[39] General Motors Company and Chrysler Group LLC are the new names that the former GM and Chrysler adopted, respectively, after emerging from bankruptcy.

[40] The Federal Reserve approved GMAC's application to become a BHC on December 24, 2008.

[41] Lifetime losses are those losses which occur from origination to the life-end of the loans.

[42] According to an April 12, 2010, GMAC press release, GMAC's mortgage subsidiary—Residential Capital, LLC—agreed to sell its European mortgage assets and businesses to Fortress Investment Group LLC. These transactions represent approximately 10 percent of Residential Capital, LLC's December 31, 2009, total assets and approximately 40 percent of total assets on a pro forma basis, adjusted for the required accounting treatment for certain off-balance sheet securitizations that are recorded on-balance sheet effective January 1, 2010, (see Financial Accounting Statement No. 167). The assets in the transactions are valued at approximately the levels established in the fourth quarter of 2009, and there is no material gain or loss expected. GMAC reported positive earnings for the first and second quarters of 2010, although it continued to show losses in certain portfolios. These were its first profits since the fourth quarter of 2008. GMAC's tier 1 common capital ratio also improved to 5 percent and 5.2 percent, respectively.

[43] Trading account assets are assets held to hedge risks or speculate on price changes for the bank or its customers. Because the more adverse scenario was plausible but unlikely to occur, the actual results were not intended and should not be expected to align with such scenario.

[44] The five BHCs are The Bank of New York Mellon Corporation; Citigroup; MetLife, Inc.; SunTrust; and U.S. Bancorp.

[45] Based on discussion with The Bank of New York Mellon Corporation officials and as stated in a October 20, 2009, company press release, the BHC's securities portfolio underwent a significant restructuring in the third quarter of 2009 in order to reduce its balance sheet risk, causing it to recognize significant losses in that period. The officials noted that the BHC sold off many of its riskiest holdings in that period, including many Alt-A residential mortgage-backed securities, so that they expect to see gains in this portfolio in the future, keeping the final 2-year loss under the SCAP projected amount. As of the second quarter of 2010 year to date, the BHC experienced a gain of $20 million in this portfolio.

[46] A counterparty loss is a loss resulting from a counterparty to a transaction failing to fulfill its financial obligation in a timely manner or from a credit valuation adjustment.

[47] These BHCs include Bank of America, Citigroup, Goldman Sachs, JPMorgan Chase & Co., and Morgan Stanley were stress tested in SCAP.

[48] Limitations of the Y-9C make it difficult to compare the actual results to the projections of SCAP. The trading and counterparty data in the Y-9C includes both customer derived revenue from transactions for BHCs that operate as broker-dealers, as well as gains and losses from proprietary trading and associated expenses. These items are presented on a net basis in the Y-9C. For the five BHCs that had their trading portfolios stressed (Goldman Sachs, Morgan Stanley, Citigroup, JPMorgan Chase & Co., and Bank of America), the trading and counterparty line item is based on projections of gains or losses from proprietary trading, but preprovision net revenue (specifically noninterest revenue) included projections of gains or losses from customer derived revenue from transactions due to operations as a broker-dealer. These items cannot be segregated based on the Y-9C data and therefore are included in the net amount in both the trading and counterparty and noninterest income line items above. As a result of this limitation, the net amount of the trading gains or losses and preprovision net revenue in the table may be over- or understated.

[49] In 2008, Lehman Brothers Holdings Inc. failed, Merrill Lynch & Co. Inc. was acquired by Bank of America, and The Bear Stearns Companies Inc. was sold to JP Morgan Chase & Co.

[50] Wholesale funding describes a class of funding used by banks to meet their liquidity needs. Wholesale funding providers include, but are not limited to, money market funds, trust funds, pension funds, corporations, banks, government agencies, and insurance companies. Wholesale funding instruments include, but are not limited to, federal funds, public funds, Federal Home Loan Bank advances, the Federal Reserve's primary credit program, foreign deposits, brokered deposits, and deposits obtained through the Internet or certificate of deposits listing services.

[51] Nonperforming loans, for the purposes of this figure, represent the total of loans that are either 90 plus days past due or in nonaccrual status. As defined by the instructions to the Y-9C, an asset is in nonaccrual status if: (1) it is maintained on a cash basis because of deterioration in the financial condition of the borrower, (2) payment in full of principal or interest is not expected, or (3) principal or interest as been in default for a period of 90 days or more unless the asset is both well secured and in the process of collection. Per the Y-9C instructions, an asset is 90 plus days past due if payment is due and unpaid for 90 days or more, and if that asset is not in nonaccrual status.

[52] Pub. L. No. 111-203, 124 Stat. 1376 (2010); Pub. L. No. 111-24, 123 Stat. 1734 (2009).

[53] Ben S. Bernanke, "The Supervisory Capital Assessment Program—One Year Later," speech delivered at the Federal Reserve Bank of Chicago 2010 46th Annual Conference on Bank Structure and Competition (Chicago, Illinois, May 6, 2010). Daniel K. Tarullo, "Lessons from the Crisis Stress Tests," speech delivered at the Federal Reserve Board 2010 International Research Forum on Monetary Policy (Washington, D.C., Mar. 26, 2010).

[54] Daniel K. Tarullo, "Involving Markets and the Public in Financial Regulation," speech delivered at the Council of Institutional Investors Meeting (Washington, D.C., Apr. 13, 2010). Bernanke "The Supervisory Capital Assessment Program—One Year Later" (2010).

[55] GAO, *Troubled Asset Relief Program: June 2009 Status of Efforts to Address Transparency and Accountability Issues*, GAO-09-658 (Washington, D.C.: June 17, 2009).

[56] The act also establishes the Financial Stability Oversight Council and Treasury's Office of Financial Research in order to further the goals of effective systemic risk measurement

[57] GAO, *Financial Regulation: Review of Regulators' Oversight of Risk Management System at a Limited Number of Large, Complex Financial Institutions*, GAO-09-499T (Washington, D.C.: Mar. 18, 2009).

[58] Basel II is an international risk-based capital framework that aims to align minimum capital requirements with enhanced risk measurement techniques and to encourage banks to develop a more disciplined approach to risk management. It was organized with three main principles of capital known as pillars: Pillar 1 relates to minimum capital requirements. Pillar 2 relates to the supervisory review of an institution's internal assessment process and capital adequacy relative to the institution's overall risk profile. Pillar 3 relates to the effective use of disclosure to strengthen market discipline as a complement to supervisory efforts.

[59] These portfolios were the only ones tested under the SCAP for which the positions were taken as of a different date than December 31, 2008. Positions were taken as of February 20, 2009, as it was both more relevant to the actual risk exposure of the BHCs at the time of SCAP and easier for the BHCs to provide.

[60] GAO, *Financial Market Regulation: Agencies Engaged in Consolidated Supervision Can Strengthen Performance Measurement and Collaboration*, GAO-07-154 (Washington, D.C.: Mar. 15, 2007).

[61] The Y-9C is a Federal Reserve reporting form that collects basic financial data from a domestic BHC on a consolidated basis in the form of a balance sheet, an income statement, and detailed supporting schedules, including a schedule of off balance-sheet items. The information is used to assess and monitor the financial condition of BHC organizations, which may include parent, bank, and nonbank entities. The Y-9C is a primary analytical tool used to monitor financial institutions between on-site inspections and is filed quarterly as of the last calendar day of March, June, September, and December. The Federal Reserve used such format to collect data from the BHCs for purposes of conducting the SCAP stress test.

[62] For a more detailed discussion about risk-management practices in place during the market turmoil, see the following reports: Senior Supervisors Group, *Observations on Risk Management Practices during the Recent Market Turbulence* (New York, Mar. 6, 2008); International Monetary Fund, *Global Financial Stability Report: Containing Systemic Risk and Restoring Financial Soundness* (Washington, D.C.: April 2008); Financial Stability Forum, *Report of the Financial Stability Forum on Enhancing Market and Institutional Resilience* (April 2008); Institute of International Finance, *Final Report of the IIF Committee on Market Best Practices: Principles of Conduct and Best Practice Recommendations* (July 2008); Credit Risk Management Policy Group III, *Containing Systemic Risk: The Road to Reform* (August 2008); Senior Supervisors Group, *Risk Management Lessons from the Global Banking Crisis of 2008* (Oct. 21, 2009); Basel Committee on Banking Supervision, *Principles for Sound Stress Testing Practices and Supervision* (Basel, Switzerland, May 2009); and the President's Working Group on Financial Markets, *Policy Statement on Financial Market Developments* (March 2008).

[63] The Office of the Thrift Supervision did not participate in conducting the stress test.

[64] On June 30, 2009, GMAC LLC changed its corporate structure and became GMAC Inc., and on May 10, 2010, GMAC Inc. changed its name to Ally Financial Inc.

[65] See GAO, *Financial Market Regulation: Agencies Engaged in Consolidated Supervision Can Strengthen Performance Measurement and Collaboration*, GAO-07-154 (Washington, D.C.: Mar. 15, 2007); *Financial Regulation: A Framework for Crafting and Assessing Proposals to Modernize the Outdated U.S. Financial Regulatory System*, GAO-09-216 (Washington, D.C.: Jan. 8, 2009); *Financial Regulation: Review of Regulators' Oversight of Risk Management Systems at a Limited Number of Large, Complex Financial Institutions*, GAO-09-499T (Washington, D.C.: Mar. 18, 2009); and *Troubled Asset Relief Program: June 2009 Status of Efforts to Address Transparency and Accountability Issues*, GAO-09-658 (Washington, D.C.: June 2009). Also, see Congressional Oversight Panel's *Stress Testing and Shoring Up Bank Capital* (June 9, 2009).

[66] The BHCs had to maintain a tier 1 capital ratio of at least 6 percent of risk-weighted assets and a tier 1 common capital ratio of at least 4 percent of risk-weighted assets at the end of 2010. PPNR is defined as net interest income plus noninterest income minus noninterest expense. Allowance for loan and lease losses is defined as the capital reserve set aside to cover anticipated losses.

[67] See GAO, *Assessing the Reliability of Computer-Processed Data, Version 1*, GAO-02-15G (Washington, D.C.: September 2002).

[68] The owned debt value adjustment is an adjustment made to BHC financial statements if the BHC chose to value its own debt on a mark-to-market basis rather than book value. As the BHC's debt becomes cheaper, this creates a positive impact on its financial statements, while, as seen in 2009, the debt becomes more expensive, it has a negative impact on the BHC's financial statements.

[69] A credit default swap spread is one measure of investors' confidence in the banking sector. It is an agreement in which a buyer pays a periodic fee to a seller, in exchange for protection from certain credit events such as bankruptcy, failure to pay debt obligations, or a restructuring related to a specific debt issuer or issues known as the reference entity. Therefore, the credit default swap spread, or market price, is a measure of the credit

risk of the reference entity, with a higher spread indicating a greater amount of credit risk. When the markets' perception of the reference entity's credit risk deteriorates or improves, the spread generally will widen or tighten, respectively.

[70] Nonperforming loans represent the total of loans that are either 90 plus days past due or in nonaccrual status. As defined by the instructions to the Y-9C, an asset is in nonaccrual status if: (1) it is maintained on a cash basis because of deterioration in the financial condition of the borrower, (2) payment in full of principal or interest is not expected, or (3) principal or interest as been in default for a period of 90 days or more unless the asset is both well secured and in the process of collection. Per the Y-9C instructions, an asset is 90 plus days past due if payment is due and unpaid for 90 days or more, and if that asset is not in nonaccrual status.

[71] The Goldman Sachs Group, Inc. and Morgan Stanley were approved by the Federal Reserve to become BHCs on September 22, 2008; American Express Company was approved on November 10, 2008; and GMAC LLC was approved on December 24, 2008.

[72] See Federal Reserve's June 1, 2009, press release that sets forth the criteria that SCAP BHCs must meet before they can pay back their TARP investments.

[73] FDIC created this facility in November 2008 to encourage liquidity in the banking system by guaranteeing newly issued senior unsecured debt of banks, thrifts, and certain holding companies and by providing full coverage of noninterest-bearing deposit transaction accounts. The facility is scheduled to end in 2010.

CHAPTER SOURCES

The following chapters have been previously published:

Chapter 1 – This is an edited, excerpted and augmented edition of a United States Department of the Treasury publication, dated October 2010.

Chapter 2 – This is an edited, excerpted and augmented edition of a United States Government Accountability Office publication, Report Order Code GAO-11-47, dated October 2010.

Chapter 3 – This is an edited, excerpted and augmented edition of a United States Congressional Research Service publication, Report Order Code R41427, dated September 21, 2010.

Chapter 4 – This is an edited, excerpted and augmented edition of a United States Government Accountability Office publication, Report Order Code GAO-10-861, dated September 2010.

INDEX

G

H

I

P

Q

R